gateway science

OCR Science for GCSE

Separate

Chemistry

Bob McDuell
David Lees
David Fowkes

Series editor: Bob McDuell

www.heinemann.co.uk
✓ Free online support
✓ Useful weblinks
✓ 24 hour online ordering

01865 888058

Heinemann
Inspiring generations

Heinemann Educational Publishers
Halley Court, Jordan Hill, Oxford OX2 8EJ
Part of Harcourt Education

Heinemann is the registered trademark of Harcourt Education
Limited

First published 2006

Harcourt Education Ltd 2006

10 09 08 07 06
10 9 8 7 6 5 4 3 2

10-digit ISBN: 0 435 67527 3
13-digit ISBN: 978 0 435 67527 1

Series editor: Bob McDuell
Designed by Wooden Ark
Typeset by HL Studios, Long Hanborough, Oxford

Original illustrations © Harcourt Education Limited, 2006

Illustrated by HL Studios
Cover design by Cooney Bains
Printed by Printer Trento S.r.l
Cover photo: © Getty Images
Picture research by Kay Altwegg and Ginny Stroud-Lewis

Acknowledgements
The authors and publisher would like to thank the following
individuals and organisations for permission to reproduce
photographs:

Page 2, Alamy Images / Robert Harding Picture Library Ltd / John Miller; 3, **T** Corbis;
3, **B** Harcourt Education / Ginny Stroud-Lewis; 4, Maximilian Stock Ltd/ABPL (x2); 5,
Tim Hill / ABPL; 6, Getty Images / Taxi; 7, **T** Harcourt Education / Ginny Stroud-Lewis;
7, **B** Harcourt Education; 8, Alamy; 9, Harcourt Education / Ginny Stroud-Lewis; 10,
Alamy Images / David Young-Wolff; 11, **T** Corbis; 11, **B** Alamy Images / Travel-Shots;
13, Harvey Pincis / SPL; 14, Digital Vision; 15, Corbis; 17, Simon Fraser / SPL; 18, Corbis
/ John Gress / Reuters; 19, T Motoring Picture Library / Alamy; 19, **B** SPL; 21, Harcourt
Education / Peter Gould; 22, Science and Society Picture Library; 23, Cordelia Molloy
/ SPL; 25, **L** Digital Vision; 25, **R** Andrew Lambert Photography / SPL; 26, Corbis /
Chinch Gryniewicz, Ecoscene; 27, **T** Alamy Images / David Lyons; 27, **M** Alamy Images
/ Paul Glendell; 27, **B** Topfoto / UPPA; 29, **T** Charles D. Winters / SPL; 29, **B** David
Taylor / SPL; 30, Alamy Images / By Ian Miles-Flashpoint Pictures; 31, Creatas; 34, Getty
Images / Photonica / Johner; 38, Rex / CNP; 39, Alamy Images / Ron Scott; 41, Klaus
Guldbrandsen / SPL; 42, Alamy Images / Mitch Diamond; 43, T Corbis / Simon Kwong
/ Reuters; 43, **B** Harcourt Education / Ginny Stroud-Lewis; 44, T George Bernard / SPL;
44, **M** Adam Hart-Davis / SPL; 44, **B** George Bernard / SPL; 45, KPT Power Photos; 46,
Digital Vision; 47, **T** Adam G. Sylvester / SPL; 47, **B** Corbis / Mohsin Raza / Reuters;
49, **T** Corbis / Layne Kennedy; 49, **B** SPL; 51, SPL / Andrew Lambert Photography;
52, Maximilian Stock Ltd / SPL; 54, Department of Geological & Mining Engineering
& Sciences, Michigan Technological University; 55, Alamy Images / Photo Japan; 57,
Alamy Images / Motoring Picture Library; 58, Iain Farley / Alamy; 59, SPL / BSIP, M.I.G.
/ BAEZA; 62, Alamy Images / FLPA; 63, T Alamy Images / foodfolio; 63, **B** Alamy Images
/ Marie-Louise Avery; 66, **T** SPL / Jonathan Watts; 66, **B** SPL / Mehau Kulyk & Victor
De Schwanberg; 67, **T** Lesley Garland Picture Library / Alamy; 67, **B** Corbis / Sygma /
Petit Claude; 68, T Harcourt Education Ltd / Peter Gould; 68, **B** SPL / Malcolm Fielding,

Johnson Matthey PLC; 69, Harcourt Education Ltd / Peter Gould; 70, SPL / Charles Bach;
74, SPL / Andrew Lambert Photography; 75, **T** SPL / Dr Mitsuo Ohtsuki; **B** Art
Directors and Trip; 78, Corbis / Ed Young; 79, T Alamy Images / Helene Rogers; **B** Corbis
/ Bob Krist; 81, SPL / Andrew Syred; 82, Alamy Images / Ange; 83, Harcourt Education /
Ginny Stroud-Lewis; 86, Art Directors and Trip; 87, **T** Alamy Images / Shout; **B** Harcourt
Education; 88, Harcourt Education / Trevor Clifford (x3); 90, Alamy Images / Peter
Defty; 91, **T** Imagebroker / Alamy; **BL** Charles D. Winters / SPL; **BM** Andrew Lambert
Photography / SPL; **BR** Andrew Lambert Photography / SPL; 92, Andrew Lambert
Photography / SPL; 94, T Archimage; BL Corbis / Reuters; **BR** Harcourt Education
/ Ginny Stroud-Lewis; 95, **T** Corbis / Bettmann; **B** Harcourt Index; 96, Science and
Society; 97, Adam Hart-Davis / SPL; 99, **T** Harcourt Education / Ginny Stroud-Lewis;
B Alamy Images / J. Schwanke; 101, Andrew Lambert Photography / SPL (x3); 102,
T Alamy Images / Jeremy Horner; **B** SPL / Astrid & Hanns-Frieder Michler; 103, Reed
International Books, Australia; 104, **T** Leslie Garland Picture Library / Alamy; **B** Corbis;
105, Getty Images / PhotoDisc; 106, Corbis; 110, Getty Images / Photodisc; 111, **T**
Getty Images / PhotoDisc; 111, **B** Greenshoots Communications / Alamy; 113, Martyn
F. Chillmaid / SPL; 114, SPL / Martyn F. Chillmaid; 115, Getty Images / Photodisc (x2);
117, Art Directors and Trip; 118, Alamy Images / David Lyons; 119, **T** Alamy Images /
Paul Glendell; **B** Alamy Images / DY Riess MD; 121, SPL / Robert Brook; 122, **TL** SPL
/ Andrew Lambert Photography; **ML** Corbis / Andrew Brookes; **BR** Art Directors and
Trip; 123, **T** Corbis; **B** Corbis / Hulton-Deutsch Collection; 125, **T** Alamy Images /
Photofusion Picture Library; 127, **T** SPL; **B** Harcourt Education Ltd; 128, Corbis; 129,
Corbis / Wolfgang Kaehler; 130, Art Directors and Trip; 131, Corbis / Bettmann; 133,
T Scott T. Smith / Corbis; **B** Erich Schrempp / SPL; 134, Frank Trapper / Corbis; 135,
T Frank Trapper / Corbis; **B** Dr Peter Harris / SPL; 137, Dr Peter Harris / SPL; 138,
Harcourt Education / Ginny Stroud-Lewis (x2); 139, **T** Alamy Images / Greenshoots
Communications; **B** WaterAid / Jon Spaull; 141, SPL / Novosti Press Agency; 142, SPL
/ Robert Brook; 146, Michael Donne / SPL; 147, Mauro Fermariello / SPL; 148, Andrew
Lambert Photography / SPL; 150, **T** Harcourt Education; 150, **B** Martin Bond / SPL;
151, Andrew Lambert Photography / SPL; 152, Charles D. Winters / SPL; 153, Harcourt
Education / Trevor Clifford; 154, SPL / Jay Lyons; 27, **M** Alamy Images
/ Paul Glendell; 154, Jesse / SPL; 155, **T** Harcourt Index; 155, **M1** Joy
Skipper / Anthony Blake Photo Library; 155, **M2** Harcourt Index; 155, **B** Trevor Clifford
/ Harcourt Education; 156, fStop / Alamy; 157, Andrew McClenaghan / SPL; 158,
Norman Hollands / Anthony Blake Photo Library; 159, **T** Martyn F. Chillmaid / SPL; 159,
B Harcourt Index; 161, Food Features; 162, CuboImages srl / Alamy; 163, Phototake
Inc. / Alamy; 166, David A. Hardy / SPL; 167, **T** Tetra Images / Alamy; 167, **B** Harcourt
Education; 168, Food Features; 171, **T** Trevor Clifford / Harcourt Education; 171, **B** David
M. Martin, M.D / SPL; 173, Trevor Clifford / Harcourt Education; 174, Simon Fraser /
SPL; 175, Lawrence Migdale / SPL; 178, Geoff Tompkinson / SPL; 182, Peter Bowater
/ Alamy; 183, **T** Harcourt Education / Trevor Clifford; 183, **BL** Time & Life Pictures /
Getty Images; 183, **BR** Harcourt Index; 185, Charles Pertwee / Alamy; 186, Justin Kase
/ Alamy; 187, **T** Harcourt Education; 187, **B** Wilmar Photography.com / Alamy; 188,
Andrew Lambert Photography / SPL; 189, **T** Manor Photography / Alamy; 189, **B** Leslie
Garland Picture Library / Alamy; 190, Mark Scheuern / Alamy; 191, **T** Food Features;
191, **B** sciencephotos / Alamy; 193, **L** Slick Shoots / Alamy; 193, **R** Harcourt Index;
194, Carphotos / Alamy; 195, Pascal Goetgheluck / SPL; 197, Trevor Clifford / Harcourt
Education; 199, Harcourt Index; 200, Imageshop / Alamy; 201, Lauren Shear / SPL;
203, L AK PhotoLibrary / Alamy; 203, **R** Reckitt Benckiser plc; 204, Harcourt Education;
206, Sheila Terry / SPL; 207, imagebroker / Alamy; 208, Andrew Lambert Photography
/ SPL; 209, T Charles D. Winters / SPL; 209, **M** Harcourt Index; 209, **B** foodfolio /
Alamy; 210, Harcourt Index; 211, **T** Harcourt Education / Trevor Clifford; 211, **B** John
Powell Photographer / Alamy; 212, Alan Williams / NHPA; 214, Harcourt Index; 220,
Gettmages/Photodisc (x2); Corbis.

The authors and publisher would like to thank the following
individuals and organisations for permission to reproduce
copyright materials:`

24 B (Structure of Gore-Tex ©) W.L. Gore and Associates. Copyright ©; 82 Bromine
extraction from water, www.amlwchdata.co.uk/copperkingdom/aoc.htm; 96 Hofmann
Voltameter – Letts Classbook Science by Baylis, published by Letts Educational Ltd; 112
pH universal indicator – Letts GCSE Classbook Science by D Baylis, published by Letts
Educational Ltd; 128, **B** Action of detergent - Chemistry Nuffield Coordinated Sciences,
published by Longman; 140 Water purification diagram – IGCSE Chemistry by Earl and
Wilford, published bty Hodder Education; 142 Reservoir capacity in England and Wales
2004/2005 – www.environment-agency.gov.uk; 170 **M** (sulphuric acid flow diagram)
www.schoolscience.co.uk; 170 **B** (graph of yield vs pressure for the Haber Process)
www.ausetute.com.au/index.html; 202 (annual production of CFCs) www.afeas.org/
production_and_sales.html; 223 (quote from Dr John Bell) The Daily Telegraph © 2006;
224 (quote from Dr Ben Feingold) www.henryspink.org/feingold_food_programme.htm.

Every effort has been made to contact copyright holders of
material reproduced in this book. Any omissions will be rectified
in subsequent printings if notice is given to the publishers.
Tel: 01865 888058   www.heinemann.co.uk

Introduction

This student book covers the new OCR Gateway Chemistry specification for Higher tier. It has been written to support you as you study for the OCR Gateway Chemistry GCSE.

This book has been written by examiners who are also teachers and who have been involved in the development of the new specification. It is supported by other material produced by Heinemann, including online teacher resource sheets and interactive learning software with exciting video clips, games and activities.

As part of GCSE Gateway Chemistry you must complete either:

a Can-do tasks in chemistry
Science in the news

OR

b Research study
Data task
Teacher assessment of your practical skills.

These are fully explained on pages 220–229.

We hope this book will help you achieve the best you can in your GCSE Chemistry Award and help you understand how much chemistry affects our everyday lives. As citizens of the 21st century you need to be informed about chemical issues. Then you can read newspapers or watch television programmes and really have views about things that affect you and your family.

Gateway Chemistry GCSE is a very good preparation for AS courses in Chemistry.

The next two pages explain the special features we have included in this book to help you to learn and understand the subject, and to be able to use it in context. At the back of the book you will also find some useful tables, as well as a glossary and index.

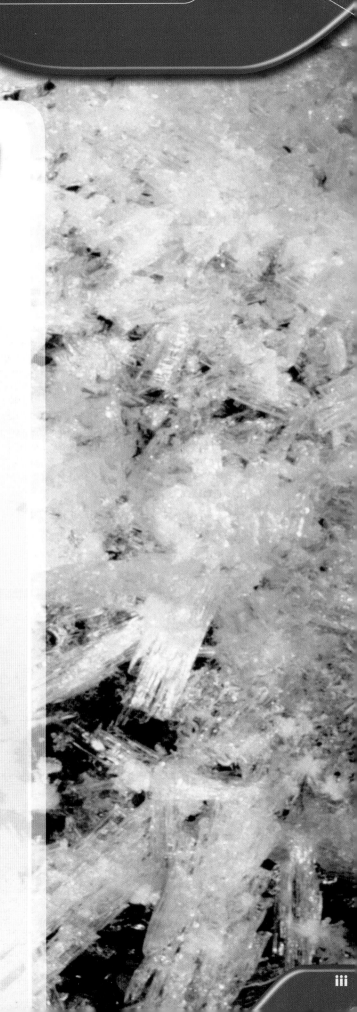

About this book

This student book has been designed to make learning chemistry fun. The book follows the layout of the OCR Gateway specification. It is divided into six sections that match the six modules in the specification for Chemistry: C1, C2, C3, C4, C5 and C6.

The module introduction page at the start of a module introduces what you are going to learn. It has some short introductory paragraphs, plus talking heads with speech bubbles that raise questions about what is going to be covered.

Each module is then broken down into eight separate items (a–h), for example, C1a, C1b, C1c, C1d, C1e, C1f, C1g, C1h.

Each item is covered in four book pages. These four pages are split into three pages covering the science content relevant to the item plus a context page places the science content just covered into context, either by news-related articles or data tasks, or by examples of scientists at work, science in everyday life or science in the news.

Throughout these four pages there are clear explanations with diagrams and photos to illustrate the science being discussed. At the end of each module there are three pages of questions to test your knowledge and understanding of the module.

There are three pages of exam-style end of module questions for each module.

The talking heads on the module introduction page raise questions about what you are going to learn.

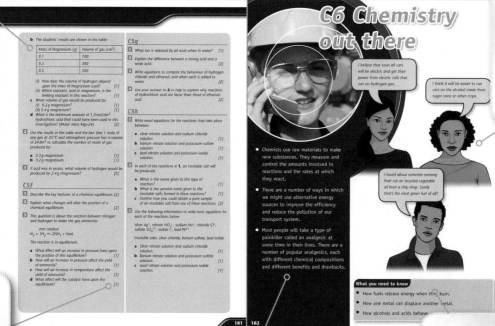

The numbers in square brackets give the marks for the question or part of the question.

The bulleted text introduces the module.

This box highlights what you need to know before you start the module.

Context pages link the science learned in the item with real life.

This box highlights what you will be learning about in this item.

General approach to the topic

Question box at the end

Some amazing facts have been included – science isn't just boring facts!

Questions in the text make sure you have understood what you have just read.

Clear diagrams to explain the science.

When a new word appears for the first time in the text, it will appear in bold type. All words in **bold** are listed with their meanings in the glossary at the back of the book.

The keywords box lists all keywords in the item.

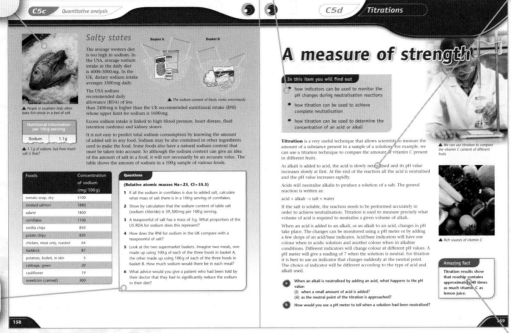

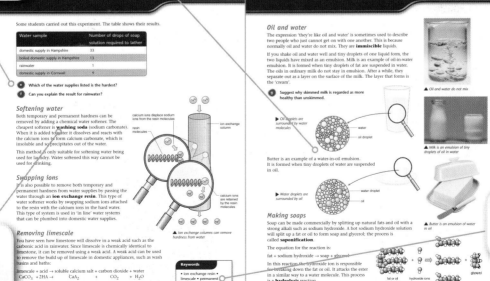

Contents

C1 Carbon chemistry

The sign says I should turn my phone off at the petrol station. Why is this necessary?

Why are tests on car emissions part of the MOT test for cars?

Combustion reactions give out energy. Do all reactions give out energy?

- The photograph shows a scene which is all too common on our roads today and planners tell us it will get worse. Every car that is in the stationary queue of traffic is burning petrol and diesel, and emitting exhaust fumes that are damaging the environment.

- Huge amounts of crude oil are used for transport, but it is also used for other things that we take for granted – clothes, furniture and household goods. The range of materials from crude oil is vast and expanding every year.

- Crude oil is an important but finite resource. It has to be managed if supplies will be available for future generations.

What you need to know

- A particle model can be used to explain solids, liquids and gases, including changes of state and diffusion.

- Mixtures are composed of constituents that are not combined.

- How to separate mixtures into constituents using distillation.

Food, glorious food

In this item you will find out

- why some foods have to be cooked before they are eaten

- what cooking does to the food

- how baking powder makes a cake rise

The next time you go to a supermarket, think about all the different varieties of foods that are available. Fresh food usually has a country of origin label. If you take a look at some of them you will find that food comes from all around the world.

a **Suggest how fresh food from South America gets to the UK without going bad.**

Look at the food in the photograph below.

Some foods can be eaten raw or cooked, but a few foods must be cooked before we can eat them.

b **Which foods in the photograph have to be cooked?**

Amazing fact

The leaves of rhubarb are poisonous as they contain oxalic acid, but the stems can be eaten.

Cooking is done for a number of reasons. It:
- kills harmful microbes because it uses high temperatures
- improves the texture of food
- improves the taste and flavour of food
- makes food easier to digest.

The cooking process

Cooking food is a chemical process involving chemical reactions. We know this because the final product is different from the raw food. The cooking process is also irreversible – it is not possible to recover the raw ingredients after cooking. Finally, cooking involves an energy change.

A hen's egg is designed to accommodate a chick embryo. It is made up of three parts: the shell, the egg white and the yolk. The egg white is made up of one-eighth protein and seven-eighths water. This provides food for the growing embryo. The yolk is a yellow (or orange) oil-in-water emulsion. It is a rich source of nutrients, especially protein. It is roughly one-third fat, one-half water and one-sixth protein.

Eggs are a complete source of food for an embryo and they are a good source of protein for humans.

 Humans need proteins, fats and carbohydrates. Which food type is not in an egg?

When an egg is heated, the protein molecules in the egg change shape. The change is permanent and cannot be reversed. This is called denaturing. The photographs show an egg before and after cooking.

▲ Before cooking

▲ After cooking

The change in the egg white is easy to see. It changes from a thick colourless liquid to a white solid, as the egg cooks. The changes to the yolk are more difficult to see, but if the egg is overcooked the yolk breaks up into a yellow powder.

Meat and potatoes

Meat is also a good source of protein. The pie diagram shows the food types in a sample of beef.

When meat is heated to 60 °C the protein molecules start to change shape. They are denatured. The meat changes colour and its texture may change depending on the method of cooking. It often shrinks.

fat (28%)

water (56%)

protein (15%)

others (1%)

▲ Food types in beef

Potatoes are **carbohydrates**. They contain cellulose, which forms the cell walls of all plants. Starch is trapped inside the potato cells. People cannot digest cellulose and uncooked starch is also difficult to digest. Cooking softens and then breaks down the cell walls releasing the starch. The starch absorbs water and becomes a gel which is more easily digested.

Baking powder

When making cakes it is important that the mixture rises during baking to give the final product a structure with lots of trapped bubbles.

When you make cakes, you use a raising agent. The simplest raising agent is **baking power** which contains sodium hydrogencarbonate. This breaks down (or decomposes) in the baking process to produce carbon dioxide.

It is the carbon dioxide which makes the cake rise and which produces lots of tiny holes.

sodium hydrogencarbonate → sodium carbonate + water + carbon dioxide

$$2NaHCO_3 \rightarrow Na_2CO_3 + H_2O + CO_2$$

▲ Trapped bubbles in a cake

A commercial baking powder contains sodium hydrogencarbonate and an acid, such as tartaric acid. When these react in the cake mixture during baking, carbon dioxide forms. Sodium tartrate also forms, but it is tasteless.

Testing for carbon dioxide

If you want to test whether a gas released during a chemical reaction is carbon dioxide, then you can bubble the gas through colourless limewater solution (calcium hydroxide). If the limewater turns cloudy, then the gas is carbon dioxide.

Limewater is calcium hydroxide solution, $Ca(OH)_2$. When carbon dioxide is bubbled through limewater, the cloudy solution is caused by calcium carbonate, $CaCO_3$.

d Write word and symbol equations for the reaction which takes place.

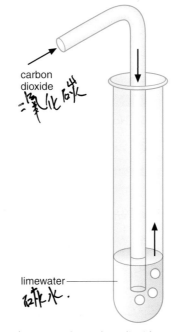

carbon dioxide 二氧化碳

limewater 石灰水.

▲ Testing for carbon dioxide

keywords

baking powder •
carbohydrate

Curried eggs

In 1988, Edwina Currie, the Junior Health Minister, drew attention to the problem of salmonella in British eggs. Overnight, sales of eggs fell by 60% and many egg producers went out of business. As a result, Edwina Currie had to resign.

But she had highlighted a problem and the British egg industry spent £20 billion putting it right. They used a programme of vaccination and other food safety measures.

Now British eggs are some of the safest in the world. In tests this year, only 0.34% of eggs tested were infected with salmonella. But the industry cannot relax its efforts.

Every day people in Britain eat about 30 million eggs of which about one-sixth are imported. Most of these imported eggs come from Spain and they are cheaper than British eggs. These eggs tend to be used by caterers rather than sold in supermarkets. You can tell a Spanish egg as it has ES stamped on it.

Last year 15 people died of salmonella in Britain and there were 80 known cases. Many of these cases could be traced back to Spanish eggs. Most people recover from food poisoning caused by salmonella, but certain groups are more vulnerable.

UK health authorities recommend that caterers should not use Spanish eggs in food for old people, the sick and young children. Also they should not be used in food where the egg is raw or only lightly cooked.

The Spanish authorities say that they export eggs to many other countries. They have no other complaints about salmonella in their eggs.

Questions

1 How many eggs are imported into Britain each day?

2 Suggest why caterers buy most of the imported eggs.

3 British eggs are much safer now than in 1988. Why must the authorities not relax their efforts?

4 Why are infected eggs more of a problem when they are raw or lightly cooked?

5 Which groups of people are more vulnerable?

6 Suggest why these groups are more vulnerable.

7 Why are the Spanish authorities surprised by British complaints about their eggs?

Eating by numbers

In this item you will find out

- about food additives and their advantages and disadvantages

- how 'intelligent' or 'active' packaging' is used for food preservation

- what emulsifiers do and how they do it

Food manufacturers add chemicals called **food additives** to food. There are different types of food additive. They are put in food for different reasons.

Food additive	Reason for using it
food colours	to make the food look more attractive
antioxidants	to slow down food reacting with oxygen and going bad
emulsifiers	to keep the different ingredients thoroughly mixed
flavour enhancers	to improve the flavour of the food

Food manufacturers can only use approved food additives that have been tested for safety.

How do we find out what the food we buy contains, so we know which food additives we are eating? Look at some packets of food in your kitchen. The ingredients are listed in order of their masses (with the largest first). Most additives are near the end of the list.

The label for a beef gravy flavour mix is shown below. The powder is mixed with hot water to make gravy.

 a What is the main ingredient in this beef flavour gravy mix?

<table>
<tr><th>Ingredients</th><th colspan="2">Nutritional information</th></tr>
<tr><td rowspan="9">Maize starch, Wheat flour, Flavourings, Salt, Skimmed milk powder, Flavour enhancer (E621), Colour (E150c), Onion powder, Hydrogenated palm oil, Sugar, Citric acid (E472c)</td><td>Typical values</td><td>Per 100 g (dry mix)</td></tr>
<tr><td>Energy</td><td>1371 kJ</td></tr>
<tr><td>Protein</td><td>11.4 g</td></tr>
<tr><td>Carbohydrate</td><td>62.6 g</td></tr>
<tr><td>of which sugars</td><td>5.1 g</td></tr>
<tr><td>Fat</td><td>1.7 g</td></tr>
<tr><td>of which saturates</td><td>0.9 g</td></tr>
<tr><td>Fibre</td><td>0.6 g</td></tr>
<tr><td>Sodium</td><td>0.5 g</td></tr>
</table>

▲ Making gravy

E-numbers

All approved food additives have **E-numbers**. The E-number tells us why the additive is used.

E-number	Purpose	Example	Example of use
E100-199	food colours	caramel	sweets, soft drinks, jellies
E200-299	preservatives	sulfur dioxide	jams, squashes
E300-399	antioxidants	vitamin C	meat pies, salad cream
E400-499	thickeners, gelling agents, emulsifiers	starch, pectin, egg yolk	sauces, jams, salad cream and mayonnaise
E600-699	flavourings, flavour enhancers	monosodium glutamate (MSG) used in Chinese food	sweets, meat products

▲ Fizzy drinks contain food colours

Antioxidants reduce the chance of oils, fats and fat-soluble vitamins from combining with oxygen and changing colour or going rancid (sour). Thickeners and gelling agents are used to thicken sauces and other foods. Emulsifiers prevent different liquids separating out.

b A fruit jelly contains E150 and E620. Suggest why it contains these two additives.

Emulsifiers

A mixture of vegetable oil and water does not mix. But it is possible to get the oil and water to mix as an **emulsion** by adding an **emulsifier** and shaking the mixture. In mayonnaise, which is an emulsion, tiny drops of oil are spread throughout the water.

The emulsifier molecules are made up of two parts. These are:

• a water-loving (**hydrophilic**) head which has an ionic charge
• an oil-loving (**hydrophobic**) tail.

The tails of the emulsifier molecules are attracted to the oil droplets. All of the heads have the same charge so there is repulsion between them. This stops the oil droplets coming together.

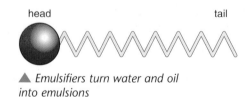

head   tail

▲ Emulsifiers turn water and oil into emulsions

All wrapped up

When you open a bag of crisps or a packet of biscuits, do you think about the wrappings? Perhaps you don't, but there are people called packaging engineers who do. Food used to be packaged in paper or cardboard. Now it is likely to be some kind of polymer film.

The purpose of any packaging is to keep the food in good condition until it is eaten. Scientists have developed active or intelligent packaging. This means that the packaging controls or reacts to changes which are taking place inside the pack to improve the safety or quality of food. This usually means keeping out oxygen (or air) and water. Keeping out water makes it more difficult for bacteria and mould to grow. Polymer films are more effective than paper and cardboard in doing this.

▲ *The polymer film keeps the meat fresh for longer*

Scientists have found that controlling the number of free radicals in food being stored is the key to keeping food in good condition for a long time. Free radicals are reactive atoms or groups of atoms that accelerate the breakdown of food.

There are two ways of controlling the numbers of free radicals in food.

Oxygen scavengers

Oxygen scavengers are chemicals in the packaging that remove any oxygen in the food by reacting with it, and so preventing free radicals forming which can be harmful.

Antioxidants

Antioxidants in the packaging also combine with the free radicals in the food before they can break down the food or the packaging.

Some film packaging (for example, for fruit) needs to allow gases to leave and enter in a controlled way. The film lets oxygen in, but ethene (which causes fruit to ripen too fast) can escape.

Another example of active or intelligent packaging is found in cans that can heat or cool their contents.

c **What type of chemical in intelligent packaging removes oxygen from food?**

Beer in cans needs to be frothy when poured out into a glass. This frothy consistency is obtained by including a small device in the can called a widget. The widget mixes air with the beer to produce the desired frothy drink.

d **What type of chemical in intelligent packaging removes any free radicals in the food?**

e **Why is one type of polymer film needed for food packaging?**

> **Amazing fact**
>
> **Fruit and vegetables contain natural antioxidants. Pomegranates and peanuts are both very good sources of antioxidants.**

> **keywords**
>
> antioxidant • emulsifier • emulsion • E-number • food additive • hydrophilic • hydrophobic

Information for the consumer

Food packaging is big business. Manufacturers spend a lot of money developing new ways to package food to keep it fresh for longer, while still being safe for us to eat.

Some people in the packaging industry believe that the way forward is in developing packaging which gives the consumer information about the food inside.

One example is packaging which changes colour depending on the temperature. This would tell the consumer if the food was getting too hot or too cold.

The VTT Technical Research Centre of Finland is developing a sensor that can be printed onto plastic packaging.

The sensor contains a substance that reacts with oxygen and lets the consumer know if food that is perishable has been packaged with oxygen.

By looking at the sensor the consumer will be able to see if the pack has been opened and is leaking oxygen.

The VTT centre is also developing methods of printing electronic data onto packs. This will help to stop counterfeit products and it will be possible to trace packs wirelessly.

It is also important in the supermarket that food is kept in the best conditions possible to prevent the food starting to breakdown. Packaging that shows when the temperature of storage is wrong by changing colour is helpful in the supermarket to show that the conditions of storage are right.

Questions

1 Suggest a use for packaging that changes colour depending on the temperature.

2 Why would a consumer want to know whether a pack is leaking oxygen?

3 Why do you think manufacturers want to be able to trace packs?

4 Suggest things that are done to ensure that a frozen chicken meal is in good condition when we buy it in the supermarket. Think about the manufacture, the transport and the storage in the supermarket.

Heaven scent

In this item you will find out

- how esters can be made and used
- why perfumes have certain properties
- why cosmetics need to be tested

An attractive smell is very powerful. The cosmetics and perfumes industries try very hard to produce smells that people will pay a lot of money to buy. Perfumes can be made by blending together natural oils (such as sandalwood or lavender), or they can be made synthetically.

But what gives perfume its smell? This is provided by a group of organic compounds called **esters**. Esters can occur naturally or they can be created synthetically.

Esters can be used as perfumes, as flavouring agents and as **solvents**. They are a very important family of organic compounds.

The mixtures of esters in a perfume are extremely expensive and the smell is very concentrated. These mixtures are diluted by adding solvents to get the perfume of the desired concentration. Perfumes can be bought in different forms, for example, eau de toilette. The more expensive products contain larger amounts of esters. Most of the perfumes produced are not used in cosmetics but are used in everyday products such as polishes or air fresheners.

Esters can even be found in sweets! The esters are added to the sweets while they are being made. The ester in pineapple chunks is methyl butanoate. This is same chemical that gives fresh pineapple its smell and taste.

▲ Lavender oil is used in a lot of perfumes and cosmetics

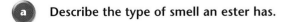

a Describe the type of smell an ester has.

Making esters

You can make an ester by warming an organic acid with an alcohol. A drop of concentrated sulfuric acid acts as a catalyst.

organic acid + alcohol → ester + water

If you react methanoic acid and ethanol you get ethyl methanoate. A sweet raspberry smell forms.

b Finish the balanced symbol equation:

$$CH_2O_2 + C_2H_6O \rightarrow ? + ?$$

The table gives the names of some common esters and the acids and alcohols used to make them. It also gives the smell of the ester.

Ester	Alcohol	Acid	Smell
methyl butanoate	methanol	butanoic acid	pineapple
ethyl ethanoate	ethanol	ethanoic acid	pear drops or nail varnish remover
methyl salicylate	methanol	salicylic acid	wintergreen
methyl benzoate	methanol	benzoic acid	marzipan

c What is the name of the ester formed from ethanoic acid and methanol?

Perfumes

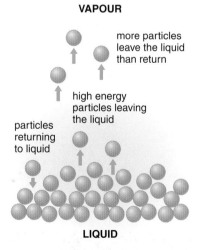

VAPOUR

more particles leave the liquid than return

high energy particles leaving the liquid

particles returning to liquid

LIQUID

Perfumes need certain properties. They need to evaporate easily, so that the perfume particles can reach the scent cells in your nose. They need to be non-toxic, so they do not poison you, and they should not irritate your skin when they are put directly on to it.

Perfumes also need to be **insoluble** in water, so they cannot be washed off easily, and they should not react with water otherwise they would react with your perspiration.

How easily a liquid evaporates is called volatility. There is only a weak attraction between the perfume particles in the liquid perfume, so it is easy to overcome this attraction. The perfume particles have lots of energy so they can escape from the other particles in the liquid. The diagram on the left shows perfume particles escaping from the liquid.

Solvents

Esters can be used as solvents. A **solution** is a mixture of a solvent and a **solute** that does not separate. Ethyl ethanoate is an ester that is a non-aqueous solvent. This means it dissolves many substances, but different substances from those dissolved by water.

Nail varnish does not dissolve in water but does dissolve in ethyl ethanoate.

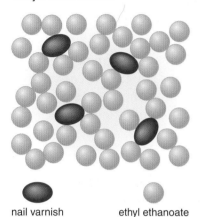

◀ *This diagram shows the particles of ethyl ethanoate and nail varnish in a solution*

 nail varnish   ● ethyl ethanoate

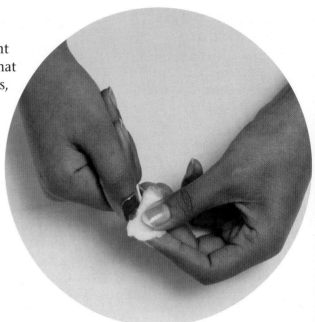

▲ *This woman is taking off nail varnish with nail varnish remover*

Water does not dissolve nail varnish. This is because the attraction between water molecules is stronger, compared with the attraction between water molecules and nail varnish particles. It is also because the attraction between nail varnish particles is stronger, compared with the attraction between water molecules and nail varnish particles.

d   **Why is it important that nail varnish does not dissolve in water?**

Testing cosmetics

Cosmetics, perfumes, other beauty products and the ingredients that are used in them, need to be tested very thoroughly before they can be sold in shops and used by people. This is so they do not harm people or cause allergic reactions.

Sometimes the products and ingredients are tested on animals. This cannot happen in the UK but it can still happen in the European Community, although it will be completely phased out by 2013. Testing on animals can only let scientists predict what effects a product or ingredient will have on humans.

However, chemicals can sometimes have different effects on different species. For example, bleach causes severe irritation to human skin, but only mild irritation to rabbit skin.

Some people feel that testing of anything on animals is wrong and should be stopped.

e   **Many people object to testing chemicals on animals. Suggest why banning testing on animals in the UK and the EU will not necessarily stop this testing.**

f   **Research shows that a chemical does not have an adverse effect on rabbits. Is this enough evidence for chemists to suggest including this chemical in cosmetics?**

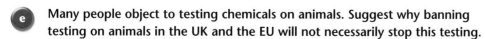

keywords

ester • insoluble • solute • solution • solvent

Taking make-up off

Dr Louise Yi works in the research laboratory of a major cosmetics firm. They have just launched a new product which is a waterproof mascara.

Waterproof mascara cannot be washed off in water and the firm has been receiving complaints that their normal eye-makeup remover does not remove all traces of mascara when people take it off.

The firm wants to develop mascara removal wipes as a new product. Dr Yi is developing the cream that the wipes will contain. She is testing the effectiveness of different chemicals in dissolving the mascara.

Her results are as follows:

Solvent	Effectiveness in removing mascara (%)	Smell	Cost
Chemical A	95	unpleasant	expensive
Chemical B	76	no smell	cheap
Chemical C	87	pleasant	expensive

Questions

1 Suggest why people want to use waterproof mascara.

2 Which chemical is most effective in removing the mascara?

3 What are the drawbacks of using this chemical?

4 Which chemical do you think Dr Li should use in the new product and why?

5 Suggest what further work should be done before the wipes are manufactured and sold.

6 Some people say that cosmetics are very expensive considering that many of the ingredients are inexpensive. How can the manufacturer justify the prices they charge?

Cracking good sense

In this item you will find out

- why crude oil is a finite resource and is non-renewable

- how crude oil can be turned into useful products by fractional distillation and cracking

- about some of the environmental and political problems caused by the oil industry

▲ *Crude oil is found in the North Sea but stocks are dwindling*

Crude oil is a **fossil fuel** and it is a **finite resource**, which means that it will not last forever. Coal and natural gas are also fossil fuels. Fossil fuels take millions of years to make. They are **non-renewable fuels** because we are using them up faster than they can be made.

Crude oil was formed millions of years ago when small sea creatures and plants died and were buried in the seabed. The high temperatures and pressures inside the Earth turned them into crude oil. This process took place in the absence of air.

The diagram on the right shows how the crude oil is trapped with natural gas. Oil cannot escape through the rocks around the oil.

 Geologists can find where crude oil is likely to be by looking for suitable rock structures. Suggest how the oil can be extracted.

Humans have known about crude oil for thousands of years. In some places crude oil is forced onto the surface of the Earth through cracks in the crust. This then partially sets, as low boiling point hydrocarbons evaporate, and the resulting black mass is called pitch. In the time of wooden ships, such as HMS Victory, pitch used to be spread over the planks of wood.

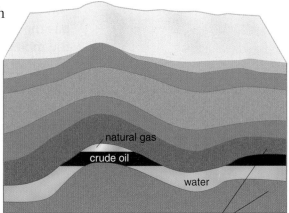

 Suggest why this was done.

In Texas, 100 years ago, farmers used to burn pitch because they did not know what to do with it.

Crude oil only became valuable when people learned how to turn it into useful products.

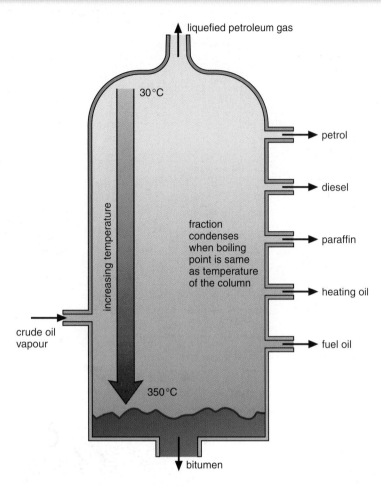

liquefied petroleum gas

30 °C

petrol

diesel

fraction condenses when boiling point is same as temperature of the column

paraffin

heating oil

increasing temperature

crude oil vapour

fuel oil

350 °C

bitumen

Making crude oil useful

Crude oil is not one pure substance. It is a mixture of many different **hydrocarbons**.

Crude oil can be split into more useful products called **fractions** by **fractional distillation**. Fractions contain mixtures of hydrocarbons. The process is carried out in an oil refinery. The diagram opposite shows a fractionating column where the separation takes place.

Fractional distillation works because a fraction contains lots of substances with similar **boiling points**. Crude oil vapour enters at the bottom left of the tower. As it passes up the tower, it cools. A fraction with a high boiling point condenses and comes off at the bottom. A fraction with a low boiling point condenses and comes off at the top.

c How is crude oil vapour produced?

d Look at the diagram. Which fraction – petrol or paraffin – condenses at the lower temperature?

The **LPG** (liquefied petroleum gases) do not condense. They contain propane and butane gases.

Breaking bonds

The diagram below shows the structures of butane and octane, which are two of the fractions in crude oil. Butane contains four carbon atoms and has the molecular formula C_4H_{10}. Octane has eight carbon atoms and has the molecular formula C_8H_{18}. The carbon atoms and hydrogen atoms in hydrocarbons are bonded together with **covalent** bonds.

The covalent bonds between carbon and hydrogen are strong bonds that are not easily broken. They are stronger than the intermolecular forces between hydrocarbon molecules. When the crude oil boils during fractional distillation, the intermolecular forces between the hydrocarbon molecules are broken.

The intermolecular forces between large hydrocarbon molecules are stronger than those between smaller hydrocarbon molecules. So hydrocarbons with large molecules have higher boiling points than hydrocarbons with smaller molecules.

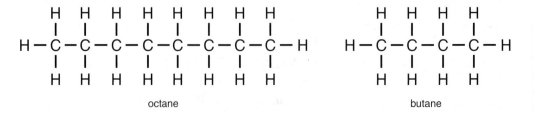

octane

butane

Supply and demand

The diagram on the right shows the uses of the different fractions in crude oil. The fractions from crude oil are used as fuels.

The table shows the supply of each fraction in crude oil and the approximate demand for each fraction by customers.

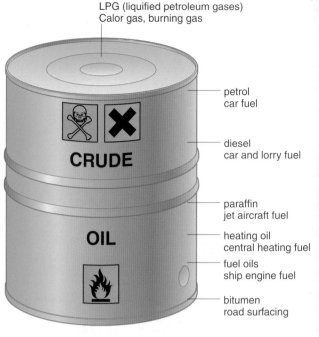

LPG (liquified petroleum gases) Calor gas, burning gas

petrol car fuel

diesel car and lorry fuel

paraffin jet aircraft fuel

heating oil central heating fuel

fuel oils ship engine fuel

bitumen road surfacing

Fraction	Supply in crude oil (%)	Demand from customers (%)
LPG	2	4
Petrol	15	27
Diesel	14	21
Paraffin	14	9
Heating oil	19	14
Fuel oil and bitumen	36	25

 Look at the rows in the table for petrol and heating oil. What do you notice about the supply and the demand for these two fractions?

Cracking

Oil companies convert high boiling-point fractions (such as heating oil) into low boiling-point fractions (such as petrol) which are in greater demand. They do this by a process called **cracking**. Cracking is carried out by heating a high boiling-point fraction with a catalyst at a high temperature. There must be no air in the apparatus.

 Why must there be no air there?

The molecules formed are smaller alkane and alkene molecules. The alkene molecules are useful because they can be used to make **polymers**.

Decane can be cracked to produce octane and ethene.

$C_{10}H_{22} \rightarrow C_8H_{18} + C_2H_4$

decane $\rightarrow$ octane + ethene

Environmental problems

Most of the problems caused by the oil industry come from leakage of crude oil, either at oil wells or when the oil is transported. Large sea tankers transport half of the world's crude oil. During routine tank cleaning, the oil is deliberately released into the sea. Oil can also spill into the sea when tankers unload at refineries.

Crude oil breaks down in the sea over a period of time. The lighter fractions of the oil evaporate at the water surface. Heavier fractions sink and form tar balls. These eventually break down with the help of bacteria in the water. However, this crude oil can kill sea birds and animals.

At oil wells it is usual to burn off waste gases. This also can cause atmospheric pollution.

▲ A spill from an oil tanker

keywords

boiling point • covalent • cracking • crude oil • finite resource • fossil fuel • fraction • fractional distillation • hydrocarbon • LPG • non-renewable fuel • polymer

The politics of oil

The Organisation of Petroleum Exporting Countries (OPEC) is mainly made up of Middle East Arab states and North African countries. It controls most of the world's production of oil and its price. Many of the largest deposits of oil are concentrated in countries in the Middle East where there is political unease.

The power of OPEC was shown in 1973 at the outbreak of the war between Israel and the Arab states. OPEC immediately quadrupled the price of crude oil. The economies of Western Europe and Japan, which relied on imported crude oil, went into decline. This led to recession and huge job losses.

This shows that oil-producing countries can make life very difficult for countries that rely on imported oil.

The US imports large quantities of foreign oil. This has kept costs down for consumers. A litre of petrol is much cheaper in the USA than in the UK.

This means that the USA is not in control of the amount of oil available or its price, which can lead to problems like the energy crisis of the 1970s.

During that time, foreign sources of oil refused to trade with the USA for political reasons and petrol was rationed. People with odd and even numbered license plates could buy petrol only on certain days. Americans became aware of how much they relied on foreign sources of oil. Since then, their dependence on foreign oil has increased, not decreased.

Questions

1 After 1973, oil companies were keen to extract oil from countries not in the Middle East, for example Nigeria and Venezuela. Suggest a reason for this.

2 Why did the crude oil price rise in 1973 affect Western Europe and Japan?

3 The price of crude oil does not just affect the price of fuel for cars and lorries. Suggest what other aspects of life are affected.

4 Petrol prices are much lower in the US than the UK. One reason is the large quantity of oil imported into the UK. Suggest one other reason why petrol prices are much higher in the UK.

Getting in line

In this item you will find out

- how to make polymers

- about alkanes and alkenes

- how to test for alkenes

Take a look around you. You should be able to see lots of objects that are made from polymers or plastics and you will be able to think of many others.

This photograph shows the inside of a modern car. Many of the things you can see are made of plastic. But how are polymers made?

Look at the single paper clips in the diagram. They are single units. Then look at the chain of paper clips. You can see it is made up of many paper clips joined together.

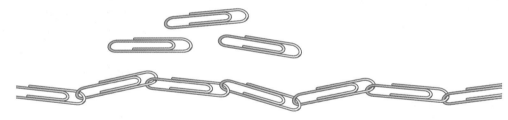

Amazing fact

The first plastic, casein, was discovered by accident when a cat knocked a bottle of formaldehyde over cheese and it set rock hard.

In the same way, polymer molecules are long chain molecules. In each chain there is a basic unit which repeats itself thousands of times.

The basic unit in a polymer is called a **monomer**. Many monomer molecules added together make up the polymer.

Poly(ethene) is the polymer made when lots of ethene monomer molecules are joined together. The picture on the right shows a poly(ethene) chain. You will notice that there are also some branches on the chain.

a Another polymer is poly(propene). What is the monomer for making poly(propene)?

b Styrene is a monomer. What is the polymer made from styrene?

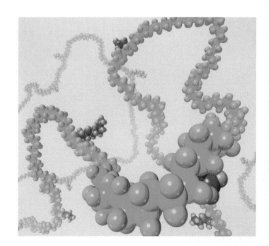

A poly(ethene) chain ▶

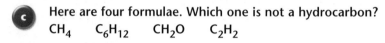

Hydrocarbons

Hydrocarbons are compounds which are made up of carbon atoms and hydrogen atoms only.

c Here are four formulae. Which one is not a hydrocarbon?
CH_4 C_6H_{12} CH_2O C_2H_2

Alkanes are one family of hydrocarbons. The simplest alkanes are methane, ethane and propane.

d What do the names of the alkanes have in common?

The diagram shows the displayed and molecular formula of the first three alkanes.

CH_4
(methane)

C_2H_6
(ethane)

C_3H_8
(propane)

All alkanes contain only single covalent bonds between their carbon atoms. Compounds that contain only single carbon-carbon bonds are called **saturated** compounds. All alkanes fit a formula C_nH_{2n+2}

Between two carbon atoms in an alkane there is a covalent bond. This is made from two electrons, one from each carbon atom. Similar covalent bonds are between carbon and hydrogen atoms. The hydrogen atoms and carbon atoms share an electron pair to form the covalent bond.

e Octane is a compound in petrol. It contains eight carbon atoms. What is the molecular formula of octane?

Alkenes are another family of hydrocarbons. The first three alkenes are ethene, propene and butene.

f What do the names of the alkenes have in common?

The diagram shows the displayed formula and the molecular formula of ethene and propene.

C_2H_4
(ethene)

C_3H_6
(propene)

All alkenes contain one or more double covalent bonds between their carbon atoms. Compounds that contain double covalent bonds are called **unsaturated** compounds.

g Butene has a molecular formula C_4H_8. What is the formula of an alkene containing *n* carbon atoms?

Testing for unsaturation

You can test whether a hydrocarbon is a saturated or an unsaturated compound. Unsaturated compounds undergo reactions that involve the breaking of one of the bonds in the carbon-carbon double bond. This is called an addition reaction, as two reactants produce a single product.

If ethene is bubbled through bromine water (a solution of bromine in water) a reaction takes place. No reaction takes place if ethane is bubbled through bromine water.

Look at the photograph on the right.

h **Describe the change you see when ethene reacts with bromine.**

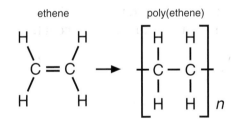

▲ *The reaction between ethene and bromine*

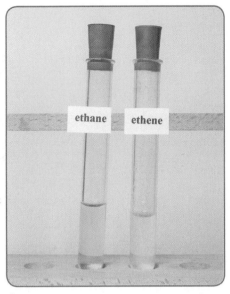

▲ *Testing for unsaturation*

Polymerisation

Addition polymerisation involves joining monomer molecules together by a series of addition reactions. Each monomer molecule is unsaturated, but the polymer is saturated. Addition polymerisation usually requires a high temperature and a suitable catalyst. The diagram summarises the process of polymerisation of ethene.

▲ *The polymerisation of ethene*

keywords

addition polymerisation
• alkane • alkene •
monomer • saturated •
unsaturated

The diagram shows ethene on the left hand side of the equation and poly(ethene) on the right. Ethene contains a double bond between the two carbon atoms and poly(ethene) contains only a single bond. Poly(ethene) does contain bonds joining the different molecules together. The letter n outside the bracket shows that a large number of ethane molecules are joined together.

Chloroethene is another unsaturated monomer that can be made into a polymer. The diagram below shows the displayed formula for chloroethene.

Examiner's tip

Don't forget the double bond in the monomer is lost when the polymer is formed.

i **Draw the displayed formula of the polymer poly(chloroethene).**

Making poly(ethene)

Poly(ethene) was first made by accident. In 1933, two chemists, Eric Fawcett and Reginald Gibson, were heating ethene gas at a very high pressure in a steel container. They did not know that some air had leaked into the apparatus. The pressure inside the apparatus kept dropping. They kept adding more ethene. When they finally opened the apparatus, they found a white waxy solid in the bottom of the apparatus.

They realised that the ethene molecules had joined together. They repeated the experiment many times over several years. They thought that oxygen was a catalyst for the joining of ethene molecules.

The poly(ethene) that they produced softened when heated and hardened again on cooling. During the Second World War, it was used as insulators for radar – which were being installed in aeroplanes. It was important that the material used was a good electrical insulator, but it also had to have a low density to reduce the weight of the plane. Without poly(ethene), the insulators would have had to be made from pottery.

Poly(ethene) was not widely available until 1950 and then it was used for making washing up bowls. Its low softening and melting temperature, however, did not make it very successful.

Chemists tried making poly(ethene) under different conditions. These samples had more desirable properties. Special metal compounds were used as catalysts. These provided a surface where the molecules could join. The resulting polymer was stronger and denser. The chains here were more regularly arranged.

Questions

1 What is the monomer used to make poly(ethene)?

2 Ethene molecules join to form poly(ethene) very slowly. Which substance in the air speeds up this process?

3 Suggest why poly(ethene) would be a better insulator for radar in aircraft than pottery.

4 Before poly(ethene), washing up bowls were usually made of painted steel. Suggest the advantages of a polymer over painted steel.

Plastics aplenty

In this item you will find out

- uses and properties of some polymers

- how the structure of a polymer relates to its properties

- problems with the disposal of polymers

Polymers are everywhere. It is now difficult to imagine life without polymers. Some of the items in the picture below are made from single polymers. Other objects are made from two or more monomers polymerised together. For example, a common form of nylon is made from two monomers polymerised together.

a Why is: (i) polystyrene used for making cups (ii) nylon used for making ropes (iii) PVC used for making wellington boots?

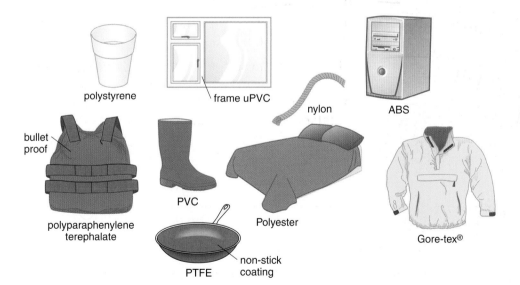

polystyrene

frame uPVC

nylon

ABS

bullet proof

PVC

polyparaphenylene terephalate

Polyester

PTFE — non-stick coating

Gore-tex®

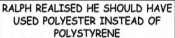

RALPH REALISED HE SHOULD HAVE USED POLYESTER INSTEAD OF POLYSTYRENE

b The computer case is made of ABS (acrylonitrile-butadiene-styrene).
(i) What three monomers are polymerised together to make ABS?
(ii) Suggest what properties ABS needs to be suitable for this use.

There is a coating of the polymer PTFE (polytetrafluoroethene) on the frying pan. It has a very slippery surface that things will not stick to.

c There are three elements in PTFE. Carbon and hydrogen are two of them. Which is the third element?

Structure of polymers

The diagram on the left shows the particles in a sample of poly(ethene).

The bonds holding the atoms together within a chain are strong covalent bonds. The intermolecular forces between the chains are weak.

Polymers that have weak **intermolecular** forces between the polymer molecules have low melting points, as little energy is needed to break the forces between the chains. They will also stretch easily because the chains can slide over each other.

This diagram shows a polymer with links between the polymer chains. This is called **cross-linking**.

The links between chains can be covalent bonds. Cross-linking changes the properties of these polymers. The chains cannot be separated by heating to a low temperature and the chains cannot slide over each other. These polymers have high melting points, are rigid and do not stretch.

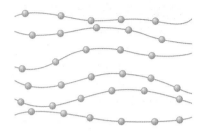

▲ *Particles in poly(ethene)*

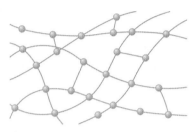

▲ *This polymer has links between the polymer chains*

Nylon and Gore-Tex®

The anorak on page 95 is made of Gore-Tex®. Before Gore-Tex® was invented, nylon would have been used for making anoraks. Nylon is tough, lightweight and keeps water and ultraviolet light out. However, it does not let water vapour out and so sweat condenses inside the anorak.

Gore-Tex® has all the positive properties of nylon but it is also breathable. Gore-Tex® is comfortable even when you get hot exercising. Any sweat is lost as water vapour through the fabric – you do not get wet even if it rains. Gore-Tex® is great for people who do outdoor activities such as cycling or mountain climbing.

Gore-Tex® is made from nylon laminated with a PTFE membrane. The holes in the PTFE are too small for water to get in, but are large enough for water vapour to pass out. The PTFE membrane is too fragile to use on its own, so it is bonded to the nylon to strengthen it.

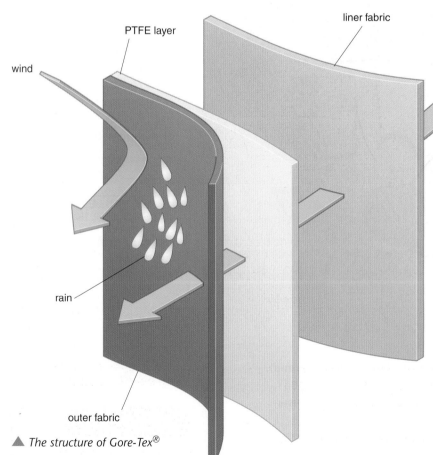

▲ *The structure of Gore-Tex®*

Disposal of polymers

Polymers are widely used but there are problems. Most polymers do not decay or decompose. These polymers are called non-biodegradable. This means they can remain in landfill sites for hundreds of years. Landfill sites are filling up and it is difficult to find new ones.

Stricter and stricter legislation is being put in place to restrict the quantity of waste and the type of waste that can be put into landfill sites. Local councils are required to achieve a reduction in waste going to landfill of 25% by 2010, 50% by 2013 and 65% by 2020. This will only be achieved if more household waste, including polymers, is recycled.

Some people suggest that one solution might be to burn them, but when polymers are burned they produce toxic gases, such as dioxin. The problem could be resolved if more polymers were **recycled**. This is difficult to do because there are so many different types. Mixed polymer waste is not very useful. It can only be made into low value products, for example, insulation blocks. Sorting polymers by hand is an expensive process. The chemical industry is helping the sorting process by stamping marks on items showing what type of polymer they are made from.

The stamped label on the right indicates that the container is made from HDPE (high density poly(ethene)). If all polymer products had similar labels they could be sorted by a person picking out the different types of polymer.

▲ The stamp on this container means it can be recycled

d Polymers are routinely separated by hand and recycled in India but not often in the UK. Suggest why.

The future is to produce polymers that rot away quickly. Many of these are made from starch and are **biodegradable**.

keywords

biodegradable • cross-linking • intermolecular • recycled

Plastic Problem in Kenya

A report published today suggested that flimsy plastic shopping bags should be banned. Also there should be a tax on thicker plastic bags. This is to remove an increasing environmental and health problem in Kenya.

People shopping at supermarkets and shops in Nairobi alone use at least two million plastic bags each year.

The bags, many of which are so thin they are simply thrown away after one trip from the shops, have become a familiar eyesore in both urban and countryside areas. Plastic bags also block gutters and drains, choke animals and pollute the soil as they only very slowly break down.

The bags, when thrown away, can fill with rainwater. This makes a breeding ground for the malaria-carrying mosquitoes.

An estimated 4000 tonnes of the thin plastic bags are produced each month in Kenya. About three-quarters of them are less than 30 micrometres thick. Some are as thin as seven micrometres.

A ban on bags less than 30 micrometres thick and the tax on thicker ones are among proposals aimed at reducing the use of polythene bags and providing funds for alternative, more environmentally friendly, carriers such as cotton bags.

These plans have been based on lessons learned from other countries in the world. In 2002, Ireland imposed a tax on plastic bags provided by stores and shops. It is estimated that this has reduced the use of plastic bags by 90%. In 2003, South Africa banned plastic bags thinner than 30 micrometres and introduced a plastics tax. It has seen a decrease in bag litter and a reduction in the manufacture of plastic bags.

Nairobi, 23 February 2005

Questions

1 Bags cause a litter problem when they are thrown away. Write down three other problems caused by these bags when they are thrown away.

2 Which countries already have already taken action against the use of thin plastic bags?

3 Kenya has no deposits of crude oil and has to buy all plastics abroad. Suggest reasons why cotton bags are better than plastic ones.

4 How many tonnes of plastic bags produced in Kenya each month of 30 micrometres or more can still be made?

5 Some supermarkets are experimenting with plastic bags made from a starch-based polymer. Suggest why this might be an alternative to a tax or a ban on plastic bags.

Up in flames

▼ *This steam engine runs on coal*

In this item you will find out

- what factors are considered when a fuel is chosen

- about the products from the combustion of carbon and carbon fuels

- about complete and incomplete combustion

Fossil fuels, such as coal, oil and gas, are used to provide most of our energy needs. Fuels are substances that react with oxygen to produce useful energy.

The three photographs show coal, oil and gas being used to power three different means of transport.

a Look at the photographs. Suggest one advantage of burning gas in the bus, rather than coal in the steam engine and diesel in the lorry.

With a choice of carbon-based fuels it is important to choose the one with the most suitable properties. We all have to make these choices in our lives. What fuel should we use to heat our houses? Should we use cars powered with petrol, diesel or LPG?

Large companies also have to make these decisions about the types of fuel that they use to produce electricity.

▲ *This lorry uses diesel as its fuel*

Humans are burning increasing amounts of fossil fuels. There are more and more cars on the roads and some large cars use a lot of petrol or diesel.

We are also transporting more goods to more places. Fresh fruit and vegetables are routinely flown all over the world and this form of transport also uses fuel.

▲ *Buses can run on LPG gas*

Choosing the best fuel

When choosing the best fuel, there are seven things that need to be considered. You can remember them if you remember the word TEACUPS:

T **toxicity** – how poisonous the fuel is
E energy value – how much energy the fuel gives out
A availability – how easy the fuel is to get hold of
C cost – how expensive the fuel is
U usability – how easy the fuel is to use
P **pollution** – how much pollution is created by the fuel
S storage – how easy the fuel is to store.

The table gives some data on three fossil fuels.

Fuel	Relative cost	Energy value	Availability	Storage	Toxity	Pollution	Ease of use
coal	cheap	medium	available	easy to store	non-toxic	smoky	difficult to catch alight
oil	expensive	high	widely available	has to be stored in a tank	leaking gas can be poisonous	little pollution	easy to burn
gas from gas main	moderate	high	only in places where there is a gas main	supply directly to house	gas non-toxic; leaks can cause explosion	little pollution	easy to burn

b Emma lives in a house in an area of a town where there is a smokeless zone. There is a gas main. Which fuel would you recommend?

c Her friend Jo lives in a block of flats. Jo is not allowed to use mains gas or bottled gas. Suggest why this is.

Burning fuels

Burning or **combustion** of all fuels needs oxygen. The combustion releases heat energy, which is very useful. When you burn a hydrocarbon fuel with lots of oxygen (air) you get carbon dioxide and water. This is called **complete combustion**.

The diagram on the opposite page shows an experiment to test what products are produced when you burn methane with lots of oxygen.

The pump sucks air through the apparatus. As the methane burns, a colourless liquid condenses and collects in the first test tube. This liquid boils at 100 °C so it is water. In the second test tube a gas is bubbled through limewater. The limewater turns cloudy, so the gas is carbon dioxide. This can be shown by the following word equation:

methane + oxygen → carbon dioxide + water

d Methane has the formula CH_4. Write the balanced symbol equation for the complete combustion of methane.

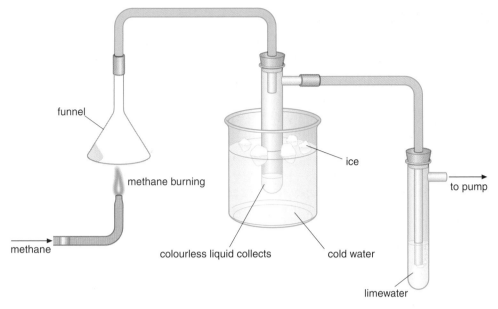

funnel

methane burning

ice

to pump

methane

colourless liquid collects

cold water

limewater

Burning methane in oxygen

The equation for the complete combustion of ethane is shown below:

$$2C_2H_6 + 7O_2 \rightarrow 4CO_2 + 6H_2O$$

 e How many molecules of oxygen are needed to burn 1 molecule of ethane completely?

Not enough oxygen

If a fuel is burned without enough oxygen then **incomplete combustion** takes place and **carbon monoxide** is produced. This is a poisonous gas. Carbon (soot) is also produced. The incomplete combustion of methane can be shown by the following word equation:

methane + oxygen → carbon monoxide + carbon + water.

f Write the balanced symbol equation for the incomplete combustion of ethane, C_2H_6.

It is better for hydrocarbon fuels to burn with complete combustion than incomplete combustion because:
• less soot is produced
• more heat is produced
• carbon monoxide is not produced.

Bunsen flames

The photographs on the right show two Bunsen burner flames. The top is the blue flame and the bottom one is the yellow flame.

When we want to heat something to a high temperature we use the blue flame. The blue flame gives out more energy than the yellow flame. This is because it involves complete combustion.

The blue flame is also a cleaner flame because it produces less soot than the yellow flame which produces lots of soot because it involves incomplete combustion.

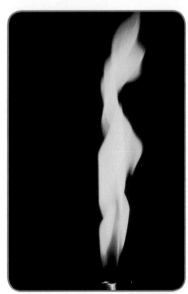

Death by carbon monoxide

Girl Dies of Carbon Monoxide Poisoning

A girl, aged nineteen, was found dead yesterday in her flat. It is believed she died of carbon monoxide poisoning. Scientists have taken away a gas fire for examination.

Every year in the UK, 50 people die of carbon monoxide poisoning. Carbon monoxide is a poisonous gas. It forms when incomplete combustion of a fuel takes place. Carbon monoxide is colourless and has no smell or taste. People die without realising they are breathing in carbon monoxide. You can now buy carbon monoxide detectors in DIY stores, but few people have them.

Carbon monoxide forms a compound called carboxyhaemoglobin with the red cells in the blood. This prevents oxygen circulating the body in the blood.

▲ A car having its MOT test

The equation shows the incomplete combustion of methane.

$$4CH_4 + 5O_2 \rightarrow 2CO + 2C + 8H_2O$$

methane + oxygen
→ carbon monoxide + carbon + water

Carbon monoxide usually forms when there is not enough ventilation for the fuel to burn completely. Servicing gas boilers and fires each year removes soot and ensures enough air can enter. This should prevent carbon monoxide from forming.

Car engines produce carbon monoxide. There are limits to how much carbon monoxide a car can give out. This is measured as part of the MOT test. Cars exceeding the limit fail the test.

Questions

1 Why is carbon monoxide such a dangerous gas?

2 Suggest ways in which the chances of carbon monoxide poisoning happening in a house can be minimised.

3 How many molecules of oxygen are needed for the incomplete combustion of one molecule of methane?

4 In long road tunnels there is sometimes a sign warning drivers to switch off their engines if they are stationary. Why?

5 Suggest one other reason why regular servicing of gas boilers should be done, apart from avoiding poisoning.

Feeling energetic

In this item you will find out

- about exothermic and endothermic reactions

- how reactions can be understood in terms of bond making and bond breaking

- how to calculate the energy output of a fuel

Fuels are materials that can release energy. Usually this is done by burning the fuel in air or oxygen.

In this forest fire, the trees are the fuel. This fire produces a huge amount of energy.

Different fuels produce different amounts of energy.

The table gives the energy released when equivalent quantities of different fuels are burned.

Fuel additive	Hexane	Methane	Methanol	Carbon	Hydrogen
State of fuel at room temperature	liquid	gas	liquid	solid	gas
Energy released (kJ)	4163	890	726	393	286

a Which liquid fuel in the table releases most energy?

b Suggest one advantage of burning methane to produce electricity rather than coal (carbon).

An **exothermic** reaction is a chemical reaction giving out energy. All of the materials in the table undergo exothermic reactions when they burn. Energy is transferred to the surroundings.

c Can you think of other exothermic reactions?

An **endothermic** reaction is a chemical reaction taking in energy from the surroundings.

Amazing fact

There are very few endothermic reactions and very many exothermic ones. At one time, people thought that endothermic reactions were impossible.

Recognising reactions

Sam carries out an experiment. He reacts water with solid calcium oxide to produce calcium hydroxide. He puts a thermometer into some water in a test tube. Then he adds a few small pieces of calcium oxide to the water. When he shakes the test tube, the temperature rises. This is an exothermic reaction because energy is given out to heat up the water. An endothermic reaction would produce a decrease in temperature.

cover

ethanol

spirit lamp

top pan balance

Comparing energy changes in combustion reactions

Combustion reactions are reactions where a fuel burns in oxygen to release energy.

Alcohols, such as methanol and ethanol, burn easily in small spirit burners.

The equation for the complete combustion of ethanol is:

$$C_2H_5OH + 3O_2 \rightarrow 2CO_2 + 3H_2O$$

The diagram on the left shows a small spirit lamp containing ethanol being weighed before the experiment.

d Why is the spirit lamp covered?

The lit spirit lamp is placed under a metal can called a **calorimeter** filled with 100 g of water. The temperature of the water is measured.

Look at the apparatus in the diagram below.

As the ethanol burns, heat energy is transferred to the water.

e What happens to the temperature of the water as the ethanol burns?

At the end of the experiment, the flame is extinguished and the spirit lamp is reweighed.

The temperature of the water at the end of the experiment is recorded.

Sample results:
   Temperature of the water
   at the start = 20 °C
   Temperature of the water
   at the end = 32 °C
   Mass of spirit lamp
   at the start = 105.57 g
   Mass of spirit lamp
   at the end = 103.47 g

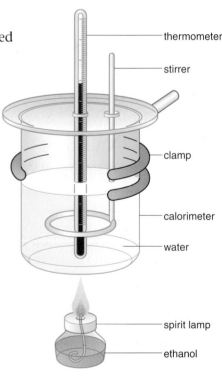

thermometer

stirrer

clamp

calorimeter

water

spirit lamp

ethanol

▲ Set up for calorimetry experiment

f What is the temperature change?

g What mass of ethanol has burned?

The amount of heat energy taken in by the water in the can is calculated by the equation:

Energy = mass (in g) × specific heat capacity of water × temperature rise (in °C)

The specific heat capacity of water is 4.2 J/g/°C.

The answer is given in joules (J). This can be converted into kilojoules (kJ) by dividing by 1000.

h Show that the energy taken in by the water in the calorimeter is ~~50.4 kJ~~. *5.04 kJ*

Energy transfer

We assume that all the energy produced when the ethanol burns goes to heat up the water in the can.

A useful comparison of the energy value of fuels, is the energy given out per gram. The equation is:

$$\text{energy per gram (in J/g)} = \frac{\text{energy supplied (in J)}}{\text{mass of fuel burned (in g)}}$$

i Calculate the energy given out by burning 1 g of ethanol.

The value from this experiment is compared with the value in a data book. The value in the data book is much higher.

j Suggest reasons why the values are different.

By convention, the energy change in an exothermic reaction is given a negative sign.

The energy per gram value in the data book is –29.7 kJ/g or –29 700 J/g.

Bond breaking and bond making.

The complete combustion of ethanol can be shown using displayed formulas:

Each of the bonds is a covalent bond. During the reaction, some bonds have to be broken and some new bonds have to be formed. Breaking a bond requires energy: the process is endothermic. Forming new bonds gives out energy: the process is exothermic.

In this reaction:

5 C—H bonds, 1 C—C bond, 1 C—O bonds, 1 O—H bond and 3 O=O bonds are broken.

4 C=O bonds and 6 O—H bonds are formed.

More energy is given out when the new bonds are formed, than when the old bonds are broken. Therefore, the reaction is exothermic.

Coffee on the run

Steve and Leah enjoy hill walking. Usually when they get thirsty, they stop for a cup of coffee which they bring with them in a flask. The flask is quite heavy so it is a nuisance to carry around sometimes.

Steve is reading a walking magazine one day when he notices an advert for a new coffee product which has just been introduced. The next time he meets Leah he tells her about it.

'This new product is ideal for people who go out for the day into the countryside but like a cup of hot coffee.

All you have to do to get hot coffee is to press the plastic button at the bottom of the can. This starts a chemical reaction inside the can. The reaction is exothermic and the energy from this reaction heats the coffee in the can.

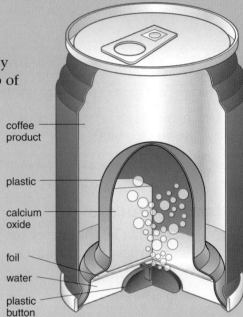

▲ *Inside the self-heating can*

The chemical reaction that heats the coffee takes place between calcium oxide and water. They are stored separately at the bottom of the can. When the plastic button is pressed, water escapes and comes into contact with the calcium oxide.

Look, here is a diagram of it. The energy released by this reaction heats up the coffee.'

Questions

1 Suggest another way of getting a hot cup of coffee if this kind of product was not available.

2 Why is it important that the calcium oxide and water are stored separately?

3 Why is it important that the coffee does not come into contact with the chemicals?

4 The equation for the reaction is: $CaO + H_2O \rightarrow Ca(OH)_2$
What is the name of the product of the reaction?

5 How many atoms are there in the formula of the product?

6 The same product is formed when calcium reacts with water. Hydrogen, H_2, is also produced. Write a balanced symbol equation for the reaction of calcium and water.

7 The reaction of calcium and water is also exothermic. Suggest why this reaction would be unsuitable for heating the coffee can.

8 In trials of the self-heating can, the coffee either did not get hot enough or got too hot. What could be changed to improve this?

C1a

1 Describe the chemical test for carbon dioxide? [2]

2 **a** Finish the word equation for the decomposition of sodium hydrogencarbonate.

sodium hydrogencarbonate → __(1)__ + __(2)__ + __(3)__ [3]

b Sodium hydrogencarbonate is heated in test tube. Does its mass increase, decrease or stay the same? Explain why. [2]

3 The formula of sodium hydrogencarbonate is $NaHCO_3$. There are four elements combined. How many atoms of each element are in the formula? [2]

4 Finish the symbol equation for the decomposition of sodium hydrogencarbonate.

$NaHCO_3$ → [4]

5 Ammonium hydrogencarbonate, NH_4HCO_3, is used as a raising agent in biscuits. On heating it decomposes to give ammonia gas (NH_3), water and carbon dioxide.

a Write a symbol equation for the decomposition of ammonium hydrogencarbonate. [4]

b Suggest a benefit of using ammonium hydrogencarbonate rather than sodium hydrogencarbonate. [2]

6 Describe and explain the changes that take place when a potato is boiled. [2]

C1b

1 What are the special features of an emulsifier molecule? [2]

2 Foods contain antioxidants.

a What does an antioxidant do in a food? [1]
b Give two foods that contain antioxidants. [2]

3 Explain why removal of water from food slows down the spoiling of food. [2]

4 Describe how an emulsifier helps to prevent oil and water separating in an emulsion. [3]

C1c

1 Ethanoic acid, CH_3CO_2H, and propanol, $CH_3CH_2CH_2OH$, react together to form an ester.

a What conditions are needed to form the ester? [2]
b What is the name of the ester? [1]
c Draw the displayed formula of this ester. [2]

2 Explain why water is not a solvent for nail varnish. Use ideas about particles in your answer. [3]

C1d

1 Arrange the four fractions in order of increasing boiling point.

fuel oil   heating oil   paraffin   petrol [3]

2 The table contains the boiling temperature range for four fractions from the fractional distillation column.

Fraction	Boiling temperature range in °C
A	70–120
B	120–170
C	170–220
D	220–270

a Which fraction contains the largest molecules? [1]
b Which fraction comes out at the highest point in the column? [1]

3 A hydrocarbon has a formula $C_{12}H_{26}$. Cracking breaks this hydrocarbon into small saturated and unsaturated products.

a Write a symbol equation for the two products each containing two carbon atoms. [3]
b Write down the names of these products. [2]

C1e

1 The linking of small ethene molecules together to form long chains is called ____. [1]

2 The displayed formula for propene is shown below.

Copy the diagram and draw a ring around the feature of the molecule that is typical of all alkenes. [1]

3 The equation for the reaction of propene and hydrogen is:

$$C_3H_6 + H_2 \rightarrow C_3H_8$$

  a Draw the displayed formula and name the
      product.   [2]
  b What type of reaction is this?   [1]

4 The diagram shows part of a polymer chain.

$$\left[\begin{array}{cc} CH_3 & H \\ | & | \\ -C & - C- \\ | & | \\ H & CH_3 \end{array}\right]_n$$

  a Why is this polymer an addition polymer?   [1]
  b Draw the displayed formula of monomer.   [1]

5 The displayed formula of tetrafluoroethene is:

$$\begin{array}{ccc} F & & F \\ \diagdown & & \diagup \\ & C = C & \\ \diagup & & \diagdown \\ F & & F \end{array}$$

Draw the displayed formula of the polymer
poly(tetrafluoroethene).   [2]

6 Describe how you could show that an alkene
is unsaturated.   [2]

C1f

1 Most polymers are not biodegradable. Suggest
two disadvantages of dumping polymer waste in
landfill sites.   [2]

2 The table gives information about three materials.

Material	Absorbs water	Sweat absorbed	Breathable
cotton	yes	absorbed	no
nylon	no	not absorbed	no
Gore-Tex®	no	escapes through material	yes

Which material is best for making an anorak for a
mountain climber? Explain your choice.   [2]

3 Explain why Gore-Tex® lets perspiration out but does not
let water in.   [2]

4 The diagrams show parts of two polymer chains.

$$-M-M-M-M-M-$$

$$\begin{array}{ccc} -M-M-M-M-M- \\ | & & | \\ X & & X \\ | & & | \\ -M-M-M-M-M- \end{array}$$

         A   B

  a The force holding two M units together in A
      is a ____ bond   [1]
  b The force between two chains in A is an
      ____ force.   [1]
  c The polymer B has ____ between chains.   [1]
  d Why does polymer A have a low melting
      point and can it be easily be stretched?   [1]
  e What are the characteristic properties of
      polymer B?   [2]

C1g

1 Landlords renting flats to students must have a
certificate each year to show that all gas appliances
have been serviced. Why is this?   [2]

2 A power station in East Anglia is using straw as a fuel
to produce electricity. The straw is left over when wheat
is grown. Suggest an advantage and a disadvantage of
using straw as a fuel.   [2]

3 Write word equations for complete and incomplete
combustion of propane.   [4]

4 Explain why every year the consumption of fossil fuels in
the world rises.   [2]

5 Write balanced symbol equations for:

  a the complete combustion of propane, C_3H_8 [2]
  b the incomplete combustion of propane ,C_3H_8 [2]

C1h

1 In an experiment to burn a small sample of fuel
weighing 0.1 g, the energy given out is 20 000 J.

How much energy would be given out if 1 g of same fuel
is burned?

A 2000 kJ
B 20 000 J
C 200 000 J
D 2 000 000 J   [1]

2 The word equation for the process of photosynthesis is shown below.

carbon dioxide + water + energy → glucose + oxygen

a Is this reaction endothermic or exothermic? Explain your answer. [2]
b Finish the word equation for respiration producing carbon dioxide and water. Include '+ energy' in your equation. [2]

3 The graph shows the energy produced when 1 formula mass of different alcohols is burned. These values are taken from a textbook.

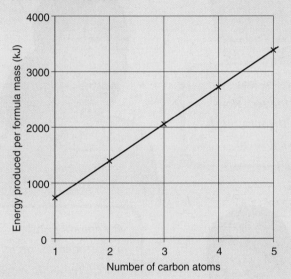

a What pattern is there in the results? [1]
b Copy the graph and sketch the line you would expect from experimental results. [1]
c The diagram shows apparatus that gives better results.

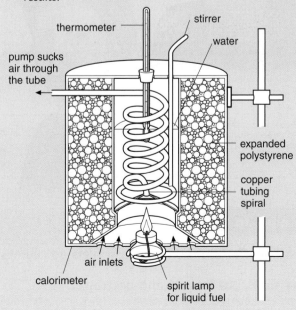

Explain why the results using this apparatus are better. [2]

4 The table gives theoretical values for the energy produced when 1 formula mass of different alcohols is burned.

Alcohol	Formula	Formula mass	Energy produced (kJ)
methanol	CH_4O	32	−726
ethanol	C_2H_6O	46	−1367
propanol	C_3H_8O	60	−2021
butanol	$C_4H_{10}O$		−2675
pentanol		88	−3329

a What are the two items missing from the table? [2]
b What is the trend in the amount of energy produced **per gram** when these alcohols burn? [2]

5 The diagram summarises the bonding changes that take place when hydrogen and chlorine react to form hydrogen chloride.

H — H   Cl — Cl   →   H — Cl   H — Cl

Explain why the reaction is exothermic. Use ideas of bond breaking and bond forming in your answer. [3]

6 In an experiment to find the energy given out when 0.25 g of X burns, the following results are obtained:

Mass of water = 100 g
Specific heat capacity of water = 4.2 J/g/°C
Temperature changes from 22 to 28 °C.

a Calculate the heat energy received by the water. [3]
b Calculate the energy given out per gram. [1]

7 Complete combustion of 32 g of methanol produces 726 kJ of energy.

a Calculate the energy produced per gram when methanol burns completely. (Look back to question 4.) [2]
b Why is it better to compare the energy released when one formula mass of each alcohol is burned, rather than the energy released when 1 g of each alcohol is burned? [1]
c Write a balanced symbol equation for the complete combustion of methanol. [3]
d Describe which bonds, and how many, are broken. Which bonds are formed when methanol burns completely? [1]

All too regularly we hear of natural disasters such as earthquakes, tsunamis and hurricanes.

Can we accurately predict where the next disaster will happen so we can take some precautions? The answer is probably no, because we do not really know enough about the structure of the Earth.

Japan suffers from earthquakes as it is at the junction of three of the large plates that make up the outer crust of the Earth. The Japanese are drilling deep into the Earth – three times deeper than anyone before, in order to find out more.

This research, and other research taking place around the world, may help us to predict natural disasters in the future.

Drivers now have to pay £8 to drive their cars into London each day. Is this to reduce atmospheric pollution in London?

A steel bridge has legs dipping into the sea. How do they stop them rusting? They can't paint them.

Are natural disasters, such as earthquakes, occurring more often or do we just hear more in the media?

What you need to know

- The possible effects of burning fossil fuels on the environment.

- The way rocks are formed and destroyed.

- Air is a mixture of gases.

Colour the world

In this item you will find out

- about different types of pigments and paint
- about dyes for fabrics

Do you like to wear colourful clothes? People wear much more colourful and brighter clothes today than they did two hundred years ago.

The dyes available to colour fabrics a couple of hundred years ago were very limited. The only dyes were natural dyes from plants and animal materials. For example, fabric was dyed yellow by boiling with water containing onion skins. These natural dyes were dull compared to modern synthetic dyes and tended to wash out of clothes.

Synthetic dyes were discovered about 130 years ago. This discovery revolutionised the dyeing industry. Clothes could now be produced which were colourfast and had a wide variety of bright colours.

The first synthetic dye was made by William Perkin. It is called mauvine and is a rich purple colour. It was made from coal tar.

Today almost all dyes used in industry are synthetic dyes.

 Apart from clothes, what are dyes used for today?

Amazing fact

It is hard to believe that the source of many brightly coloured dyes is black coal tar.

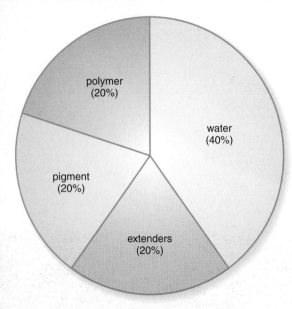

▲ *Composition of water-based paint*

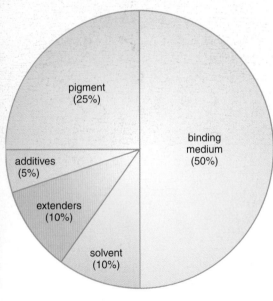

▲ *Composition of oil-based paint*

Paint particles

All paints contain particles of coloured pigments. They also contain a solvent and a binding medium. The solvent thins the paint while the binding medium hardens as it reacts with oxygen to form a layer of paint.

Paint is a mixture called a **colloid**. This is where solid particles are mixed with liquid particles but are not dissolved. The pigment particles and binding medium particles are dispersed throughout the liquid solvent particles. The different component particles of the paint do not separate out because they are scattered throughout the mixture. The particles are also small enough so that they do not settle at the bottom.

Water or oil?

Most paints are applied as a thin surface which dries when the solvent evaporates. Different paints have different solvents.

Emulsion paints are water-based paints. They consist of tiny drops of a liquid polymer (the binding medium) spread out in water (the solvent). After the paint is applied, the water in the paint evaporates and the polymer particles fuse together to form a continuous film.

 How would you clean paint brushes used for emulsion paint?

Oil paints use hydrocarbon oil as the solvent and consist of pigments spread throughout the oil. They often contain an extra solvent that dissolves the oil to form a solution. After the paint is applied, the solvent evaporates and the binding medium reacts with oxygen from the air (oxidises) to form a paint film.

Gloss paints used to be made from a hardening oil such as linseed oil. These harden to form a thin layer by reaction with oxygen. Linseed oil is still used to treat cricket bats. This hardening, however, is very slow taking several days. We like paints to dry to a hard film quickly. A drying time of a couple of hours is preferable.

Brushes used with linseed oil paints are more difficult to clean.

Modern gloss paints used an alkyd resin binding medium. The alkyd resin is a polymer formed by reacting a vegetable oil, such as linseed oil, with an alcohol and an organic acid. Brushes used for modern oil paints are easier to clean providing the paint is not allowed to dry.

 Suggest why gloss paint should be used in a well-ventilated room?

 Suggest why is it better to have several thin coats of paint rather than one thick coat.

Special paints

There are now special paints available. Some paints contain special pigments whose colour changes as the temperature changes. These pigments are called **thermochromic pigments** and the paints are called thermochromic paints. The paints could be used to coat a cup, for example. The colour of the cup will change when hot liquid is put into it.

e Why would a cup that changes colour be an advantage?

Thermochromic paints could also be used on the outside of a kettle. The paint would change colour when the water inside the kettle was hot.

f Why would this be a safety feature of the kettle?

Thermochromic paints can also be added to acrylic paints to give even more colour changes.

There are other paints that glow in the dark. They contain **phosphorescent pigments**. These pigments absorb and store light energy and then release it as light over several hours. This means you can see the pigments in the dark.

Beer is best drunk cold. A new brand of beer is sold in special cans. The cans are labelled by printing using an ink containing a thermochromic pigment. At ordinary temperatures the labelling is red, but if the can is cooled to the correct drinking temperature the printing goes blue. A blue can is ready for drinking.

Before phosphorescent pigments were used for such purposes, radioactive materials used to be used on watch faces. If a Geiger counter was passed over the face of one of these watches there would be a rapid clicking sound showing radiation was being detected. The amounts of radiation were small but significant.

Modern paint technologists are striving to produce new paints for specific purposes.

You can buy paints with special finishes e.g. a paint with a suede finish or paints for special surfaces e.g. for bathroom tiles or for hot surfaces. Paint technologists have to modify the composition of paints and test them thoroughly before they can be sold.

g Why would these paints be useful for seeing road signs at night on country roads?

h Suggest why phosphorescent paints are safer than paints containing radioactive substances which also glow in the dark.

i Why would phosphorescent paint be unsuitable for a sign warning people inside a dark underground cavern about a possible danger?

Keywords

colloid • phosphorescent pigment • thermochromic pigment

Eco-friendly paint

Shari and Ahmed are decorating a nursery for their baby which is due in March. Shari wants to paint the room in bright colours. They pay a visit to a local DIY store to look at paint. They pick up some tins of gloss paint from a well-known brand.

'I'm worried about what's in these paints,' says Shari, 'Babies are more likely to be poisoned by the chemicals in paint than adults.'

They pick up a leaflet which explains what is in the gloss paint.

'I think this contains too many chemicals,' says Shari.

She asks for help in the store and the assistant explains that when the paints have dried the resulting paint film is tough and hard.

A couple of days later, Shari sees a website on the Internet which is advertising eco-friendly gloss paints. They contain natural ingredients such as plant oil, earth pigments and wood resin. Shari notices that the range of colours is smaller than for normal gloss paints and they are less bright. The eco-friendly paints are biodegradable. This means they will rot down when they are disposed of.

GLOSS PAINT

Hydrocarbon solvent
Acrylic pigment
Alkyd resin binder
Extenders
Additives to speed up drying

▲ Normal gloss paint

GLOSS PAINT

Plant oil
Earth pigments
Wood resin
Extenders

▲ Eco-friendly gloss paint

Questions

1 Why is Shari concerned about the ingredients in normal gloss paint?

2 Which paint would dry faster? Explain your answer.

3 Suggest why the eco-friendly paint comes in fewer colours than normal gloss paints?

Building basics

In this item you will find out

- about materials used in construction

- about sedimentary, metamorphic and igneous rocks

- how limestone can be used to make cement and concrete

The photograph on the right shows the tallest skyscraper in the world. It is the Taipei 101 tower in Taiwan. It is over 508 m high. This is more than ten times the height of Nelson's column in London.

This skyscraper is made mainly from steel-reinforced concrete and glass. These **construction materials** are made from other materials taken from the earth.

Steel is made from iron which is extracted from **ores**. Aluminium, which is another popular building material, is also extracted from ores. Glass is made by heating sand to very high temperatures.

The skyscraper also contains bricks. They are made from baked clay.

Concrete is made from **limestone**. Limestone used to be an important building material.

▲ The Taipei 101 tower in Taiwan

The wall in the photograph is in the Peak District in Derbyshire. It was made from pieces of limestone rock from a nearby quarry. Today, most limestone is used to make other construction materials.

a Suggest one advantage of using rocks close to where they are quarried.

Amazing fact

The Taipei 101 tower is built to resist an earthquake of 7 on the Richter scale. During construction it withstood an earthquake of 6.8 successfully.

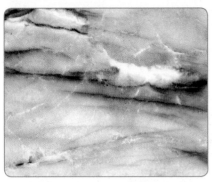
▲ Limestone

▲ Marble

▲ Granite

Granite, limestone and marble

The photographs show samples of **granite**, limestone and **marble**. They are three rocks used as construction materials.

Limestone is a sedimentary rock. It is formed when small sea creatures die, sink to the bottom of the ocean and are buried. Over a long period of time the rock is formed. The remains of the sea creatures from millions of years ago may be seen as fossils in limestone today.

Marble is a metamorphic rock. It is made by the action of high pressures and high temperatures on limestone. During the process, limestone melts and crystallises.

Granite is an **igneous** rock. It is a crystalline rock formed when molten rock from inside the Earth cools and crystallises within the Earth.

Granite is much harder than marble. Marble is much harder than limestone. In limestone the tiny grains are cemented together but can be separated quite easily. In marble there is some fusion of the grains together under the effects of high pressures and temperatures, making it harder. Granite is hardest because it is crystalline.

Decomposition of limestone

Limestone and marble are both forms of calcium carbonate, $CaCO_3$.

Thermal decomposition is a reaction where one substance is chemically changed, by heating, into at least two new substances. Calcium carbonate splits up (thermally decomposes) to form calcium oxide and carbon dioxide when it is heated.

calcium carbonate → calcium oxide + carbon dioxide

$$CaCO_3 \quad \rightarrow \quad CaO \quad + \quad CO_2$$

The process of heating limestone to produce calcium oxide (sometimes called quicklime) and carbon dioxide goes back many centuries. Originally it was done in large kilns heated by burning wood. These kilns were usually covered with earth. They produced calcium oxide in batches. The kiln had to be emptied and refilled after each batch.

Later, stone kilns using coal as the fuel were developed which enabled calcium oxide to be produced continuously. Today, modern gas-fired kilns are used.

b The kilns need to get temperatures above 900 °C. Suggest a reason for covering the kiln with earth.

c What is the advantage of a continuous process over a batch process?

Lime is still important for manufacturing sodium carbonate, steel manufacture, water purification and treatment. Over half of the output in the UK comes from the area around Buxton in Derbyshire.

Cement and concrete

A lot of limestone is made into **cement**. To do this limestone and clay are heated together. The product is then crushed. When cement is mixed with sand and water, it sets hard. It can be used to stick bricks together when building.

Cement can be used to make concrete. Cement, sand, gravel (small stones) and water are mixed together to make concrete.

Concrete is a very useful construction material for making railway sleepers or lamp posts. It is not very strong, however, unless it is reinforced.

Reinforcing concrete makes a **composite** material. Reinforcing the concrete with steel rods or a steel framework makes concrete a better construction material. It combines the hardness of concrete with the flexibility of steel. The forces are transferred sideways which makes the beam stronger. In the diagram below the vertical force is turned into a horizontal one.

The photograph above shows concrete bridges where steel is used to reinforce the concrete.

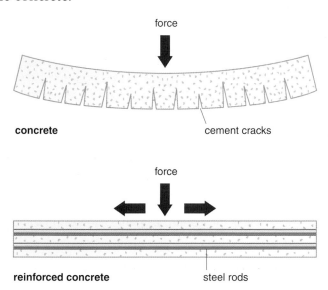

concrete   cement cracks

reinforced concrete   steel rods

▲ *Steel rods make concrete stronger*

Amazing fact

Salt put onto concrete bridge roads to clear ice can lead to the concrete cracking. The steel reinforcing rods can rust if water seeps through cracks in the concrete.

Keywords

cement • composite • concrete • construction material • granite • igneous • limestone • marble • ore • thermal decomposition

Uses of limestone

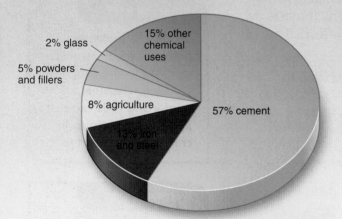

Every year 100 millions tonnes of limestone are quarried in the UK.

The pie diagram below shows the main uses of limestone.

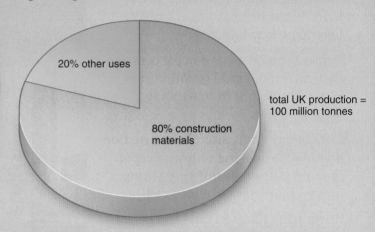

20% other uses

80% construction materials

total UK production = 100 million tonnes

Much of the limestone used as a construction material is known as aggregate. It is limestone that is crushed into small pieces. This is used where solid foundations are needed, for example for concrete floors, roads or railway tracks.

The second pie diagram shows how the limestone not used as a construction material is used.

A lot of the limestone is converted to calcium oxide and carbon dioxide by thermal decomposition. Calcium oxide is sometimes called quicklime. If calcium oxide is reacted with water, calcium hydroxide, $Ca(OH)_2$, is formed. This is sometimes called slaked lime. Farmers use calcium hydroxide to neutralise the soil.

2% glass

5% powders and fillers

8% agriculture

15% other chemical uses

57% cement

13% iron and steel

Questions

1 How many atoms are there of each element in the formula of calcium hydroxide.

2 Suggest why is it easier to transport the aggregate than large lumps of limestone?

3 What mass of limestone is turned into cement each year in the UK? Use the two pie charts to help you.

4 Suggest why the mass of calcium oxide produced by heating calcium carbonate is always less than the mass of calcium carbonate used.

5 Write a balanced equation for the reaction of calcium oxide and water.

6 Calcium hydroxide can be used to make lime mortar. When this sets it reacts with carbon dioxide from the air. The product is calcium carbonate. Write a symbol equation for this reaction.

Restless Earth

In this item you will find out

- about the structure of the Earth

- what causes earthquakes and volcanoes

- about volcanic rocks

A volcanic eruption can cause widespread damage. Geologists study **volcanoes** for several reasons.

They carry out experiments to find out more about what is happening inside a volcano. The results of their experiments may reveal information about what is inside the Earth and also enable them to make predictions about when an eruption of a volcano may take place.

It is also possible to monitor, with sensitive equipment, the areas where earthquakes are likely to happen. Slight changes within the Earth can be detected.

This kind of monitoring of possible earthquake and volcano sites is very expensive and needs to be carried out over long periods of time if useful predictions are to be made.

a Suggest why there is much more monitoring in the US than in Indonesia.

To understand these natural phenomena better we need to know more about the Earth and its structure. But there are problems with studying the structure of the Earth. We cannot just slice it open and look inside. The Earth has a diameter of about 12 700 km. The deepest that we have been able to drill into the Earth is 15 km.

▶ *Earthquakes can cause devastation and loss of life*

Amazing fact

On the small island of Bali in Indonesia there are 149 active volcanoes.

Structure of the Earth

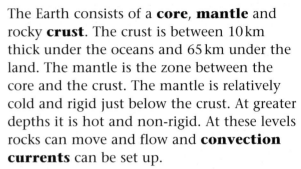

Some people used to think that the Earth was like a solid rubber ball with the same material throughout. We now know that it isn't. The diagram shows the structure of the Earth.

crust
mantle
liquid outer core
solid inner core

The Earth consists of a **core**, **mantle** and rocky **crust**. The crust is between 10 km thick under the oceans and 65 km under the land. The mantle is the zone between the core and the crust. The mantle is relatively cold and rigid just below the crust. At greater depths it is hot and non-rigid. At these levels rocks can move and flow and **convection currents** can be set up.

The outer 100 km of the Earth, consisting of the crust and the upper part of the mantle, is called the **lithosphere**. It is relatively cold and rigid.

b Where would be the best place to drill down into the crust to reach the mantle?

Tectonic plates and earthquakes

The lithosphere is made up of a number of large sections called **tectonic plates**. There are two types of tectonic plates: oceanic and continental. The oceanic plates lie under the oceans and the continental plates form the continents. These plates float on the mantle because they are less dense than it. They move a few centimetres each year.

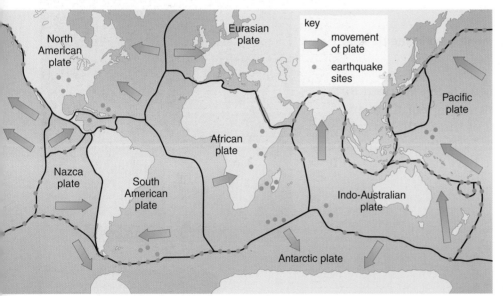

key
→ movement of plate
• earthquake sites

North American plate
Eurasian plate
African plate
Pacific plate
Nazca plate
South American plate
Indo-Australian plate
Antarctic plate

The diagram shows the plates that cover the Earth.

You will notice the orange dots on the map. These represent places where earthquakes occur.

c Can you suggest a theory about where earthquakes occur?

d Does this theory fit all cases?

Earthquakes occur where two plates join. The sliding of one plate against the other builds up stresses and strains. When these become too much the result is an earthquake.

Theory of plate tectonics

When two plates collide, the rocks are squeezed together. This is shown in the diagram. As the two plates collide the oceanic plate is forced under the continental plate. The rocks in the oceanic plate partly melt and return to the **magma** (molten rock) in the mantle. This is called **subduction**. The result is an oceanic trench, where the oceanic plate dips, and a mountain chain caused by folding of rocks on the continental plate.

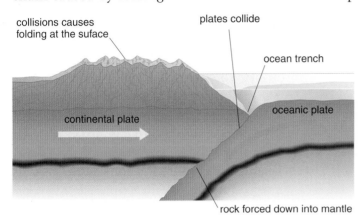

collisions causes folding at the suface

plates collide

ocean trench

oceanic plate

continental plate

rock forced down into mantle

▲ *Rhyolite*

The continental plate has an average density of $2.7\,g/cm^3$. The oceanic plate is more dense and has a density of $3.3\,g/cm^3$. The convection currents caused by energy transfer in the mantle cause the plates to move slowly.

Volcanic rock

Where there are weaknesses in the Earth's crust such as cracks or volcanoes, molten rock can make its way through to the surface. The magma rises to the surface, usually because it is less dense than the mantle. But if there is enough pressure the magma can rise even if it is denser than the mantle.

Magma cools and crystallises on the surface to form igneous rock. The magma can have different compositions and this affects what types of rock are formed.

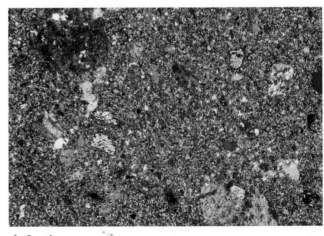

▲ *Basalt*

Lava with a low silica content is runny. It flows steadily so its movement is predictable and fairly 'safe'. It quickly cools forming iron-rich rocks like **basalt**, which have only very tiny crystals.

A high silica content prevents lava flowing easily so it piles up forming rocks like **rhyolite** (pumice stone), which is used as an abrasive. High silica content also stops lava from losing trapped gas. This gas makes the lava explode out of volcanoes as dangerous and unpredictable lava bombs.

Igneous rocks can also cool slowly inside the Earth. Here, very slow cooling allows large interlocking crystals to form in rocks such as granite. Slightly faster cooling gives smaller interlocking crystals in rocks such as gabbro.

Keywords

basalt • convection currents • core • crust • lithosphere • magma • mantle • rhyolite • subduction • techtonic plate • volcano

Developing the theory of plate tectonics

The theory of plate tectonics on page 121 has been developed fairly recently. In 1915, a German geophysicist, Alfred Wegener, published a book. He was one of the first people to suggest that continents moved. He suggested that a supercontinent, which he called *Pangaea*, had existed. He thought that it had broken up, starting 200 million years ago, and that the pieces had 'drifted' to their present positions.

The diagram on the left shows *Pangea*.

The book was not translated into English until 1924 when it was criticised by scientists. The president of the prestigious American Philosophical Society said of Wegener's ideas. 'Utter, damned rot!' A leading British geologist said, 'Anyone who valued his reputation for scientific sanity would never dare support such a theory.'

If Wegener's ideas were true, South America was once joined to Africa. He also noted that when you fit Africa and South America together, mountain ranges (and coal deposits) run uninterrupted across both continents.

Wegener compared the fossils from Africa and South America. These are shown in the diagram.

The problem with Wegener's hypothesis was that he could not provide evidence to support his theories or explain what caused the movement of the plates. The rotation of the Earth and tidal-type waves were two ideas that did not seem credible.

By 1954 scientists realised that there were convection currents in the mantle inside the Earth. It was possible to make much more accurate measurements, including measurements of magnetic fields. By about 1960, scientists generally agreed with Wegener's theory. They realised that Alfred Wegener was right in most of his major ideas.

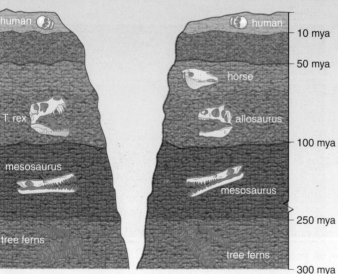

KEY
mya = million years ago

Questions

1 Alfred Wegener was a geophysicist. Which sciences does a geophysicist specialise in?

2 What does the fossil evidence in the diagram above suggest?

3 Suggest why there was opposition to his ideas in 1924?

4 Why was there little opposition by 1960?

Make mine metals

In this item you will find out

- how copper is purified
- about alloys
- the use of smart alloys

The photograph shows some objects that are made of the metal copper. At the front of the picture on the left is malachite. This is an ore of copper.

Copper is an expensive metal although it is relatively easy to extract from its ore. It is expensive for the following reasons:

- There is a huge demand for copper for electrical wires and water pipes.
- There are very limited stocks of ores, such as malachite, in the Earth.
- Most of these ores contain only a small percentage of copper.

a Explain why it is worth using ores containing a very low percentage of copper.

Recycling copper from electrical wires, water pipes and **alloys**, for example, is cheaper than extracting copper from copper ore. Recycling also makes our scarce resources last longer. But local councils arrange for the collection of a range of materials, such as glass and paper, for recycling. They do not collect copper even though waste copper is much more valuable than waste glass or paper.

b Suggest reasons why they do not collect waste copper.

> **Amazing fact**
>
> 'Silver' coins such as 50p pieces contain a lot of copper but no silver. The coins are made from an alloy of copper and nickel.

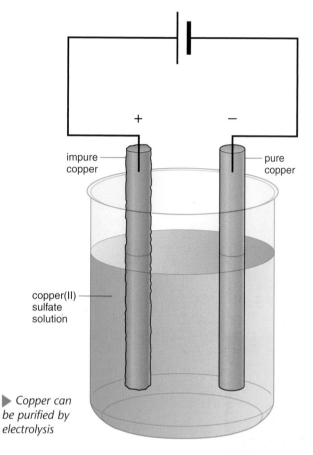

▶ *Copper can be purified by electrolysis*

◀ *Purification of copper on a large scale*

Purification of copper

Copper is easily extracted from its ore by heating the ore with carbon. This is because it is low in the reactivity series (page 130). Its ores are unstable and split up easily by reduction.

Copper must be very pure if it is to be used to make electricity wires – at least 99.95% pure. Any impurities will increase the resistance of the wire.

Copper can be purified by **electrolysis**. The apparatus is shown in the diagram on the left.

The copper(II) sulfate solution is the **electrolyte** and contains:

copper(II) ions	sulfate ions	hydrogen ions	hydroxide ions
Cu^{2+}	SO_4^{2-}	H^+	OH^-

c The copper(II) ions and the sulfate ions come from the copper(II) sulfate. Where do the hydrogen and hydroxide ions come from?

During the electrolysis, copper atoms from the positive electrode (**anode**) lose electrons and form copper(II) ions in solution.

copper atom $\rightarrow$ copper(II) ion + 2 electrons

$$Cu \rightarrow Cu^{2+} + 2e^-$$

At the negative electrode (**cathode**), a copper(II) ion picks up two electrons and becomes a copper atom.

copper(II) ion + 2 electrons $\rightarrow$ copper atom

$$Cu^{2+} + 2e^- \rightarrow Cu$$

So copper transfers from the anode to the cathode. The impurities drop to the bottom of the beaker.

The photograph shows a factory where purification of copper is taking place. The man is walking over the copper electrodes.

Alloys

We don't use very many metals in their pure form. Metals are more useful to us when they are made into alloys. An alloy is a mixture of two elements where at least one is a metal.

The table gives information about some common alloys.

Alloy	Main metal in alloy	Use
amalgam	mercury	tooth fillings
brass	copper and zinc	hinges, screws, ornaments
solder	tin and lead	joining metals

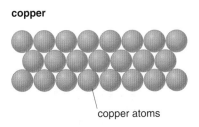

copper

copper atoms

The diagram on the right shows the arrangement of atoms in pure copper and in brass.

The properties of brass are different from the properties of the copper and zinc that make it up. In copper, the layers of copper atoms can slide over each other, In brass, the copper and zinc atoms are different sizes. The layers do not slide over each other easily. Brass is harder than copper or zinc. This makes it more useful. Brass can be used for door handles, but copper and zinc would not be strong enough.

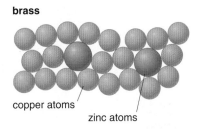

brass

copper atoms

zinc atoms

 d **Suggest what properties amalgam needs to have to be used as fillings.**

Smart alloys

Nitinol is one of the names for a family of nickel-titanium alloys that are **smart alloys** or shape-memory alloys (SMA). The alloy was named after the Nickel Titanium Naval Ordnance Laboratory where it was discovered in 1961.

It is a mixture of approximately equal amounts of nickel and titanium. It can remember its original shape. A piece of nitinol wire can be bent into the shape of a paper clip. It works well as a paper clip. However, it goes back to being a straight piece of wire if an electric current passes through it or it is put into hot water.

The actual discovery of the shape memory property of Nitinol came about by accident. At a laboratory management meeting, a strip of Nitinol that was bent out of shape many times was presented. One of the people present heated it with his pipe lighter, and surprisingly, the strip stretched back to its original form.

Originally developed for military uses, smart alloys are now widely used including in a number of medical applications. Spectacle frames made of nitinol may go out of shape in use. Putting them in hot water will restore the original shape. Nitinol is also used to make hooks on wires that hold tendons to the bone in shoulder surgery.

Other smart alloys include:

- copper-aluminum-nickel alloys
- copper-zinc-aluminum alloys
- iron-manganese-silicon alloys.

Keywords

alloy • anode • cathode • electrolysis • electrolyte • smart alloy

The search for copper

Copper is an extremely important metal and scientists are always looking for new supplies of it.

Divers recently recovered a 17 tonne boulder of nearly pure copper on the bed of Lake Superior in Canada. Similar boulders have been found in the past, but this is the largest.

Copper boulders are purified on the side of the lake by electrolysis. The diagram shows how this is done.

Today, copper purification usually takes place where there are relatively cheap supplies of electricity available. This is because very large amounts of electricity are required to make one tonne of copper. Often this purification is near hydroelectric power stations or where the manufacturer can negotiate an economical rate for electricity.

▼ Boulder of copper

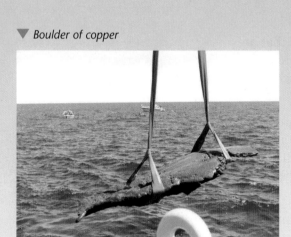

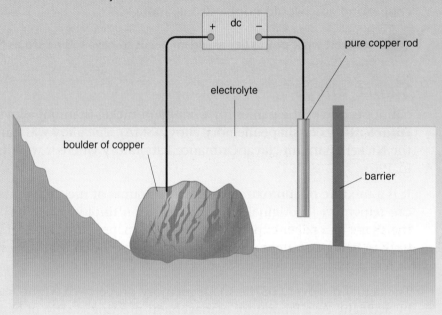

Questions

1 Suggest why it is possible for copper to remain on the bed of a lake without reacting with anything.

2 What is the advantage of purifying copper at the lakeside?

3 Use the diagram to explain how the copper is purified by electrolysis by the side of the lake.

4 Write ionic equations for the reactions that take place during the electrolysis.

5 Chemists have shown by analysis that the boulder from Lake Superior contains 80% copper. What is the maximum mass of pure copper that can be obtained from the boulder. Hint: 1 tonne = 1000 kg.

6 What are the incentives to recycle more copper?

Problem or resource?

In this item you will find out

- about rusting

- the advantages and disadvantages of building car bodies from aluminium or steel

- about recycling car materials

The manufacturers of some new cars recycle materials from old cars to help reduce costs and to avoid using up scarce resources. Cars are built from steel, copper, aluminium, glass, plastics and fibres.

a Suggest what properties of glass need to be used for car windscreens.

b Aluminium is light but strong. Why do you think is it good for making car bodies?

Old cars at breaker's yards can provide spare parts for other cars. Some manufacturers buy old engines or gear boxes and remanufacture them up to the original specifications. The rest of the car is crushed and much of it is recycled. The table shows the percentage of different materials currently recycled.

Material	Percentage (by weight) recycled
iron and steel	62
copper	50
aluminium	40
glass	60
polymers including fabrics	50

A modern car usually has a steel body which is much thinner than the steel used 30 years ago. This is possible because steel makers can make steel sheet with a very uniform thickness. Also, the car makers are able to use rust-proofing techniques which stop car bodies rusting as they used to. The benefit to the manufacturer is a reduction of costs of production and the benefits to the car-owner is better fuel economy because the car is lighter and a longer life for the car.

Recycling materials is good because it saves resources and cuts down on the disposal of waste. But the value of an old car for scrap barely covers the cost of collecting it. For this reason cars are sometimes seen abandoned. When a car is broken up, not all the materials in the car are re-used.

Makers of new cars in the future will have to design their cars so that more of the materials in the car can be recycled. When they sell a new car they will have to agree to take it back at the end of its life. By January 2007 they will have to plan to recycle 85% of the car and by 2015 at least 95%.

Rusting

The diagram shows an experiment to find what is needed for **rusting** (**corrosion**) of iron to take place.

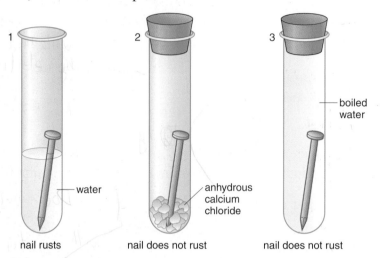

Test tube 1 is a control experiment. It shows that an iron nail rusts with air and water. Test tube 2 contains a nail inside a test tube with dry air. The anhydrous calcium chloride removes any water vapour. No rusting takes place here. Test tube 3 contains a nail in water but with no oxygen or air there. The nail does not rust. This experiment shows that rusting takes places when iron is in contact with water and oxygen (air). Rusting is speeded up by salt water or **acid rain**.

The rusting of iron is an **oxidation** reaction. Iron reacts with oxygen and water to form hydrated iron(II) oxide, $Fe(OH)_3.xH_2O$. When iron rusts the hydrated iron(III) oxide flakes off revealing a fresh surface for rusting. The rusting process can be shown by the word equation:

iron + oxygen + water → hydrated iron(III) oxide

Aluminium does not corrode even in damp conditions. This is because there is a thin coating of aluminium oxide on the surface of aluminium which does not flake off. This protects the surface from corrosion. Aluminium does corrode when it comes into contact with salt.

Car bodies

Alloys usually have different properties from the metals they are made from, which makes them more useful. Steel is an alloy containing iron with a very small percentage of carbon. Steel is harder and stronger than iron. It is also less likely to corrode than iron.

 The steel used today to make car bodies is much thinner than the steel used 30 years ago. Suggest advantages of this to both the car manufacturer and the car buyer.

Stainless steel is an alloy that does not rust at all. About 25 years ago a car was produced with a stainless steel body. This was more expensive than using normal steel but the car did not need painting. The photograph on the next page shows the stainless steel DeLorean sports car.

Some cars now have bodies made from aluminium rather than steel. This has several advantages. The same car made with an aluminium body rather than a steel body will be lighter because aluminium is less dense and so the owner will get better fuel economy. An aluminium car body will corrode less than a steel body and so the car will last longer.

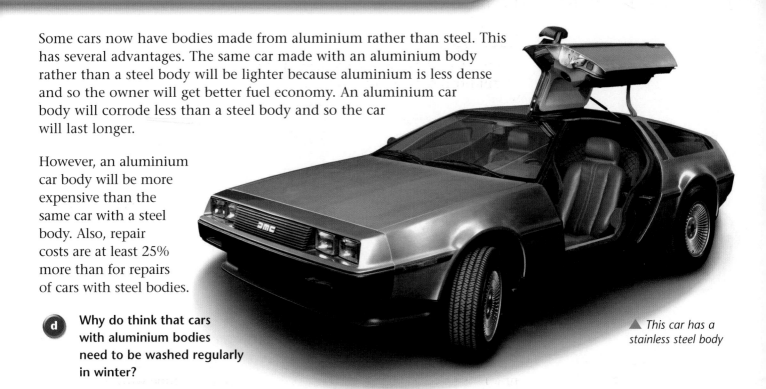

However, an aluminium car body will be more expensive than the same car with a steel body. Also, repair costs are at least 25% more than for repairs of cars with steel bodies.

d Why do think that cars with aluminium bodies need to be washed regularly in winter?

▲ *This car has a stainless steel body*

Corrosion of two metals together

There are times when two metals might come in contact in a car. This can sometimes cause problems, for example, a car manufacturer is considering using metal rivets to fix panels of steel together. Either zinc or copper rivets could be used. Some experiments can be carried out to investigate what happens when the two metals are in contact. The following three experiments can be set up:

A one with an iron nail
B one with an iron nail in contact with a piece of zinc
C one with an iron nail in contact with a piece of copper.

Ferroxyl indicator can be used to show where rusting of iron is taking place. Areas that are pink are protected from corrosion. Areas that are green show where corrosion is taking place.

The diagram shows the results.

e What can you conclude from the results of the experiments with the three nails?

f Which rivets would you suggest are used? Explain your choice.

g The manufacturer also makes the car with an aluminum body. He is planning to bolt body panels together. Aluminium bolts are not strong enough. Would you suggest iron bolts? Explain your answer.

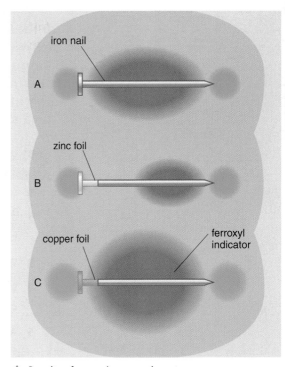

▲ *Results of corrosion experiment*

Keywords

acid rain • corrosion • oxidation • rusting

Rusty cars

Thirty years ago cars rusted far more than they do today. There have been great advances in the treatment of steel to prevent rusting. Car manufacturers are able to give guarantees that the cars will not rust within 12 years.

Steel used for car making today is coated with zinc. This is called galvanising. The steel is usually dipped into a bath of molten zinc. This gives the steel protection against rusting.

Zinc is a reactive metal, which is more reactive than iron. It may seem strange that zinc should be able to protect steel from corrosion when it is more reactive and should need all the protection it can get. When oxygen in the air reacts with the surface of zinc, a very dense and impermeable coating of zinc oxide is formed. It is this physical barrier that protects the zinc surface from further attack.

If the surface of the galvanised steel becomes scratched, you would expect the exposed steel area to corrode. But the zinc and iron form an electrolytic cell. Rusting of iron involves losing electrons. In the electrolytic cell, zinc loses electrons more readily than iron. So the rusting of steel is reduced when zinc in is contact with the steel. If a metal lower in the reactivity series than iron was used to protect steel instead of zinc, corrosion would be speeded up.

Reactivity series of metals

Potassium	most reactive
Sodium	
Calcium	
Magnesium	
Aluminium	
Carbon	
Zinc	
Iron	
Tin	
Lead	
Hydrogen	
Copper	
Silver	
Gold	
Platinum	least reactive

(elements in italics, though non-metals, have been included for comparison)

▲ *Reactivity series*

Questions

1 What name is given to the protection of steel with zinc?

2 Zinc is more reactive than iron. Why does the zinc on the surface of the steel not corrode?

3 Write an ionic equation for the rusting of iron to produce iron(III) ions.

4 Which of the metals in the list, in contact with iron would speed up corrosion: aluminium, magnesium or lead?

5 A car manufacturer wants to use a metal washer between two lengths of steel exhaust pipe. Copper and zinc washers are available. Which washer should he use and why?

Air fit to breathe

In this item you will find out

- the composition of clean air
- how air pollutants are formed and their effects
- how atmospheric pollution is controlled

The photograph shows an aerial view of Santiago in Chile. This city has one of the biggest **atmospheric pollution** problems in the world.

The city is in a deep valley with high mountains around it. The direction of the wind does not usually blow the pollution out of the valley. It is difficult to see any distance because of atmospheric pollution.

So what causes atmospheric pollution? The table shows some of the common pollutants in the air, how they are formed and what effects they have.

Pollutant	How it forms	Effects
carbon monoxide	incomplete combustion in petrol or diesel engine	poisonous gas
oxides of nitrogen	formed in car engines from reaction of nitrogen and oxygen	acid rain and photochemical smog
sulfur dioxide	combustion of fuels containing sulfur, e.g. petrol	acid rain

Atmospheric pollution is caused by emissions from houses, vehicles and factories. As the population grows and industry develops the problem can get out of control. Motor cars and other vehicles are today regarded as the major cause of atmospheric pollution in towns and cities.

a Some countries are getting petrol companies to remove all sulfur from petrol. How will this reduce atmospheric pollution problems?

In Santiago, some cars are banned from using the roads on certain days. On one day all cars with registrations ending in 2 or 3 may be banned. On another day those ending in 7, 8 and 0 might be banned.

b Why does this reduce the atmospheric pollution levels?

The bar chart on the right shows the level of nitrogen oxides in the atmosphere in Santiago over the period of a week.

c Suggest what might have happened on Wednesday to change the level of nitrogen oxides in the atmosphere.

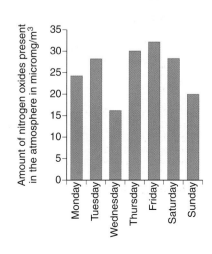

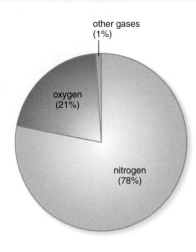

other gases
(1%)

oxygen
(21%)

nitrogen
(78%)

What is in air?

We all take air for granted as it is always there. We know today that air is a mixture of gases. However, two hundred years ago many people believed that air was an element and not a mixture at all. Two scientists, Priestley and Lavoisier, did experiments to show that air was a mixture of gases. Their ideas were not accepted immediately.

d Why do you think new ideas in science are often rejected at first by other scientists?

The pie diagram on the left shows the percentage composition by volume of clean dry air.

e Which gas is in the atmosphere in the largest amounts? The table gives the typical composition of a sample of dry air.

Gas	nitrogen	oxygen	carbon dioxide	argon	other gases
Percentage	78.0	21.0	0.03	0.9	0.07

f Which is the reactive gas in the air?

g Which gas in the table is a compound?

Argon is one of a family of gases including helium, neon, krypton and xenon. These are called noble gases. They used to be called rare gases.

h Why do you think rare gas is a poor name for argon?

An electric light bulb contains a mixture of nitrogen and argon. A fluorescent light tube usually contains neon.

Because air is a mixture, its composition can vary from place to place. But the composition never varies much from that shown.

Carbon dioxide and oxygen balance

The percentage of carbon dioxide and oxygen in the air remains constant.

The diagram on the left shows a simple carbon cycle, which explains why the percentages remain constant. The processes of combustion, especially of carbon fuels, and **respiration** both use up oxygen and produce carbon dioxide.

$$C + O_2 \rightarrow CO_2$$
$$C_6H_{12}O_6 + 6O_2 \rightarrow 6CO_2 + 6H_2O$$

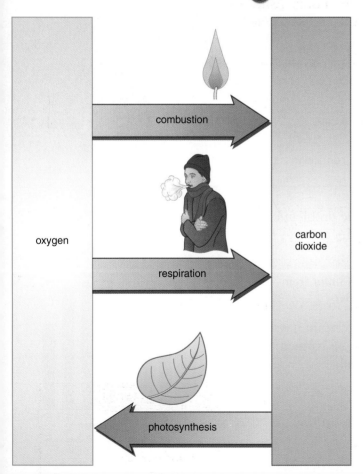

oxygen

combustion

respiration

carbon dioxide

photosynthesis

▲ Keeping oxygen and carbon dioxide in balance

Photosynthesis in green plants uses up carbon dioxide and produces oxygen.

$$6CO_2 + 6H_2O \rightarrow C_6H_{12}O_6 + 6O_2$$

There is a balance between respiration/combustion and photosynthesis that keeps the composition of the atmosphere constant.

The balance of carbon dioxide and oxygen in the air can be disturbed by human influences:

- **deforestation** – The burning of timber uses up oxygen and produces carbon dioxide.
- increasing energy consumption – The more fossil fuels that are burned the more carbon dioxide is produced.
- population increase – More oxygen is used in respiration and there is increased burning of fossil fuels.

The origin of the atmosphere

There have been many theories about how the Earth's atmosphere came to be. This is the most widely accepted one.

The Earth's original atmosphere, billions of years ago, probably came from gases that escaped from inside the Earth. These gases included carbon dioxide and steam, with smaller amounts of methane and ammonia. As the Earth cooled, the water vapour condensed to form the oceans. Some of the carbon dioxide dissolved in the water.

Then about 3000 million years ago, simple plant life in the sea converted carbon dioxide into oxygen by photosynthesis. Ammonia in the early atmosphere was converted into atmospheric nitrogen by bacteria. Nitrogen remains in the atmosphere because of its lack of reactivity.

Reducing atmospheric pollution

The World Health Organisation makes recommendations for air quality. In Lahore in Pakistan the levels of pollutants are 20 times greater than the WHO maximums. In a recent year, 6.4 million people in Pakistan were admitted to hospital with illnesses caused by air pollution. It is important to control atmospheric pollution because of the effect it has on humans and the environment.

A catalytic converter can be fitted to the car exhaust system to remove the pollutants carbon monoxide and nitrogen monoxide. It converts poisonous carbon monoxide and nitrogen monoxide in the exhaust gases into carbon dioxide and nitrogen.

carbon monoxide + nitrogen monoxide → nitrogen + carbon dioxide

$$2CO + 2NO \rightarrow N_2 + 2CO_2$$

ⓘ Some people say that producing carbon dioxide is not acceptable. Suggest why.

Keywords

atmospheric pollution
• deforestation •
photosynthesis •
respiration

Photochemical smog

Photochemical smog is a type of air pollution. It forms when sunlight acts upon motor vehicle exhaust gases to form harmful substances such as ozone (O_3). Ozone causes breathing difficulties and can make respiratory problems worse. Photochemical smog can irritate the eyes, causing them to water and sting.

Motor vehicles produce exhaust gases containing oxides of nitrogen such as nitrogen dioxide (NO_2) and nitrogen monoxide (NO). When the nitrogen dioxide concentration is above clean air levels and there is plenty of sunlight, an oxygen atom splits off from the nitrogen dioxide molecule and reacts with oxygen molecules in the air to form ozone.

Nitrogen monoxide can remove ozone by reacting with ozone to form nitrogen dioxide and oxygen. When the ratio of NO_2 to NO is greater than three, the formation of ozone is the dominant reaction. If the ratio is less than 0.3, then the nitrogen monoxide reaction destroys the ozone at about the same rate as it is formed, keeping the ozone concentration below harmful levels.

Scientists measure the concentration of nitrogen oxides in the atmosphere and the hours of sunshine. Here are their results for one week.

	Monday	Tuesday	Wednesday	Thursday	Friday	Saturday	Sunday
NOx (ppb*)	80	80	160	90	80	90	50
Hours of sunshine	4	4	7	4	1	3	3
* ppb = parts per billion							

Questions

1 Nitrogen (N_2) and oxygen (O_2) combine in the car engine to form nitrogen monoxide. Write a symbol equation for this reaction.

2 Photochemical smog is more of a problem in Santiago or Pakistan than in the UK. Suggest why.

3 Nitrogen monoxide reacts with more oxygen to form nitrogen dioxide. Write a symbol equation for this reaction.

4 Write the symbol equation for the reaction of nitrogen monoxide and ozone.

5 Why do chemists monitor the NO_2:NO ratio?

6 Why do you think the level of photochemical smog and ozone is higher on Wednesday than Saturday? Refer to the data in the table.

7 The average value for the concentration of nitrogen oxides is 90 ppb. Why is this value alone not very useful when comparing the air pollution in different cities? What extra information should be given?

Closer and hotter

In this item you will find out

- that chemical reactions take place at different rates

- how temperature affects the rate of reaction

- how concentration affects the rate of reaction

Have you ever eaten chilli con carne? It is a famous dish made from beef, tomatoes and kidney beans. You can buy kidney beans in cans, but if you want to used dried beans then you have to soak them overnight and boil them in a saucepan in lots of water for about two hours.

If you have a pressure cooker, you can speed up the cooking of the dried beans. In a pressure cooker, the beans are cooked in about one-quarter of the time. The steam produced by the boiling water cannot escape and so the pressure inside the pressure cooker builds up. As the pressure builds up, the temperature of the boiling point of water increases above 120°C. At this higher temperature the cooking process is speeded up.

This example shows that reactions can be speeded up by using a higher temperature or a higher pressure.

▶ *Using a pressure cooker speeds up cooking times*

Amazing fact

You may think that a pressure cooker is a new invention. The first pressure cooker was used over 500 years ago.

Increasing the temperature

A reaction takes place when particles of the **reactants** collide with each other. The more collisions that take place the faster will be the reaction. One way of speeding up a chemical reaction is by increasing the temperature. Increasing the temperature makes the particles move faster. This is shown in the diagram.

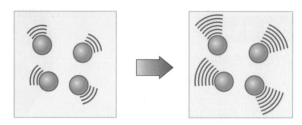

 More collisions as the temperature rises

if the acid is heated the particles move faster

Examiner's tip

At higher tier it is important you write about collision frequency (i.e. number of collisions per second) and not just the number of collisions.

As a result there is a greater frequency of collisions (more collisions each second). When a collision occurs, a reaction only takes place when the colliding particles have more than a certain amount of energy (called the activation energy). At a higher temperature the particles possess more energy and so more collisions will have enough energy to undergo reaction. This results in a faster reaction.

a Choose the correct words to complete these sentences:
   (i) As temperature increases the average energy of the particles increases/decreases/stays the same.
   (ii) The number of effective collisions increases/decreases.
   (iii) This makes the reaction faster/slower.

Increasing the concentration

Another way of increasing the **rate of reaction** is to increase the **concentration** of one of the reactants. Increasing the concentration means there are more particles in a given volume. The particles are closer together. Again, more collisions will happen each second – the frequency of the collisions will be greater.

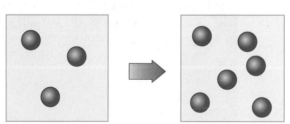

 More particles means more collisions

if the concentration of the acid is increased, there are more acid particles in the same volume of water

If the reactants are gases, for example hydrogen and oxygen, then increasing the pressure is the same as increasing the concentration. Both result in the particles being more crowded together which speeds up the reaction.

b Choose the correct words to complete these sentences:
   (i) As concentration increases the average energy of the particles increases/decreases/stays the same but the number of effective collisions increases/decreases.
   (ii) This makes the reaction faster/slower.

Investigating rate of reaction

The diagram on the right shows the apparatus that can be used to investigate the rate of a reaction. We are going to react marble chippings (calcium carbonate) and dilute hydrochloric acid together to produce calcium chloride, water and carbon dioxide.

calcium carbonate + hydrochloric acid → calcium chloride
+ water + carbon dioxide

$$CaCO_3 + 2HCl \rightarrow CaCl_2 + H_2O + CO_2$$

The solid line on the graph below shows the results.

The graph that we get is a curve. The graph starts steeply. As the reaction proceeds the gradient of the graph reduces and reduces. Finally when the reaction has stopped the graph is horizontal. The reaction stops when one of the reactants is used up.

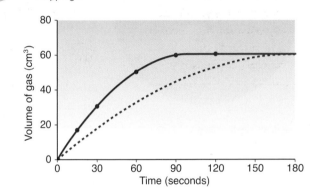

 c   After how long does the reaction stop?

We repeat the reaction. This time the hydrochloric acid is mixed with an equal volume of water. The concentration of hydrochloric acid is half what it was in the first experiment.

The results are shown by the dotted line on the graph. Now that the concentration is less, the reaction takes longer. It is a slower reaction. The graph is less steep and takes longer to become horizontal. The same volume of the gas carbon dioxide is produced because the same mass of calcium carbonate is used. The amount of **product** depends upon the quantity of reactant used.

 d   In the first experiment 0.17 g of calcium carbonate was used. What would be the final volume of gas collected if 0.34 g was used?

The rate of the reaction at any point can be calculated by measuring the slope (gradient) of the curve at that point. The initial rate of the first reaction can be obtained using the following formula.

$$\text{Initial rate} = \frac{\text{volume of gas}}{\text{time}} = \frac{40}{30} = 1.3 \, cm^3/s$$

As the reaction progresses the slope decreases.

 e   What is the slope when the reaction has finished?

The table gives the time taken to complete a reaction at different temperatures.

Temperature (°C)	10	20	30	40	50
Time (s)	180	90	40	15	5

Keywords

concentration • product • rate of reaction • reactant

 f   People sometimes say that increasing the temperature of the reaction doubles the rate of reaction. Look at the table. Is this statement always true?

Fireworks

In the UK fireworks are graded. Party poppers are graded 1. This means they can be safely used indoors. Garden fireworks are graded 2 or 3 and large display fireworks are graded 4 or 5. The grading depends mainly on the power of the explosive mixture.

Party poppers are indoor fireworks. They contain small amounts of an explosive. The explosive is a mixture of a fuel, a chemical that supplies oxygen and other chemicals to give special effects.

When the string is pulled, the explosive is ignited. The explosion takes only a tiny fraction of a second. It produces a sound, some heat energy and a large volume of gaseous products. It is this that forces out the streamers.

Sparklers should be used outside because they burn at very high temperatures. They are a grade 2 firework. A sparkler mixture does not contain an explosive. The usual mixture for making the sparkler is iron filings, aluminium powder, barium nitrate and a glue to hold the materials together. A slurry of the ingredients is made and iron wire is dipped in and pulled out. This is repeated a number of times. Finally some primer paint is put on the end of the sparkler to make it easier to catch alight.

Once alight, the products include solid barium oxide, oxygen and nitrogen gases. The aluminium burns in the oxygen produced to form aluminium oxide, Al_2O_3. The gases cause the iron filings to be ejected. They catch alight in the high temperatures to produce the sparkle.

Garden and display fireworks are often bright colours. Small amounts of metal or metal compound give the firework the characteristic colour.

The table gives some colours produced by different metal or metal compound.

Metal or metal compound	Colour
lithium	red
sodium	orange/yellow
potassium	lilac
copper	blue/green
magnesium	white

Questions

1 There is a smell associated with a party popper but not with a sparkler. What do you think causes this smell?

2 A small amount of explosive that explodes in a confined space can cause serious problems. Why does this not cause a problem in a party popper?

3 Which chemical in the sparkler provides the oxygen needed?

4 Write a balanced symbol equation for the burning of aluminium in oxygen.

5 Write a balanced symbol equation for the burning of iron in oxygen to form the iron oxide Fe_3O_4.

6 Balance the equation for the reaction in the sparkler:
$Al + Ba(NO_3)_2 \rightarrow BaO + N_2 + Al_2O_3 + O_2$.

7 Why is unwise to let young children hold sparklers?

8 What colour would you expect a firework to be if the following are added to the explosive mixture?
 a sodium and magnesium
 b magnesium and copper

Explosions and catalysts

In this item you will find out

- how catalysts change the rate of chemical reactions

- how increasing the surface area of a reactant speeds up a reaction

- about explosions

An **explosion** is a very fast reaction that releases a large amount of products as gases.

We expect explosions to be caused by high explosives such as trinitrotoluene (TNT) or dynamite. Chemicals such as ammonium nitrate can also be explosive. On 21 September 2001 a huge explosion occurred in a fertiliser factory in Toulouse in France involving 200–300 tonnes of stored ammonium nitrate. As a result 31 people died and the explosion caused damage over a wide area.

However, serious explosions can happen in factories where flour, custard powder or sulfur are used. The photograph shows the results of an explosion at Blaye in France in 1997.

The explosion at Blaye was caused when dust from the grain used to make flour formed an explosive mixture with air. In this accident 11 people were killed.

There are important guidelines to be followed in factories and storage facilities that handle powders.

1   Workers must wear special boots which do not cause friction against the floors.

2   There must be no flames, no smoking and no hot surfaces.

▲ *Explosion at Blaye*

3   Factories must have efficient ventilation systems which remove the air and replace it with fresh filtered air.

a   Which guidelines are intended to stop the ignition of explosive mixtures?

b   Which guidelines are intended to stop a build up of explosive mixtures in the factory?

Amazing fact

In one week in 2005 over 100 people were killed in China in explosions in coal mines involving explosive mixtures of coal dust and air.

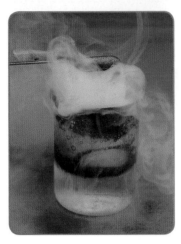

Catalysts

Hydrogen peroxide is widely used as a bleach. Some people use it to bleach hair.

Like water, it is compound of hydrogen and oxygen. It has a formula H_2O_2.

It decomposes very, very slowly to form water and oxygen. The photographs on the left show some hydrogen peroxide in a beaker before and after adding powdered manganese(IV) oxide.

The manganese(IV) oxide acts as a **catalyst**. A catalyst speeds up chemical reactions.

The manganese(IV) oxide speeds up the reaction of hydrogen peroxide. A catalyst is not used up and remains unchanged at the end of a reaction. Only a small amount of catalyst is needed to speed up the reaction of a large amount of reactants. A catalyst is also specific to a particular reaction. A catalyst for one reaction may not catalyse a different reaction. Catalysts do not alter the amount of product being made in a reaction, they just allow the reaction to happen more quickly.

> **Examiner's tip**
>
> Candidates often think that all catalysts are enzymes. Enzymes are only one type of catalyst.

c What is the benefit to a manufacturer of producing the same amount of product more quickly?

The equation for the hydrogen peroxide reaction is:

hydrogen peroxide $\rightarrow$ water + oxygen
$$2H_2O_2 \rightarrow 2H_2O + O_2$$

The graph on the left shows the decomposition of $25\,cm^3$ of hydrogen peroxide with $0.2\,g$ of manganese(IV) oxide.

d Read the volume of gas collected after 30 s from the graph.

e What is the total volume of gas collected when all the hydrogen peroxide has reacted?

f How can you tell from the graph that the reaction is faster after 30 s than it is after 60 s?

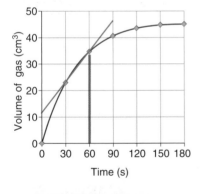

Industrial catalysts

The table gives some examples of catalysts used in industrial processes.

Catalyst	Reaction
titanium(IV) chloride	polymerisation of ethene
vanadium(V) oxide	contact process to make sulfuric acid
iron	Haber process to make ammonia
nickel/rhodium alloy	hardening vegetable oils to make margarine
platinum	making nitric acid from ammonia

▲ Platinum gauze used as a catalyst in making nitric acid

Increasing surface area

In the last item we looked the reaction between marble and hydrochloric acid (page 137). We are going to repeat the experiment but this time with the same mass of powdered calcium carbonate.

The line graph on the left shows the results. The graph line for the original experiment is there for comparison.

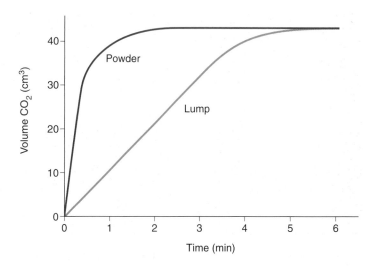

 g Is this reaction faster than the original experiment? How can you tell from the graph?

The photographs below shows the difference between a lump reacting and a powder reacting.

The reaction is faster because the powder has a larger **surface area** for the acid particles to collide with. There are more collisions per second (a greater frequency of collisions) so the reaction happens faster. This is shown in the diagram below.

If the limestone is crushed, the surface area is bigger because more surface is exposed

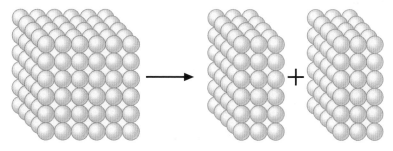

▲ A larger surface area means more collisions. In each case, the acid particles collide with the limestone more frequently, and so the reaction will get faster

 h Catalysts are often in the form of fine meshes or pellets. Suggest why this is better than large solid lumps.

Making tablets dissolve

Amanda works for a pharmaceuticals company that makes painkillers that can be bought over the counter. One particular painkiller can be bought as a round pill, as a lozenge-shaped pill with a sugar coating or as a powder.

These painkillers work by dissolving in the stomach. The painkilling active ingredients are then able to attack the source of the pain.

Some people prefer to use pills because they are handy to carry around and they are easier to swallow. The powders have to be mixed with water and drunk and they usually taste horrible.

Amanda carries out an experiment to find out how quickly each painkiller dissolves.

She test three different products A, B and C. She drops a single dose of each painkiller into acid similar in concentration to the acid in the stomach. She uses the same volume of acid each time.

Her results are shown on the graph. Three lines A, B and C are plotted.

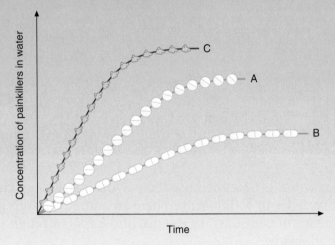

Questions

1 Why do you think it is an advantage for painkillers to dissolve quickly?

2 Which type of painkiller has the fastest rate of reaction?

3 Explain why this painkiller dissolves the quickest.

4 Suggest a reason why the sugar-coated lozenge dissolves slowly.

5 It is important to take the correct dose of painkiller. Suggest why pills are better than powders for doing this.

6 In the photograph there are some capsules containing very tiny pellets. When these are swallowed the outside of the capsule quickly breaks down and the tiny pellets escape. Explain why do you think these are better than a tablet?

7 What evidence is there in the graph that the different products contain different amounts of painkiller?

C2a

1 Years ago gloss paints had to be stirred before use and from time to time during use. It is not necessary today. Suggest why. [2]

2 For many centuries cloths have been dyed using plant dyes such as woad. Now synthetic dyes are used.

Suggest two reasons why synthetic dyes have replaced natural dyes. [2]

3 A wood varnish consists of a natural resin dissolved in an organic solvent.

Describe the change that takes place when the varnish dries. [1]

4 Describe two things that happen when a gloss paint dries. [2]

5 The table gives the percentage composition of two oil-based paints.

Paint	Binding medium	Solvent	Pigment
undercoat	40	20	20
top coat	60	20	10

Undercoat must provide a good base colour, covering up any paint underneath. Top coat must give a tough, shiny, final finish.

Describe how the composition of these paints makes them suitable for their purpose. [4]

C2b

1 Write down the name of a construction material made from:

a bauxite (aluminum ore) [1]
b clay [1]
c sand. [1]

2 Put these three rocks in order of increasing hardness:

granite   limestone   marble [2]

3 Which two materials heated together produce cement? [2]

4 Use chemicals from the list to write the word equation for the thermal decomposition of limestone.

**calcium carbonate   calcium oxide
carbon dioxide   water** [2]

5 Explain why steel-reinforced concrete can be used for weight-bearing beams in construction. [3]

6 Write a balanced symbol equation for the thermal decomposition of calcium carbonate, $CaCO_3$. [2]

7 Granite, limestone and marble are three rocks used in the construction industry.

a Which rock is produced by the crystallization of molten rock from the magna? [1]
b Which rock is produced by the action of high temperatures and pressures on existing rocks? [1]
c Which rock is sedimentary? [1]
d Which rock cannot contain fossils? [1]

C2c

1 a What causes an earthquake? [1]
  b Where on the Earth are earthquakes most likely to happen? [1]

2 Explain why some igneous rocks are made up of small crystals and others of large crystals. [2]

3 The theory of plate tectonics is a fairly recent one. Suggest difficulties scientists have had discovering the truth about the Earth's crust. [3]

C2d

1 Brass is an alloy used for making screws for fixing wood.

a Which metals are used to make brass? [2]
b Suggest two properties of brass that make it suitable for this use. [2]

2 a Describe some of the problems of recycling copper. [2]
  b Why is it particularly important to recycle copper? [2]

3 Duralumin is an alloy made from aluminium and copper. It is denser than pure aluminium but stronger than pure aluminium or pure copper.

a Despite being denser than pure aluminium, duralumin is used for building aircraft rather than pure aluminium. Why is this? [1]
b Overhead power cables are made from pure aluminium rather than duralumin. Suggest why. [1]
c Pure aluminium costs £800 and pure copper costs £1 200 per tonne. Work out the cost of the metals used to produce 1 tonne of duralumin containing 10% copper. [2]

4 Silver can be purified in a similar way to copper. The electrolyte is silver nitrate solution, $AgNO_3$.

a Write down the symbols for the ions in silver nitrate solution. [2]

b Write the ionic equation for the change at the positive electrode. [2]

c Write the ionic equation for the change at the negative electrode. [2]

C2e

1 Explain why steel ship hulls have to be examined frequently for rusting. [2]

2 Suggest reasons why steel is used instead of iron for car bodies. [3]

3 Write the word equation for the rusting of iron. [2]

4 Explain the advantages and disadvantages of using aluminium rather than steel for car bodies. [4]

C2f

1 Look at the graph showing the number of deaths each day in London between 1st December and 15th December 1952. It also shows the concentrations of smoke and sulfur dioxide.

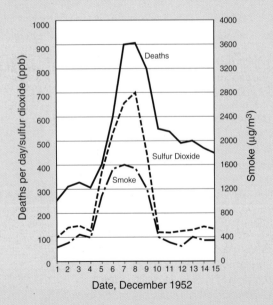

Date, December 1952

a How many deaths occurred on 5th December 1952? [1]

b What is the relationship between the number of deaths and the concentration of sulfur dioxide? [2]

c Is there a similar correlation between the number of deaths and the concentration of smoke? Explain your answer. [2]

2 The original atmosphere of the Earth included hydrogen and helium. Why did they escape from the atmosphere? [1]

3 a How are nitrogen oxides formed in a car engine? [1]

b Why does this reaction not take place when a splint is burning in ordinary air? [1]

4 The diagram summarises an experiment using iron filings.

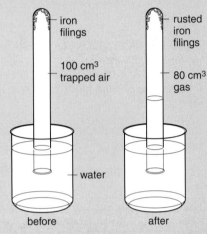

before   after

Explain the results of the experiment. [2]

5 Write a balanced equation for the reaction that takes place in a catalytic converter to remove carbon monoxide and nitrogen monoxide. [3]

6 The percentage of nitrogen has remained constant for a long time. Why is this? [3]

C2g

1 The graph shows the volume of hydrogen collected at intervals in an experiment with dilute sulfuric acid.

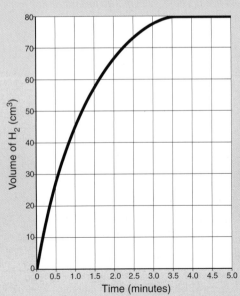

Time (minutes)

a After how long is the reaction complete? [1]
b After how long are half the reactants used up? [1]
c Calculate the average volume of gas produced each second in the first minute. [2]
d Why is your answer to **c** not a useful measure of the rate of reaction? [1]

2 Refer to question **1**.

Draw a tangent to the curve at one minute and calculate the rate of reaction at this time. [4]

3 Which one of the following graphs would be most useful in establishing that the rate of reaction is directly proportional to concentration (c) of the reactant? (T represents time.)

A c against T
B 1/c against 1/T
C c against 1/ T
D c against c × T [1]

C2h

1 The mass of a catalyst was determined at intervals during a reaction. Which one of the graphs A–D would be obtained? [1]

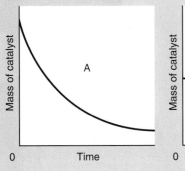
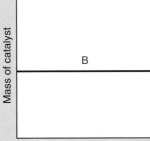
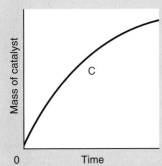
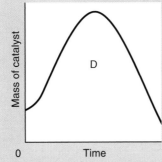

2 An experiment was carried out using marble chips and dilute hydrochloric acid to investigate the effects of particle size on the rate of reaction.

$$CaCO_3 + 2HCl \rightarrow CaCl_2 + CO_2 + H_2O$$

A large marble chip (mass 0.4 g) was placed in a conical flask and the flask placed on a top pan balance. $25\ cm^3$ of hydrochloric acid was added to the flask and a plug of cotton wool was placed in the neck of the flask. The reading on the balance was noted at intervals.

The results are shown in the table.

Time (min)	0	2	4	6	8	10	11	12
Total loss in mass (g)	0.0	2.2	2.9	3.3	3.6	3.7	3.7	3.7

a Plot a graph of the total loss of mass (on the y-axis) against time. [3]
b When was the reaction fastest? [1]
c After how many minutes was the reaction completed? [1]

The reaction was repeated using 0.4 g of powdered marble and a fresh $25\ cm^3$ sample of dilute hydrochloric acid.

d On the same graph, sketch the graph that would be obtained with powdered marble. [3]
e What can be concluded from these two experiments? [1]
f Explain your conclusion in **e**. Use ideas about particles in your answer. [2]

3 In an experiment to compare different ions as a catalyst for a certain reaction, the following results were obtained.

	Temperature (°C)	Substance tested as a catalyst	Time for reaction to be completed (s)
A	20	cobalt(II) chloride	18
B	20	sodium nitrate	36
C	20	cobalt(II) nitrate	12
D	30	cobalt(II) nitrate	8
E	20	sodium chloride	40

a Why should D not be used in any comparison? [1]
b Which substance gives the greatest increase in the rate of reaction? [1]
c Which substance is least effective as catalyst? [1]
d Which ion is most effective as a catalyst? [1]

73

C3 The Periodic Table

I've seen a Periodic Table on the wall in our school laboratory. I know it shows all of the chemical elements, but what's the point? They are not even in alphabetical order.

It's a way of putting the elements in order to show how they behave. It's all to do with the properties that each element has, and which elements have similar properties.

- 200 years ago chemists knew that some elements have properties that are quite different from each other, while others have similar properties. But they could not see any logic or order to the properties of the elements.

- A Periodic Table of the elements was put together by Dmitri Mendeleev in 1869. He placed elements in order of increasing atomic mass. His brilliant idea was to leave gaps for elements that had not yet been discovered. Today we use a modern version of Mendeleev's Periodic Table.

And the properties of each element are decided by the structure of the atoms in that element. So it all makes sense when you look at a Periodic Table.

What you need to know

- All substances are made from elements.

- Elements are made up of atoms.

- Elements have different properties.

Atoms and elements

In this item you will find out

- about sub-atomic particles and their place in atoms

- the connections between atomic structure and the Periodic Table

- about the structure of isotopes

Have you ever seen an atom? You may think that atoms are too small to see, but using modern technology we can view images of some of the very largest atoms. The electron micrograph shows atoms in a crystal of uranium.

It is difficult to imagine how small atoms are. A 2 cm cube of iron contains about 600 000 000 000 000 000 000 000 iron atoms.

In the centre of an **atom** is the nucleus. This is where the **protons** are. **Electrons** are outside the nucleus, arranged in shells. Most atoms also contain **neutrons** in the nucleus.

These three sub-atomic particles have different properties.

Sub-atomic particle	Where found	Relative mass	Relative charge
proton	in the nucleus	1	+1
neutron	in the nucleus	1	0
electron	outside the nucleus	0.000 5	−1

Because an atom has equal numbers of positive protons and negative electrons, the whole atom is neutral.

a Electrons were discovered in 1887 and protons in 1911, but neutrons were not discovered until 1932. Suggest why it took longer for neutrons to be discovered.

> **Amazing fact**
>
> About 2500 years ago the Greek philosopher Democritus proposed that the physical world consisted of atoms. He had no scientific evidence to support these ideas, which were discounted by Aristotle, the most influential man of this time.

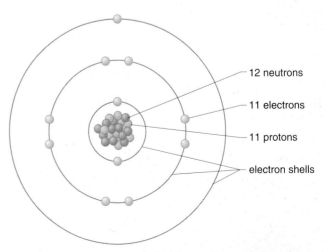

12 neutrons
11 electrons
11 protons
electron shells

▲ *Inside a sodium atom*

Putting elements in order

Each element contains just one type of atom. Each atom in an element contains the same number of protons. This is called the **atomic number** of the element. It can also be called the **proton number**.

In the Periodic Table, elements are arranged in order of their atomic number.

These are the elements in the second row of the Periodic Table.

Element	Lithium	Beryllium	Boron	Carbon	Nitrogen	Oxygen	Fluorine	Neon
symbol	Li	Be	B	C	N	O	F	Ne
protons	3	4	5	6	7	8	9	10
electrons	3	4	5	6	7	8	9	10

The nucleus of an atom of beryllium contains four protons and five neutrons. If you add them together they come to nine. This is the **mass number** of beryllium. It can also be called the **nucleon number**. The mass number of an element is found by adding together the number of protons and neutrons.

 An atom of fluorine has 9 protons and 10 neutrons. What is the mass number of fluorine?

Electron structures

As you found out earlier, electrons are arranged in shells around the nucleus of each atom. Each electron shell can hold a maximum number of electrons. The first shell can hold one or two electrons while the second and third shells can hold from one to eight.

When one shell is full, electrons start to fill the next shell. Since the number of electrons in a neutral atom is the same as the number of protons, the electron structures can be worked out from the atomic number of the element.

Some examples are given in the table.

Element	Symbol	Atomic number	Electrons	Electron arrangement
lithium	Li	3	3	2,1
carbon	C	6	6	2,4
neon	Ne	10	10	2,8
sodium	Na	11	11	2,8,1
chlorine	Cl	17	17	2,8,7
calcium	Ca	20	20	2,8,8,2

 Use a Periodic Table to help you work out the electron structures of each of these elements:

argon   magnesium   oxygen   potassium   silicon

Chemical shorthand

You can use a shorthand convention to give details of the sub-atomic particles in an atom. The diagram on the right shows the shorthand notation for an atom of carbon, which has six protons and six neutrons. The total number of protons and neutrons adds up to a mass number of 12.

When atoms gain or lose electrons they form ions. Each positive charge indicates the loss of one electron from an atom. Each negative charge indicates the gain of one electron by an atom.

A sodium atom $^{23}_{11}Na$ has 11 protons, 11 electrons and 12 neutrons.

A sodium ion $^{23}_{11}Na^{+}$ has 11 protons, 10 electrons and 12 neutrons.

d **Work out the number of protons, electrons and neutrons in these particles:**

$^{14}_{7}N$ $^{19}_{9}F$ $^{27}_{13}Al$ $^{7}_{3}Li$ $^{35}_{17}Cl$ $^{24}_{12}Mg^{2+}$ $^{16}_{8}O^{2-}$ $^{27}_{13}Al^{3+}$

$$^{12}_{6}C$$

▲ *Shorthand notation for carbon-12*

Isotopes

In each element every atom has the same number of protons. But in most elements some of the atoms have a different number of neutrons from others. Atoms of the same element with the same atomic number but with different numbers of neutrons, and so different mass numbers, are called **isotopes**.

Here is some information about the isotopes of carbon.

Isotope	Carbon-12	Carbon-13	Carbon-14
Atomic number	6	6	6
Mass number	12	13	14
Percentage of isotope	98.9	1.1	trace

Some isotopes, such as carbon-14, are radioactive. Over a period of time they decay to form other elements, becoming less radioactive as they do so.

From information in the table it is possible to work out the numbers of each sub-atomic particle in these atoms. For example, an atom of carbon-14 has six protons, so it must also have six electrons. It has 14 – 6 = 8 neutrons.

e **Use the numbers of protons, electrons and neutrons shown below to work out the identity of each isotope.**

(i) 8 protons, 8 electrons, 10 neutrons

(ii) 19 protons, 19 electrons, 22 neutrons

(iii) 7 protons, 7 electrons, 8 neutrons

(iv) 92 protons, 92 electrons, 143 neutrons

Examiner's tip

The atomic number of an element tells you how many protons are in an atom, which is the same as the number of electrons. A positive ion will have fewer, and a negative ion more, than this number of electrons.

Keywords

atom • atomic number • electron • isotope • mass number • neutron • nucleon number • proton • proton number

New elements from old

▶ *This cyclotron was used to make the new superheavy elements*

Two new 'superheavy' elements were recently made by bombarding lead atoms with energy-packed krypton atoms at the rate of two trillion per second.

After 11 days, the scientists working at the Lawrence Berkeley National Laboratory, USA, had produced just three atoms of element 118. They each contained 118 protons and 175 neutrons in their nuclei.

The new atoms decayed almost instantly to element 116, which was also short-lived. But for that brief moment, they were the only three atoms of these elements ever to have existed on Earth.

In nature, no element heavier than uranium, with 92 protons and 146 neutrons, can normally be found. Scientists can make heavier ones by colliding two large nuclei together and hoping that they will form a new, heavier nucleus for a short time.

Synthetic elements are often short-lived but provide scientists with valuable insights into the structure of atomic nuclei. They also offer opportunities to study the chemical properties of the elements heavier than uranium.

Element 118 takes less than a thousandth of a second to decay by emitting an alpha particle. This leaves behind an isotope of element 116 which contains 116 protons and 173 neutrons. This element is also radioactive, alpha-decaying to an isotope of element 114. The chain of successive alpha decays continues until you get element 106.

Questions

1 How do scientists make elements heavier than uranium?

2 Why is it useful to make these elements?

3 For how long did the new element 118 last?

4 What happened to this new element?

Interesting ions

In this item you will find out

- how to describe the formation of ions in terms of electron arrangement

- how to work out formulae for ionic compounds

- how to explain the properties of ionic compounds

In the time of the Roman Empire soldiers were often paid with salt. If you did a good job you were 'worth your salt'. We still use this expression today.

Can you imagine a world without salt? Not only would your potato crisps or chips taste odd, but lots of other things would be difficult to do.

▲ Food would be boring without salt

Only about five per cent of the world's annual salt production ends up as seasoning at the dinner table. The vast majority is used in numerous commercial applications like manufacturing pulp and paper, setting dyes in textiles and fabric, and producing soaps and detergents.

Sodium chloride is an ionic compound. This means that the sodium and chlorine are joined together by **ionic bonding**. When the compound is formed, the atoms form positive and negative ions.

Amazing fact

Over 5 million tonnes of salt are produced in the United Kingdom each year.

There are lots of ionic compounds. Sodium chloride is just one example. Some other examples are sodium oxide, magnesium chloride and magnesium oxide.

(a) Why is salt important?

(b) Salt is mined as rock salt, a mixture of sodium chloride and grit. Many tons of rock salt are spread on roads during the winter. Suggest why this is done.

▶ Making soap

LOST ELECTRONS

LOST PROPERTY

Forming ions

Ions are atoms with a positive or a negative charge. Positive ions are formed when an atom loses one or more electrons.

A sodium atom loses one electron to form a sodium ion. Since one negative electron has been lost, and no positive protons have been lost, the ion has a single positive charge, Na^+.

When a magnesium atom forms an ion, it loses two electrons. This gives the magnesium ion a 2+ charge, Mg^{2+}.

Metal ions have positive charges. Non-metal ions have negative charges. A chlorine atom gains one electron but does not gain a proton. So a chloride ion has a negative charge, Cl^-. An oxygen atom gains two electrons to form an oxide ion, O^{2-}.

Atom or ion	Formula	Protons	Electrons	Electron arrangement
sodium atom	Na	11	11	2,8,1
sodium ion	Na^+	11	10	2,8
chlorine atom	Cl	17	17	2,8,7
chloride ion	Cl^-	17	18	2,8,8
magnesium atom	Mg	12	12	2,8,2
magnesium ion	Mg^{2+}	12	10	2,8
oxygen atom	O	8	8	2,6
oxide ion	O^{2-}	8	10	2,8

The table shows the way that the electron structures of some atoms change when they form ions.

When an atom forms an ion, it achieves a full outer shell of electrons, called a **stable octet**.

Metals atoms have one, two or three electrons in their outer shell. When they form ions all of the electrons in the outer shell are lost. The next shell, which is full, becomes the outer shell. Non-metal atoms have four or more electrons in the outer shell. They gain the correct number of electrons to fill this shell. Each ion has the same electron arrangement as a noble gas – for an oxide ion it is that of neon. The ion does not, however, have the same number of protons as the atoms of this noble gas.

c Why do atoms of different elements lose or gain different numbers of electrons to form ions?

d Work out the charges and write down the formulas for the ions formed from the following atoms:

Li   Al   F   Ca   N   K

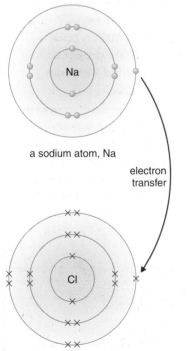

a sodium atom, Na

electron transfer

a chlorine atom, Cl

▲ *Transferring electrons in the formation of sodium chloride*

Ionic bonding

An **ionic compound** is formed by transfer of one or more electrons from a metal to a non-metal. When sodium chloride is formed, each sodium atom transfers one electron to a chlorine atom. This forms a positive sodium ion, Na^+, and a negative chloride ion, Cl^-. These ions are then attracted to one another.

In the formation of the ionic compound magnesium oxide, both of the electrons lost from a magnesium atom are received by a single oxygen atom. This makes the ions Mg^{2+} and O^{2-}.

e Draw a 'dot and cross' diagram, similar to those shown for sodium chloride and magnesium oxide, to show the transfer of electrons in the formation of magnesium chloride.

f Work out the electron structures and formulae of the ions in sodium oxide. Then find the formula for this ionic compound and draw a 'dot and cross' diagram to show how the compound is formed.

More about salts

The ions in sodium chloride or magnesium oxide form a regular arrangement called a giant **ionic lattice**. This is held together because the positive ions are **electrostatically attracted** to the negative ions.

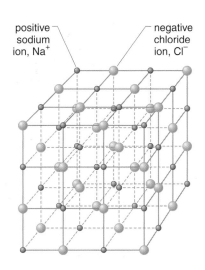

▲ The arrangement of ions in a sodium chloride lattice

▲ Sodium chloride crystals

Because of the strong electrostatic attraction between the ions in sodium chloride and magnesium oxide, a lot of energy is needed to pull the ions apart. This means that these compounds have high melting points.

Ionic compounds cannot conduct electricity when solid. This is because the electrons in the ions are firmly held – electrons cannot flow through the solid ionic compound to carry an electric current. Also, the strong electrostatic attraction between positive and negative ions prevents them moving to carry the current.

When sodium chloride or magnesium oxide is melted, the ions move apart and are able to move. This means that molten sodium chloride and molten magnesium oxide can conduct electricity.

The ions in sodium chloride or magnesium oxide are attracted to charges on water molecules so they are soluble in water. The ions separate when they dissolve so the solution conducts electricity. This is true of most ionic compounds.

g Solid calcium chloride does not conduct electricity. Explain why.

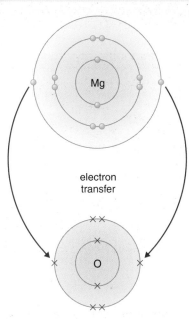

▲ Transferring electrons in the formation of magnesium oxide

Beside the sea

Dr Sally Minto is a chemical engineer. She works at Amlwch on the island of Anglesey in North Wales where there is a factory that extracts the element bromine from seawater.

Bromine is a very poisonous and corrosive red-brown liquid. Bromine compounds are widely distributed on Earth but are normally found in low concentration. Dissolved bromide ions in seawater represent a considerable concentration of the element compared with sources on land.

Bromine is present in seawater at only 0.006 5% (65 parts per million). It takes 22 000 tonnes of seawater to make one tonne of bromine. The site at Amlwch has six large seawater pumps capable of pumping 500 000 000 gallons of seawater into the process every day.

The seawater is treated with chlorine which converts sodium bromide into free bromine by this reaction.

$$2NaBr + Cl_2 \rightarrow 2NaCl + Br_2$$

Bromine is a very volatile liquid which means that it easily vaporises into a gas. At Amlwch the bromine is literally blown out of the seawater using large fans.

Questions

1 Write a word equation for the reaction that produces bromine from seawater.

2 Apart from the plentiful supply of seawater, suggest what other advantages there are for building a factory that makes bromine near to the coast?

3 Why do you think the concentration of bromine (as bromide ions) in seawater is higher than in any location on land?

4 Why is the extraction of bromine important to the chemical industry?

5 What precautions do you think Sally and the other workers at the Amlwch factory should take:
  (a) to ensure their own safety
  (b) to ensure the safety of people living on the island?

Diagram labels: fan, sulfur dioxide gas, acidified chlorinated seawater, fresh water, primary acid liquor, absorber packing, packing, seawater inlet, seawater outlet

▲ *Extracting bromine from seawater*

The bromine vapour is then condensed back into a liquid. From here the bromine can be purified and used to produce a range of useful products.

Bromine has a number of uses including the purification of water and the manufacture of dyes and medicines, fire retardants for plastics, and fumigants for killing pest infestations. Silver bromide is an important chemical in photographic film.

Bonding and beyond

In this item you will find out

- how non-metal atoms join by covalent bonding to make molecules

- why covalent molecules have specific properties

- how elements are grouped in the Periodic Table

▲ Natural gas is methane

When you turn on the fire or sit next to a hot radiator, do you think about the gas that lots of us use for our heating? Natural gas is the compound methane. This compound contains atoms of carbon and hydrogen, joined together by **covalent bonding**.

When an atom of a metal joins with an atom of a non-metal an ionic bond is formed. But when two non-metal atoms combine together, they share electrons to form a covalent bond. The atoms join to form a **molecule**.

Covalent compounds contain molecules with a number of different non-metal atoms joined together. A molecule of methane contains one carbon atom and four hydrogen atoms, so methane has the formula CH_4. Carbon dioxide, CO_2, and water, H_2O, are also covalent molecules. The diagram shows the formulas of some covalent molecules.

$$H-\underset{\underset{H}{|}}{\overset{\overset{H}{|}}{C}}-H$$

methane

$$O=C=O$$

carbon dioxide

$$H\diagdown O \diagup H$$

water

$$H-H$$

hydrogen

$$Cl-Cl$$

chlorine

Some elements also have atoms joined by covalent bonds. For example, hydrogen consists of H_2 molecules and chlorine consists of Cl_2 molecules.

a What are the states (gas, liquid or solid) of methane, carbon dioxide, water, hydrogen and chlorine?

b Water has unusual properties for a small covalent molecule. Use your answer to question a to suggest one unusual property.

Amazing fact

Many small covalent molecules are gases with very low boiling points. Hydrogen has a boiling point of −253 °C. This is just 20 degrees above absolute zero, the coldest possible temperature.

Forming simple molecules

Each covalent bond involves the sharing of a pair of electrons, one electron coming from each atom. These 'dot and cross' diagrams on the right show the covalent bonds in hydrogen and chlorine.

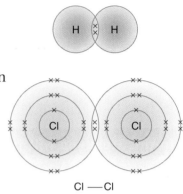

▶ *Covalent bonds in hydrogen and chlorine*

In the molecules of non-metal elements such as hydrogen and chlorine, two atoms from the same element share a pair of electrons in a covalent bond. One electron in this pair comes form each atom in the molecule.

When non-metal elements form compounds such as carbon dioxide and methane, in each molecule of the compound atoms from different elements share pairs of electrons in covalent bonds. Again one electron comes from each atom that is sharing the pair of electrons.

By sharing pairs of electrons each atom has a full outer shell: a duplet (two electrons) for the first shell and an octet (eight electrons) for the second and third shells. This is the stable electron arrangement found in the outer shells of the noble gases.

c Draw a 'dot and cross' diagram to show the covalent bonds in a molecule of water.

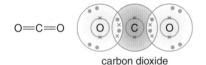

carbon dioxide

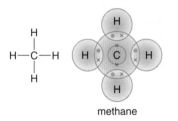

methane

▲ *Covalent bonds in carbon dioxide and methane*

More about carbon dioxide and water

Covalent bonds are immensely strong and require a very large amount of energy to break them. However, the forces of attraction between molecules are much weaker. There is enough energy at low temperatures to break the weak **intermolecular forces** between most small covalent molecules.

This means that most simple covalent compounds have low melting points and boiling points and are gases or liquids at room temperature.

Covalent compound	Formula of molecule	Melting point (°C)	Boiling point (°C)
methane	CH_4	–183	–162
water	H_2O	0	100

Water is unusual in that it has higher melting and boiling points than most other covalent compound with small molecules.

Covalent molecules, such as water and carbon dioxide, are not charged particles. There are no ions or free electrons present in these compounds so they do not conduct electricity.

> **Examiner's tip**
>
> When drawing a dot and cross diagram of a covalent molecule, use the dots and crosses to show which electrons in the bonds are from which atom.

Here is the displayed formula for the covalent compound dibromoethane.

$$\begin{array}{c} \text{Br} \quad \text{Br} \\ \mid \quad \mid \\ \text{H}-\text{C}-\text{C}-\text{H} \\ \mid \quad \mid \\ \text{H} \quad \text{H} \end{array}$$

(d) **How many atoms of each element are in a molecule of dibromoethane?**

Grouped together

The diagram on the right shows a shortened version of the Periodic Table.

The numbers across the top of the Periodic Table show the vertical **Groups** of elements. Group 1 contains the metals lithium to francium. Group 7 contains fluorine to astatine. Group 8 (sometimes called Group 0) contains helium to radon. The elements in each group have similar chemical properties.

The number of the Group that an element belongs to tells you how many electrons are in the outer shell of an atom of that element. All of the elements in Group 1 have one electron in the outer shell. All of the elements in Group 7 have seven electrons in the outer shell. All of the elements in Group 8 have eight electrons in the outer shell, except helium which has two. Going down a Group, each successive element has one additional complete shell to the element above it.

1	2	3	4	5	6	7	8
1 **H** Hydrogen 1							4 **He** Helium 2
7 **Li** Lithium 3	9 **Be** Beryllium 4	11 **B** Boron 5	12 **C** Carbon 6	14 **N** Nitrogen 7	16 **O** Oxygen 8	19 **F** Fluorine 9	20 **Ne** Neon 10
23 **Na** Sodium 11	24 **Mg** Magnesium 12	27 **Al** Aluminium 13	28 **Si** Silicon 14	31 **P** Phosphorus 15	32 **S** Sulfur 16	35.5 **Cl** Chlorine 17	40 **Ar** Argon 18
39 **K** Potassium 19	40 **Ca** Calcium 20	70 **Ga** Galium 31	73 **Ge** Germanium 32	75 **As** Arsenic 33	79 **Se** Selenium 34	80 **Br** Bromine 35	84 **Kr** Krypton 36
85 **Rb** Rubidium 37	88 **Sr** Strontium 38	115 **In** Indium 49	119 **Sn** Tin 50	122 **Sb** Antimony 51	128 **Te** Tellurium 52	127 **I** Iodine 53	131 **Xe** Xenon 54
133 **Cs** Caesium 55	137 **Ba** Barium 56	204 **Tl** Thalium 81	207 **Pb** Lead 82	209 **Bi** Bismuth 83	209 **Po** Polonium 84	210 **At** Astatine 85	222 **Rn** Radon 86
223 **Fr** Francium 87	226 **Ra** Radium 88						

(e) **What is the name of the element that has two electron shells and has five electrons in its outer shell?**

(f) **To which Group does the element with the electron structure 2,8,4 belong?**

Periods

The horizontal rows of the Periodic Table are called **Periods**. The first Period contains only hydrogen and helium. The second Period contains eight elements, from lithium to neon. The third has another eight elements, from sodium to argon.

Each Period begins with an element in Group 1, with one electron in the outer shell, and ends with an element in Group 8, with a full outer shell. The number of the Period that an element is in is the same as the number of occupied shells in the atoms of that element. Magnesium is in Period 3 so an atom of magnesium has three shells of electrons.

(g) **In which Period does the element with the electron structure 2,8,5 belong?**

> **Keywords**
>
> covalent bonding • Group • intermolecular force • molecule • Period

A new Periodic Table

Chemistry students are used to seeing the modern Periodic Table.

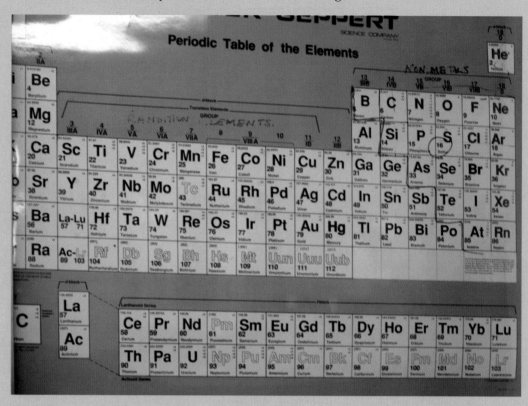

A new copy of the Periodic Table has been made for use by geology students. It shows how chemical elements are distributed in nature, sorting them by electrical charge rather than by numbers of protons and electrons.

The Earth's minerals consist mainly of charged elements, or ions. These behave differently from the original Periodic Table's neutral atoms. The new table groups ions with similar charge according to where they are found. Some elements appear several times with different charges. Sulfur appears four times.

Geologists know that a mineral's properties, such as melting point and solubility in water, depend on the size, charge and structure of its ions. It is possible to group ions according to their properties and occurrence on the Earth. Ions with similar chemical behaviour, and which are found in similar natural environments, can be put into the same group.

The new table has five families which represent minerals in the Earth's crust, the Earth's mantle, in solution in water, in the atmosphere and forming the basic nutrients of life.

Living things prefer ions with a single charge, like potassium in fertiliser and sodium in salt. Ions that can have more than one charge, like aluminium, can form resilient minerals that might be found in the Earth's crust or mantle.

Questions

1 What decides the Group that an element goes into in the modern Periodic Table used by chemistry students?

2 What decides how elements are grouped in the new geology Periodic Table?

3 Many of the compounds studied by chemists are covalent. Why would the geology Periodic Table cause problems for the study of covalent compounds?

4 In the new geology Periodic Table, sulfur appears four times. Explain why sulfur only appears once in the chemistry Periodic Table.

The alkali metals

In this item you will find out

- how and why the metals in Group 1 react in a similar way

- how and why the reactivity in Group 1 increases down the Group

- how to use flame tests to identify Group 1 metal ions

The engine on your boat has failed and you are drifting towards dangerous rocks. How can you make sure that the lifeboat crew see and rescue you? One way is to set off a distress flare.

Distress flares are very bright. The light they give off is often a particular colour. Red indicates danger or 'stop'. Green indicates safety or 'go'.

What makes these flares different colours? Metal compounds are added to the mixture of chemicals in the flare. When the flare burns the very high temperature vaporises the metal ions. They absorb heat energy and re-emit it as light of a particular wavelength. This gives a colour to the flame.

In the laboratory this property of metal ions can be used to test for metals in compounds. A moistened nichrome wire is dipped into a solid sample of the compound containing the metal ion, and then put into a very hot Bunsen flame. The photograph on the right shows a **flame test** being carried out.

Light emitted by the metal gives the flame a colour. For example, each of the metals in Group 1 of the Periodic Table gives the flame a different colour.

The colour of the flame can then be used to identify the metal ion present in a compound.

▲ Distress flare

▲ Flame test

a Suggest why different metals give different colours to the flame.

b Which metal may be used in a distress flare to indicate danger or 'stop'?

Group I element	Symbol	Flame colour
lithium	Li	carmine red
sodium	Na	golden yellow
potassium	K	lilac
rubidium	Rb	red
caesium	Cs	blue

87

The alkali metals

The elements in Group 1 of the Periodic Table are called the **alkali metals**. Three of the alkali metals are lithium, sodium and potassium.

The reactivity of the Group 1 metals increases down the Group, so lithium is the least reactive alkali metal. Reactions of these metals with water can be seen when a small cube of each metal is added to water in a trough.

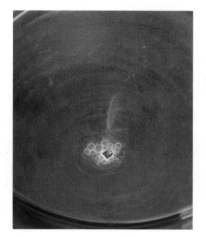

▲ Lithium reacting with water

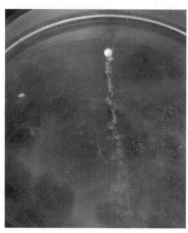

▲ Sodium reacting with water

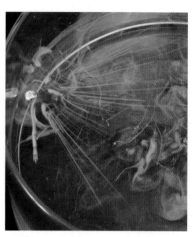

▲ Potassium reacting with water

The table shows observations made during this experiment.

Group 1 metal	Observations when the metal is added to water	Colour of Universal Indicator added to the water
lithium	• floats on the water • remains as a cube shape • fizzes slowly • disappears slowly	purple
sodium	• floats on the water • melts to form a ball of metal • fizzes quickly • whizzes around on the surface • disappears quickly	purple
potassium	• floats on the water • melts to form a ball of metal • fizzes furiously • whizzes around on the surface • burns with a lilac flame • disappears very quickly	purple

c **What evidence does this experiment provide for the change in reactivity of the alkali metals down Group 1?**

In each of the three experiments, water in the trough turns Universal Indicator purple. This shows that an alkali is formed during the reaction. This alkali is the metal hydroxide.

The fizzing in these reactions shows that a gas is given off. If you collect some of this gas in a test tube and put in a lighted splint, then the gas explodes with a squeaky pop sound. This shows the gas is hydrogen.

We can write symbol equations and word equations for these reactions.

$2Li \quad + \quad 2H_2O \quad \rightarrow \quad 2LiOH \quad + \quad H_2$
lithium + water → lithium hydroxide + hydrogen

$2Na \quad + \quad 2H_2O \quad \rightarrow \quad 2NaOH \quad + \quad H_2$
sodium + water → sodium hydroxide + hydrogen

d Write a balanced symbol equation for the reaction of potassium with water.

e Rubidium is the next Group 1 metal after potassium. Use information from the table to predict how rubidium reacts with water.

f Write a balanced symbol equation for this reaction.

Physical properties

Group 1 metals also show a trend in physical properties down the Group.

g Predict the melting point and hardness of caesium, the metal below rubidium in Group 1.

Group 1 metal	Melting point (°C)	Hardness
lithium	181	fairly hard
sodium	98	fairly soft
potassium	64	soft
rubidium	39	very soft

Group 1 metals and their electrons

The table on the right shows the arrangement of electrons in the first three Group 1 elements.

The number of electrons in the outer shell of an atom determines how it will react. Each element in Group 1 has one electron in its outer shell. This means that Group 1 elements have similar properties.

Group 1 element	Electron arrangement
lithium	2,1
sodium	2,8,1
potassium	2,8,8,1

When these atoms react each loses the one electron in its outer shell to form a positive ion. This loss of electrons is called oxidation.

For example, for sodium:

$Na \rightarrow Na^+ + e^-$

This ionic equation shows that an atom of sodium loses an electron during the reaction. This shows that the sodium atom has been oxidised. The next electron shell now becomes the outer electron shell of the ion. This shell is full, giving the ion a stable electronic structure.

As we move down Group 1, each successive element is more reactive. This is because it is easier for this element to lose an electron than the element above it in the Group. It is more easily oxidised.

Keywords

alkali metal • flame test

Investigating a 'hit and run' car accident

Police called to a 'hit and run' accident found shards of paint at the scene. They also found a damaged car not far from the scene.

Samples of paint from the scene and the car were sent to Dr Peter Brown, a forensic scientist. He used a technique called flame emission spectroscopy to analyse the paint.

When metal atoms are heated in a flame the energy they gain is given out as light. Each metal element gives out light of a characteristic colour or wavelength.

Although the colour of the flame as seen by the human eye can be used to identify which metal is present, this does not give a measure of the amount of each metal present.

The emitted light is analysed by a machine that can distinguish and measure light wavelengths far better than the human eye.

This is one of the most sensitive of all analytical methods. A few milligrams of a solid sample is usually enough for the detection of metallic elements present at a concentration of a few parts per million or less.

Here are some of Dr Brown's results.

Concentration in sample (ppm)		
Metal element	Paint from scene	Paint from car
barium	584	588
copper	1066	1072
lead	722	519
strontium	98	101

Questions

1 Suggest why it would not be good enough simply to compare the colour of the paint to see if the samples match.

2 Why did Dr Brown use flame emission spectroscopy instead of simply doing a flame test with a Bunsen burner?

3 Do Dr Brown's results prove that the paint came from the car? Explain your answer.

The halogens

In this item you will find out

- how halogens react with alkali metals

- how the reactivity of halogens changes down the Group

- how to predict the properties of other halogens

▲ The water in swimming pools is sterilised with chlorine

Elements in Group 7 are called the **halogens**. These are very important elements with a variety of uses. Chlorine, fluorine, bromine and iodine are all halogens.

We use chlorine to sterilise the water used in swimming pools and supplied to the taps in our homes. It is also used in the manufacture of pesticides and plastics. Iodine is used to sterilise wounds. When painted onto a cut it prevents infection by bacteria.

As you can see from the photograph below, the elements in this group differ a great deal in their appearance.

Amazing fact

You need iodine in your diet to stay healthy. If you don't get enough iodine, your thyroid gland swells to form a goitre.

◀ Chlorine, bromine and iodine

We can summarise the appearance of these halogens at room temperature in a table.

a The appearance of these three halogens shows a trend going down the Group. Describe this trend.

b Fluorine is also a halogen. It is above chlorine in Group 7. Would you expect fluorine to be a gas, liquid or solid?

c Astatine is also in Group 7, below iodine. What colour would you expect astatine to be?

Halogen	State	Colour
chlorine	gas	green
bromine	liquid	orange-red
iodine	solid	grey

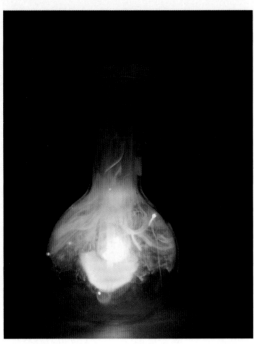

▲ Chlorine reacting with sodium

Halogens and alkali metals

The alkali metals react with the halogens to form salts called metal **halides**. For example, sodium reacts with chlorine to make sodium chloride (as in the photograph), with bromine to make sodium bromide, and with iodine to make sodium iodide. The other alkali metals react with halogens in a similar way.

d What is the name of the alkali halide formed when potassium reacts with iodine?

Here are symbol and word equations for the reaction between sodium and chlorine.

$$2Na \quad + \quad Cl_2 \quad \rightarrow \quad 2NaCl$$
sodium + chlorine → sodium chloride

e Write a symbol equation for the reaction between sodium and bromine.

f Write a symbol equation for the reaction between potassium and chlorine.

Reactivity of halogens

The reactivity of the halogens decreases down the Group. You can see this in the **displacement** reactions between halogens and metal halides. When chlorine gas is bubbled through a solution of potassium bromide, a red colour appears in the solution. This is the element bromine that has been displaced by the more reactive chlorine. The symbol and word equations for this reaction are shown below.

$$Cl_2 \quad + \quad 2KBr \quad \rightarrow \quad Br_2 \quad + \quad 2KCl$$
chlorine + potassium bromide → bromine + potassium chloride

A series of similar experiments gives the results in the table.

Halogen	Halide solution	Result	Halogen displaced
chlorine	potassium bromide	red solution	bromine
chlorine	potassium iodide	brown solution	iodine
bromine	potassium chloride	none	none
bromine	potassium iodide	brown solution	iodine
iodine	potassium chloride	none	none
iodine	potassium bromide	none	none

In these reactions a more reactive halogen displaces a less reactive halogen from a solution of its halide.

- Chorine displaces both bromides and iodides.
- Bromine displaces iodides.

g Use information in the table to put the three halogens in order of reactivity, starting with the most reactive.

h Write a symbol equation for the reaction between bromine and potassium iodide.

Predicting properties of halogens

Since the trend in reactivity of Group 7 elements goes from the top to the bottom, we can use results from the displacement reactions of chlorine, bromine and iodine to predict how other elements in the Group will react.

Fluorine is at the top of the Group, above chlorine. We can therefore predict that fluorine will displace chlorides, bromides and iodides. Fluorine is the most reactive halogen.

i Astatine is below iodine in Group 7. How would astatine react in the displacement of metal halides? What does this show about the reactivity of astatine?

Halogens and electronic structure

The halogens react in a similar way because they each have atoms with seven electrons in the outer shell. When these atoms react, each gains an electron to form a negative ion. The gaining of an electron is called **reduction**. The negative ion formed has a stable electronic structure. This is why the halogens all have similar properties.

For example for a chlorine molecule:

$Cl_2 + 2e^- \rightarrow 2Cl^-$

This ionic equation shows that each atom of chlorine gains an electron during the reaction. This shows that each chlorine atom has been reduced.

Halogen	Atom	Electron structure	Ion	Electron structure
fluorine	F	2,7	F⁻	2,8
chlorine	Cl	2,8,7	Cl⁻	2,8,8
bromine	Br	2,8,18,7	Br⁻	?

 j Look at the table. What is the electronic structure of a bromide ion?

As we saw earlier, the reactivity of the halogens decreases down the Group. The higher up the Group a halogen is the more reactive it is, and the easier it is for one of its atoms to gain an electron.

▲ Water treatment plant

Chlorine to the rescue

Cholera used to be a major health problem in the United Kingdom. An outbreak in 1882 killed 32 000 people.

Today, chlorine added to drinking water kills harmful bacteria and prevents the spread of waterborne diseases. Although chlorine is very poisonous, and was used as a weapon in the First World War, the low concentration in drinking water is harmless to humans. However, it is deadly to microorganisms.

The concentration of chlorine in tap water is less than that used in swimming pools. One reason for this is that we drink lots of tap water, so a higher concentration of chlorine could be harmful. We do not drink much of the water in swimming pools, so a higher concentration of chlorine is safe to use.

Cholera is still rife in many countries, such as India, where sewage is not adequately separated from drinking water sources, and chlorine is not added to water before it is pumped to houses. When travelling abroad it is important to make your drinking water safe.

The simplest way is to drink only bottled water. If water is purchased locally it is essential to ensure that the cap still has the manufacturer's seal, and the bottle has not been re-filled with contaminated water. Local water can be purified by boiling, adding iodine or adding chlorine. Silver-based tablets are also available from chemists and specialised travel equipment shops. These effectively kill bacteria in the water, making it safe to drink, though it may have an unusual taste.

▲ Well water can contain bacteria

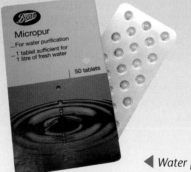

◀ Water purification tablets

Questions

1 Why is cholera no longer a problem in the United Kingdom?

2 Suggest how disease-causing organisms get into the water supply in countries such as India.

3 Describe two ways to avoid getting a disease from contaminated water.

Getting the metal

In this item you will find out

- what happens during the electrolysis of molten salts and solutions

- the products that can be made by the electrolysis of sodium chloride

- how electrolysis is used in the extraction of aluminium

▲ Early aircraft

Would you like to travel in an aircraft made of wood and string? Early aircraft used thin wooden spars, kept in place by strings or wires. This type of construction was light enough to be powered into the air by the engines in use at that time. The design was not very strong, and accidents were common.

Modern aircraft are sleek, safe and comfortable. The body of a modern aircraft is made from Duralumin. This is a strong, hard, lightweight alloy of aluminium.

Although aluminium is a fairly reactive metal, it has a coating of aluminium oxide that prevents corrosion when it is exposed to the air. Aluminium is used to make greenhouse frames because it can withstand bad weather without damage to its surface. The oxide coating of aluminium can be polished to give an attractive, shiny appearance. This makes the metal a good choice for door handles.

▲ Modern passenger jet

Aluminium is more expensive than steel because you need to use large amounts of electricity to extract it from its ore. The industrial extraction of aluminium uses a process called electrolysis.

a Suggest why aluminium is better than wood for making an aeroplane.

b Why is aluminium a better choice than steel (iron) for making a greenhouse frame?

Amazing fact

Recycling aluminium uses only 5% of the energy used to make new aluminium. Each year over 12 million tons of aluminium is recycled, much of it from drinks cans.

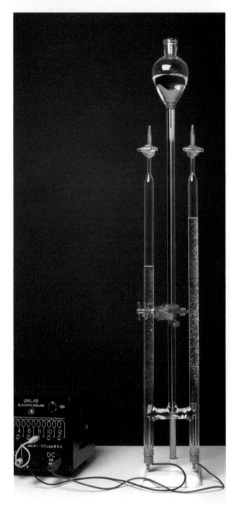

▲ Hofmann voltameter

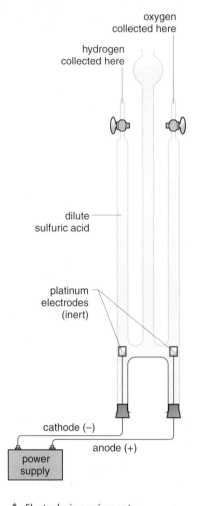

oxygen collected here

hydrogen collected here

dilute sulfuric acid

platinum electrodes (inert)

cathode (−)

anode (+)

power supply

▲ Electrolysis equipment

Electrolysis of dilute sulfuric acid

In the laboratory electricity can be passed through an electrolyte of a dilute solution of sulfuric acid using a set of apparatus called a Hofmann voltameter. This is shown in the photograph and the diagram on the left.

Hydrogen and oxygen gases are released, and collected separately in the apparatus.

You can find out which gas is which by collecting them in test tubes and carrying out these tests:

- if the gas burns with a squeaky pop when a lighted splint is brought to the mouth of the test tube then the gas is hydrogen.
- if a glowing splint relights when it is lowered into the test tube then the gas is oxygen.

Electrode reactions

Sulfuric acid contains positive hydrogen ions, H^+, and negative sulfate ions, SO_4^{2-}. It also contains negative hydroxide ions, OH^-, from the water. Electricity is passed through the solution using platinum **electrodes**.

Since opposite charges are attracted to each other, the ions move to electrodes of opposite charge. Negative ions move to the positive electrode (anode) and positive ions move to the negative electrode (cathode). This is why negative ions are called anions and positive ions are called cations.

Hydrogen ions move to the cathode. Each hydrogen ion collects an electron from the cathode, becoming a hydrogen atom. Pairs of these atoms form molecules of hydrogen gas.

$$2H^+ + 2e^- \rightarrow H_2$$

Hydroxide ions move to the anode. As these ions give up electrons to the anode, oxygen gas is formed.

$$4OH^- \rightarrow O_2 + 2H_2O + 4e^-$$

Sulfate ions are not affected by the electrolysis, and remain in solution. The result of this electrolysis is therefore the decomposition of water into its elements.

$$2H_2O \rightarrow 2H_2 + O_2$$

 c **The volume of hydrogen given off is twice that of the oxygen. How is this consistent with the overall equation for the electrolysis?**

Extracting aluminium

Aluminium is found in the mineral bauxite which contains mostly aluminium oxide, Al_2O_3. Aluminium is extracted from purified aluminium oxide by electrolysis.

You can only carry out electrolysis using molten ionic compounds or their solutions in water. This poses a major problem for the extraction of aluminium, since a temperature of $2030\,°C$ is needed to melt aluminium oxide. This is a difficult and uneconomic temperature to maintain. Also, aluminium oxide is insoluble in water. This problem is solved by dissolving aluminium oxide in molten cryolite. This mineral has a melting point just below $1000\,°C$.

carbon lining forming negative electrode

solid crust of electrolyte

carbon positive electrodes

insulation   molten electrolyte   molten aluminium

▲ *Electrolytic cell used in aluminium manufacture*

Aluminium and oxygen

In the electrolytic cell both the anode and the cathode are made of **graphite** which is a form of carbon. A cell is shown in the diagram on the right.

Positive aluminium ions, Al^{3+}, are attracted to the cathode which is the graphite lining of the electrolytic cell. Each aluminium ion gains three electrons from the cathode, forming an aluminium atom.

$$Al^{3+} + 3e^- \rightarrow Al$$

Molten aluminium forms and collects at the bottom of the cell. This is tapped off into moulds and allowed to cool to form solid ingots.

Negative oxide ions, O^{2-}, are attracted to the graphite anodes. Each oxide ion gives two electrons to the anode, forming an oxygen atom. Pairs of oxygen atoms join to form the molecules in oxygen gas.

$$2O^{2-} \rightarrow O_2 + 4e^-$$

The oxygen reacts with the graphite anodes, forming carbon dioxide. This means that the anodes have to be replaced frequently.

▲ *Ingots of aluminium*

 d **Work out how many aluminium atoms and oxygen molecules are discharged from the solution for each 12 electrons that flow around the circuit.**

You can see that electrolysis splits aluminium oxide into its elements.

$$2Al_2O_3 \rightarrow 4Al + 3O_2$$
aluminium oxide $\rightarrow$ aluminium + oxygen

Keywords

electrode • graphite

Who got there first?

Two unknown young scientists, Paul Héroult and Charles Hall, simultaneously invented a new electrolytic process, which is the basis for all aluminium production today. They worked separately thousands of miles apart, and were unaware of each other's work. Both inventors discovered that if they dissolved aluminium oxide (alumina) in a bath of molten cryolite and passed a powerful electric current through it, then molten aluminium would be deposited at the bottom of the bath.

Charles Hall lived in the USA. On 23 February 1886, in the woodshed behind his family's home, he produced globules of aluminium metal by the electrolysis of aluminium oxide dissolved in a cryolite–aluminium fluoride mixture and repeated this experiment the next day for his sister Julia to witness. This achievement was the culmination of several years of intensive work on this problem.

Paul Héroult lived in France. His was a world of country folk and cottage industries. While a student at the École des Mines, Paris, he began working on the electrolysis of aluminium compounds. His father, Patrice, managed a small tannery, which Paul inherited. Paul used the tannery buildings for his experiments. His mother gives him her last 50 000 francs to acquire a dynamo to produce the electric current that he used in 1886 to produce aluminium.

On 9 July 1886, Hall filed a patent for his process. In July 1888 his application was found to be in interference with the application filed on 23 April 1886 by Paul L. T. Héroult. The Héroult process is essentially identical to the one discovered by Hall in the same year.

Héroult was the same age as Hall. For many years the two inventors battled in the courts to decide who had made the discovery first. Eventually an agreement was reached between the two inventors, who shared the legal rights to the process.

▲ Paul Héroult

Charles Hall ▶

Questions

1 Hall and Héroult were unaware of each other's discovery. Suggest why this was not surprising in the year 1886.

2 It is unlikely that two scientists working on the same topic in the 21st century would be unaware of each other. Suggest why.

3 Both Hall and Héroult were amateur inventors, working with simple apparatus in makeshift laboratories. Most modern scientific advances are made in large university or industrial laboratories. Suggest why.

4 Suggest why the two inventors spent years arguing over who made the invention first.

Transition elements

In this item you will find out

- about the properties and uses of transition metals

- about the properties of transition metal compounds

- how to identify transition metal ions

▲ *Margarine is manufactured using a catalyst*

Margarine is made by the hydrogenation of vegetable oils. The addition of hydrogen to the molecules in the oils turns them from liquids to solids.

Ammonia is made by the Haber Process. Nitrogen and hydrogen combine under conditions of high pressure and high temperature.

What have these two important industrial processes got in common? They both use catalysts to speed up the reaction. A catalyst is not changed during the reaction, and so can be used for a long time before it needs to be replaced. The manufacture of margarine uses a nickel catalyst. The Haber Process uses a catalyst made of iron.

Amazing fact

Metal coins were not the first things to be used as money. The currency in China in the eighth century BC consisted of miniature farming tools.

Both nickel and iron belong to a large group of metals called **transition elements** or **transition metals**. These are found in a 'block' in the middle of the Periodic Table. Most of the catalysts used in industry are transition elements.

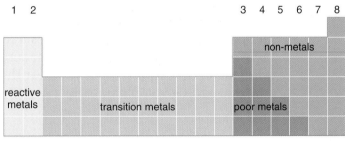

◀ *Where the transition elements are*

The transition metals have typical metal properties such as shiny appearance, conduction of electricity and conduction of heat. There are additional properties that are characteristic of most transition metals such as high melting point, high density, extreme hardness, low reactivity and coloured compounds.

Transition metals have many uses as pure compounds, but they are particularly useful when mixed in alloys.

The screw in the photograph on the right is used to drive a ship. It is made from Monel, an alloy of the transition metals nickel and copper. It is extremely resistant to corrosion, even from seawater. Because of their durability, transition metal alloys are also used to make coins.

▼ *This screw is made from transition metals*

a Write down the names and uses of three other transition elements that are not mentioned above.

Transition metal compounds

The compounds of transition elements are often coloured. The table shows the colours of some of them.

Transition metal ion	Colour of compounds	Example
copper(II)	blue	copper(II) sulfate
iron(II)	light green	iron(II) nitrate
iron(III)	orange/brown	iron(III) chloride

▶ Copper(II), iron(II) and iron(III) compounds

Each transition metal gives a particular colour to most of its compounds. Copper(II) sulfate crystals are blue because they contain copper(II) ions.

 b **What colour would you expect crystals of iron(II) sulfate to be?**

Thermal decomposition

Many transition metal compounds also show characteristic chemical properties. Thermal decomposition is a reaction in which a substance is broken down into two or more other substances by heat. Transition metal carbonates decompose when you heat them. In these reactions carbon dioxide gas is given off and a metal oxide is formed.

For example:

$$CuCO_3 \rightarrow CuO + CO_2$$
copper(II) carbonate → copper(II) oxide + carbon dioxide

$$MnCO_3 \rightarrow MnO + CO_2$$
manganese(II) carbonate → manganese(II) oxide + carbon dioxide

A test for the carbon dioxide gas given off is to bubble it through lime water. The lime water will turn milky.

Similar reactions take place when iron(II) carbonate and zinc carbonate are heated. In each of these decomposition reactions there is a colour change as the reaction takes place.

c Write symbol equations for the thermal decomposition of iron(II) carbonate and zinc carbonate.

Identifying transition metal ions

Precipitation is a reaction that produces an insoluble solid when two solutions are mixed. When you add sodium hydroxide solution to a solution of a transition metal compound, the metal ions and hydroxide ions form a **precipitate** of the metal hydroxide. The colour of this hydroxide can be used to identify the transition metal.

You can see the colours of copper(II), iron(II) and iron(III) hydroxides in the photographs below.

▲ Copper(II) hydroxide   ▲ Iron(II) hydroxide   ▲ Iron(III) hydroxide

Transition metal ion	Formula of transition metal ion	Colour of metal hydroxide precipitate
copper(II)	Cu^{2+}	blue
iron(II)	Fe^{2+}	grey/green
iron(III)	Fe^{3+}	orange

For the reaction between iron(II) ions and hydroxide ions, the symbol equation is:

$Fe^{2+} + 2OH^- \rightarrow Fe(OH)_2$

d Write symbol equations for the precipitation of copper(II) hydroxide and iron(III) hydroxide.

e A student adds sodium hydroxide to a solution of iron(III) nitrate. Describe how the appearance of the solution changes as the sodium hydroxide is added.

f Write word and symbol equations for the reaction in question e.

Keywords

precipitate • transition element • transition metal

Less exhausted

▲ People in Tokyo often wear smog masks

When petrol is burned in a car engine, the pollutant gases carbon monoxide and nitrogen monoxide are made. These are released into the air from the car exhaust.

Carbon monoxide is a very poisonous gas. It interferes with the transport of oxygen in the blood. As little as one per cent of carbon monoxide in the air can be fatal.

Nitrogen monoxide is also poisonous. It causes acid rain and city smog.

To reduce this pollution, every new car sold in the United Kingdom is fitted with a catalytic converter.

This contains the transition elements platinum and rhodium. These are very efficient catalysts for reactions that convert carbon monoxide and nitrogen monoxide into the less harmful gases carbon dioxide and nitrogen.

However, using a catalytic converter makes a car engine less efficient. The car will use more fuel to travel the same distance as a similar car without a catalytic converter.

Many catalysts, including platinum and rhodium, are 'poisoned' by small quantities of heavy metals such as lead. Cars fitted with catalytic converters must only use unleaded petrol.

Even when only unleaded petrol is used, the efficiency of the catalysts slowly decreases as the car is driven. Once a car is three years old, it has to be tested each year to see if the catalytic converter is reducing the concentrations of pollutant gases to a minimum standard. If too much carbon monoxide or nitrogen monoxide is detected in the mixture of gases from the car exhaust, the catalytic converter is replaced.

▲ Catalytic converter

Questions

1 Suggest why the efficiency of the catalyst decreases even though unleaded petrol is used.

2 Why do you think the efficiency of the catalytic converter is not tested until a new car is three years old?

3 The increase in the percentage of carbon dioxide in the air during the past century is a cause of global warming.
   (a) Suggest why the use of catalytic converters will not reduce global warming.
   (b) Why do you think using catalytic converters may increase global warming?

Metals

In this item you will find out

- how the properties of metals are related to their uses

- how the nature of metallic bonding explains the properties of metals

- about superconducting metals

▲ *Saucepans are often made with copper bases*

What properties should the materials used to make a saucepan have?

The material must be hard, durable, easy to shape, attractive, easy to clean, cheap to make, but most of all it must be a good conductor of heat. All metals are good conductors of heat, but not every metal would be good for making a saucepan. The alloy stainless steel has all of the qualities listed above, and is widely used to make saucepans.

Copper is a better conductor of heat than stainless steel, and some saucepans are made completely from this metal. But copper is a fairly soft metal so it is easily damaged. It also discolours in use and is not easy to clean. The ideal solution is to make a saucepan using stainless steel, but with a copper base.

Metals are used to make many articles. In each case a metal with the correct properties for the job is chosen.

Here are some examples:

- aluminium has a very low density and is used in the manufacture of aircraft frames
- tungsten is very hard and is used to make the sharp edges of cutting tools such as drills and saws.

a Explain how a copper saucepan is in some ways better and in some ways worse than a stainless-steel saucepan.

b You can buy saucepans made from aluminium. What advantage would one of these saucepans have over a saucepan made of stainless steel?

c Suggest another product that aluminium would be suitable for, and explain your choice.

Amazing fact

Over 17 million tons of copper metal are extracted from copper ores each year.

▲ You can see crystals on the surface of this post

Metallic bonding

Metals have a number of characteristic properties. Most are shiny (lustrous), hard, have a high density, high tensile strength, high melting and boiling points, and are good conductors of heat and electricity.

All metals are made of crystals. If you were standing close enough you could see crystals of zinc on the surface of the galvanised barrier in the photograph on the left. In these crystals, metal ions are held in a regular arrangement by very strong **metallic bonding**.

▶ Metallic bonding

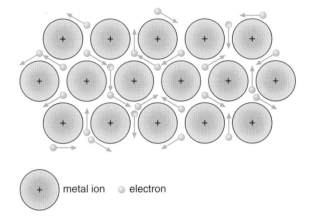

⊕ metal ion   ◯ electron

▲ Iron is good for making bridges

Positive metal ions are surrounded by a 'sea' of mobile negative electrons. Electrostatic attraction holds together the negative delocalised electrons and the positive ions very strongly. Because the particles are hard to pull away from each other, most metals are hard and strong. They also have high tensile strength, which means they do not easily break when pulled. These properties make iron, for example, a good material for the construction of road and rail bridges and car bodies.

Mixing metals to make alloys can give even more useful properties. Mixing iron with carbon to make steel increases its strength and hardness. Mixing copper with tin to make brass prevents corrosion.

Melting and boiling points

Metal	Melting point (°C)	Boiling point (°C)
aluminium	661	2467
gold	1064	2807
tungsten	3407	5927
iron	1535	2750
Non-metal		
phosphorus	44	280
sulfur	113	445
iodine	114	185

As you've already found out, most metals have a high melting point and boiling point. Compare the data for some metals and some non-metals in the table on the previous page.

You can see that the metals have much higher melting and boiling points than the non-metals. This is because of the strong metallic bonds between the metal atoms.

To melt a metal the strong attraction between delocalised electrons and positive metal ions in the metallic bonding has to be overcome. This requires a lot of energy and so a high temperature. In a similar way, you also need a lot of energy to boil a metal so they have high boiling points.

The very high melting point of tungsten means that it can be used for the filament of electric light bulbs. It glows white-hot without melting.

There are, however, some metals that do not have a high melting point. Caesium melts if a glass tube containing the metal is held in the hand.

 Suggest why some metals have a much lower melting point than others.

Moving electrons

When metals conduct electricity, electrons move through them. Because the delocalised electrons are able to move easily through the regular arrangement of metal ions, metals are good conductors of electricity.

Because it is such a good conductor of electricity, copper is used for the wiring in houses. But even copper has some electrical resistance so energy is lost in heating up the wire.

▲ *Tungsten electric lamp filament*

Superconductors

At very low temperatures some metals, including mercury, lead and tin, can be **superconductors**. These conduct electricity with little or no resistance which means the electricity can move through them with no loss of energy. This is called loss-free power transmission.

Superconductors can be used to make super-fast electronic circuits and very powerful electromagnets.

One of the main problems with superconducting metals is that they only work at very low temperatures: about –269 °C. If we want to use them for practical purposes, we need to find a way to make superconductors work at 20 °C.

 Why are low temperature superconductors not suitable for most practical purposes?

Keywords

metallic bonding •
superconductor

A superconducting future

The future of superconductors is bright and scientists are excited about superconductivity in a compound called magnesium diboride, MgB_2. This is because the temperature at which it has zero resistance is above what is normally expected for a superconductor.

It also has properties that other high temperature superconductors don't have. Normally these superconductors are brittle and hard to work with, which makes them hard to use for wires, but this new superconductor isn't like this. It's easy to bend and shape and it's cheap and plentiful. The amount of current it can carry is high and wires can easily be made out of it. This makes it ideal for industrial use. However, use of magnesium diboride for wires presents other problems, and further research is needed before commercial use of this superconductor is possible.

One of the main possibilities of superconductors being used in the future is in power lines. At present about 10% of the electricity we use is lost heating up the wires. The price of a superconductor has dropped so much that we may soon be able to afford to replace power lines with a superconducting wire.

The current carried by a superconducting wire is also much higher than that of a conventional copper wire. This means that a superconducting power cable could carry a lot more current than a conventional wire, with no loss of power transmission.

Superconductors could also allow for the development of magnetically levitated trains. Free of friction, they could glide along at high speeds using a fraction of the energy trains now use.

Questions

1 Magnesium diboride has zero resistance at a temperature above that normally expected for a superconductor. Why is this important?

2 What other useful properties does magnesium diboride have?

3 Why may the future use of superconductors in power transmission cables be a good idea?

4 What other applications of superconductors may be possible in the future?

C3a

1 *Explain what is meant by the following terms:*

   a atomic (proton) number   [1]
   b mass (nucleon) number   [1]
   c isotope   [1]

2 *How are elements arranged in the Periodic Table?*   [2]

3 *Copy and complete this table about elements and sub-atomic particles.*

Element	Atomic number	Mass number	Number of protons	Number of electrons	Number of neutrons
lithium	3	7			4
	7	14	7	7	
aluminium		27	13		14
argon			18	18	22

[8]

4 *The electronic structure of potassium is 2,8,8,1:*

Use a Periodic Table to help you work out the electronic structure of the following elements:

   a carbon   [1]   **b** fluorine   [1]
   c neon   [1]   **d** magnesium   [1]

5 *The table shows information about the isotopes of an element. Copy and complete the table, and name the element.*

Mass number	Number of protons	Number of electrons	Number of neutrons
16	8	8	
17		8	9
	8	8	10

[4]

6 *Aluminium, atomic number 27, was discovered by Hans Christian Oersted in Copenhagen, Denmark, in 1825. In 2001, a team of scientists working in Berkeley, USA announced the discovery of a new element with atomic number 118. The discovery of element 118 was later retracted after other scientists reported that they were unable to reproduce the results of the Berkeley team.*

   a *Scientists around the world learned of the discovery of element 118 within hours of the announcement in 2001. The discovery of aluminium was not widely known for several years. Explain this difference.*   [3]
   b *Why is it important for the details of new scientific discoveries to be passed on to other scientists?*   [2]

C3b

1 *Which statements about how sodium chloride conducts electricity are true?*

   A conducts electricity when solid
   B does not conduct electricity when solid
   C conducts electricity when molten
   D does not conduct electricity when molten
   E conducts electricity when in solution in water
   F does not conduct electricity when in solution in water   [3]

2 *Explain how metal and non-metal atoms combine. Use ideas about electrons, ions and attraction in your answer.*   [3]

3 *Draw 'dot and cross' models to show the ionic bonding in the following compounds.*

   a sodium chloride   [3]   **b** magnesium oxide   [3]

4 *Potassium ions have the formula K^+. Aluminium ions have the formula Al^{3+}. Chloride ions have the formula Cl^-. Oxide ions have the formula O^{2-}. What is the formula of each of the following compounds?*

   a potassium chloride   [1]   **b** potassium oxide   [1]
   c aluminium chloride   [1]   **d** aluminium oxide   [1]

5 *Use ideas about the structure of magnesium oxide to explain each of the following facts.*

   a Magnesium oxide has a high melting point.   [2]
   b Solid magnesium oxide does not conduct electricity. [2]
   c Molten magnesium oxide does conduct electricity. [2]

C3c

1 *Non-metals combine together by sharing electrons. What is the name given to this type of bonding?*   [1]

2 *Copy and complete this table about Groups and Periods in the Periodic Table.*

Symbol of element	Group number	Period number	Number of electrons in outer shell
Li		2	1
Cl	7	3	
Na	1		1
Ne		2	8
F	7		7
Ar	8	3	

[6]

3 *Draw 'dot and cross' diagrams to show the bonding in the following molecules.*

   a hydrogen, H_2 [2]   **b** methane, CH_4 [3]

4 *Use ideas about forces between molecules to explain the following facts.*

   a carbon dioxide is a gas at room temperature   [2]
   b pure water does not conduct electricity   [2]

5 The electronic structures of some elements are shown below.

To which Group and Period does each of these elements belong?

a 2,1   [1]   b 2,8,8   [1]   c 2,8,7   [1]
d 2,4   [1]   e 2,8,2   [1]

C3d

1 a Describe two things that you **see** when a small piece of potassium is dropped into a trough of water. [2]
  b Write word and symbol equations for this reaction. [4]
  c Other elements in Group 1 react with water in a similar way. Use ideas about the electronic arrangement of these elements to explain why. [2]

2 A student carries out a flame test on a white powder. The flame has a lilac colour.

  a Describe how this flame test is carried out. [4]
  b Which Group 1 metal is present in the white powder? [1]

3 The table shows some of the properties of four Group 1 metals.

Group 1 element	Reaction with water	Melting point (°C)	Density (g/cm³)
lithium	slow	181	0.54
sodium	fast	98	0.97
potassium	very fast	63	0.86
rubidium		39	1.53

Use information in the table to predict the following. For each one, explain your answer.

  a The way that rubidium reacts with water. [1]
  b Whether caesium will float on water. [1]
  c Whether caesium will melt if held in the hand. [1]

4 The reactivity of the elements increases down Group 1. Use ideas about electronic structure and bonding to explain this. [4]

5 When an ion is formed from an atom of potassium, an electron is lost.

  a Write a symbol equation for the formation of a potassium ion. [2]
  b The formation of a potassium ion is described as an oxidation. Explain why. [2]

C3e

1 Potassium reacts violently when in contact with fluorine.

  a Name the compound formed in this reaction. [1]
  b Write word and symbol equations for this reaction. [2]

2 The table shows results of some experiments where a halogen was added to the solution of a halide.

Halogen	Halide solution	Result	Halogen displaced
chlorine	potassium bromide	red solution	bromine
chlorine	potassium iodide	brown solution	iodine
bromine	potassium chloride	none	none
bromine	potassium iodide		
iodine	potassium chloride		
iodine	potassium bromide		

  a Copy the table and fill in the blank boxes to complete it. [6]
  b Explain how these results show the trend in reactivity in Group 7. [3]

3 Predict and explain what you would see in each of the following.

  a fluorine is added to a solution of potassium iodide [2]
  b fluorine is added to a solution of potassium bromide [2]
  c fluorine is added to a solution of potassium chloride [2]

4 The table gives information about some physical properties of three halogens.

Halogen	Boiling point (°C)	Melting point (°C)	Density (g/cm³)
chlorine	−34	−101	1.56
bromine	59	−7	3.12
iodine	185	114	4.93

  a Predict the density of astatine. [1]
  b What is the state of astatine at room temperature? [1]
  c Predict the boiling point of fluorine. [1]

5 a Write an equation to show the formation of a fluoride ion from a fluorine molecule. [2]
  b Why is this called a reduction reaction? [2]
  c Use this reaction to help you explain why the halogens have similar properties. [2]
  d Use this reaction to help you explain the trend in reactivity in Group 7. [4]

C3f

1 During the electrolysis of dilute sulfuric acid a gas is given off at each electrode.

  a Which gas is given off at the cathode? [1]
  b Which gas is given off at the anode? [1]

2 Aluminium is extracted by the electrolysis of aluminium oxide.

   a What gas is formed at the anodes? [1]

   b The anodes are made of carbon (graphite). Why do they need frequent replacement? [1]

   c Write a word equation for the decomposition of aluminium oxide that takes place in this electrolysis. [2]

3 Write equations for the reactions that take place at the electrodes during the electrolysis of dilute sulfuric acid. [6]

4 **a** Aluminium oxide is dissolved in molten cryolyte to make the electrolyte used in the extraction of aluminium. Why is this used instead of just molten aluminium oxide? [2]

   b Electrolysis is an expensive way to extract a metal from a mineral. Explain why. [2]

5 Write equations for the reactions that take place at the electrodes during the extraction of aluminium from aluminium oxide. [6]

C3g

1 Transition metals are often used as catalysts. Describe how one transition metal is used in this way. [2]

2 The table shows the colours of precipitates made when sodium hydroxide is added to some transition metal ions in solution.

Transition metal ion	Formula of transition metal ion	Colour of metal hydroxide precipitate
copper(II)	Cu^{2+}	blue
iron(II)	Fe^{2+}	grey/green
iron(III)	Fe^{3+}	orange/brown

Sodium hydroxide solution is added to solution X containing a transition metal sulphate. A green precipitate is formed.

   a Name the transition metal compound in solution X. [1]

   b Write a word equation for the reaction between the transition metal compound and sodium hydroxide. [2]

3 Many carbonates containing transition elements undergo thermal decomposition when heated. Carbon dioxide is given off and the transition metal oxide formed.

   a What do you **see** when a transition metal carbonate is heated? [2]

   b Write a symbol equation for the thermal decomposition of copper(II) carbonate. [2]

4 When sodium hydroxide solution is added to a solution containing a transition metal ion, a coloured precipitate is formed. What does this suggest about the solubility of transition metal hydroxides? [1]

5 Write a symbol equation for the reaction between iron(III) ions and hydroxide ions. [3]

C3h

1 Most metals have high melting and boiling points. Use ideas about the bonding in metals to explain these facts. [2]

2 Superconductors are better conductors of electricity than other metals.

   a How does a metal conduct electricity? [1]

   b Why do superconductors conduct electricity so well? [1]

   c State two uses of superconductors. [2]

3 This table shows properties of some metals

Metal	Electrical conductivity	Heat conductivity	Density (g/cm³)
aluminium	good	good	2.70
copper	excellent	excellent	8.92
iron	good	good	7.87

   a Suggest why saucepans made from iron often have copper bases. [1]

   b Why is house wiring made of copper instead of aluminium? [1]

   c Why are the overhead power cables that stretch between pylons made from aluminium instead of copper? [2]

4 **a** Describe the bonding in a metal. [2]

   b Use ideas about this bonding to explain why metals have high melting points. [2]

   c Use ideas about this bonding to explain why metals are good conductors of electricity. [1]

5 What are the disadvantages of using superconducting metals? [4]

6 Scientists tested the hardness of a metal by measuring the force needed to produce a 3 mm deep dent in each of six samples.

Sample number	1	2	3	4	5	6
Force/N	455	458	398	455	456	454

   a Suggest why the scientists tested six samples rather than one. [2]

   b The scientists used their results to calculate an average. They did not include the result for sample 3 in this calculation. Explain why. [2]

C4 Chemical economics

Today I saw a farmer spreading fertiliser on a field. He is using huge bags of the fertiliser. Surely they cost a lot of money, and I thought that using fertiliser was supposed to help farmers grow cheaper food.

Fertiliser is a bulk chemical. It is made in very large quantities and so can be made cheaply. Without cheap fertiliser farmers could not grow as much, so food would be more expensive.

And the huge demand for fertiliser means that it is worth setting up factories to make large amounts at low cost.

- During the past century the discoveries of chemists have changed the way we live. Methods have been found to extract metals such as aluminium from the Earth, new materials with exciting properties have been invented, and new ways of using well-known materials have been discovered.

- Millions of tons of commonly used metals, such as iron and aluminium, are produced each year. Reagents such as ammonia and nitric acid are made continuously to provide reactants for chemical processes. Vast quantities of fertilisers and polymers are manufactured.

- Other chemicals are needed in much smaller quantities and may be very expensive to make. Many of the new medicines invented by chemists each year are manufactured as they are required to treat diseases.

What you need to know

- Reactants are turned into products in a chemical reaction.

- Accurate measurements can be made using a burette or pipette.

- The use of techniques such as filtration, evaporation, crystallisation and chromatography.

Salt and acid please

In this item you will find out

- how acids are neutralised by bases, alkalis and carbonates
- how salts are formed during neutralisation reactions
- how to write balanced equations for neutralisation reactions

▲ These fruits contain citric acid

Citrus fruits like oranges, lemons and limes have a sharp taste. This is caused by an acid called citric acid that is contained in these fruits. Citric acid is a weak acid so it is safe to eat.

Vinegar is a solution of ethanoic acid, also called acetic acid. You can put a dilute solution of ethanoic acid on your food without harming yourself because it is also a weak acid. Boric acid is so weak it is even used in eye drops to treat infections.

But not all acids are weak and harmless. On 6 August 1949, John George Haigh was executed. He had been found guilty of murdering five people. He disposed of the bodies of his victims by dissolving them in sulfuric acid.

Haigh mistakenly believed that a corpse could be completely disposed of by using the acid. But his last victim's gallstones and false teeth did not dissolve as quickly as the rest of the body. This gave police enough evidence to convict Haigh.

Sulfuric acid is a strong acid. It is very corrosive and will attack many materials including skin and bones. Because of its corrosive properties, this acid is used to clean metal surfaces before they are coated with other metals by electroplating.

a Suggest why it is important to remove grease and dirt before the metal surface is coated with another metal.

b Suggest why some acids are safe to eat but others are not.

▲ Metal surfaces can be cleaned by sulfuric acid

The pH scale

We can measure how acidic a solution is by using Universal Indicator. When this **indicator** is added to a solution it changes colour to show the level of acidity. This is shown in the diagram.

colour of Universal Indicator			red		orange	yellow	green	blue	blue-purple		purple		
pH	1	2	3	4	5	6	7	8	9	10	11	12	13	14
	strong acids				weak acids		neutral	weak alkalis		strong alkalis			

The acidity is shown by a number on the **pH** scale.

 Describe a solution with pH 8.

Neutralisation

A **base** is a substance that neutralises an acid. Bases are solids but some dissolve in water to form an alkali, for example sodium hydroxide. A base always has a metal part, in this case sodium, and a non-metal part, in this case hydroxide.

When an alkali is added a little at a time to an acidic solution, the pH of the solution gradually changes from acidic to neutral to alkaline. When an acid is added to an alkali the opposite change takes place. Adding an alkali increases the pH. Adding more acid decreases the pH.

The reaction between an acid and an alkali is called **neutralisation**, and always makes a salt and water.

acid + base → salt + water

For example:

$$H_2SO_4 \quad + \quad 2NaOH \quad \rightarrow \quad Na_2SO_4 \quad + \quad 2H_2O$$
sulfuric acid + sodium hydroxide → sodium sulfate + water

The name of the salt formed during a neutralisation reaction comes from the name of the metal in the base and the name of the acid.

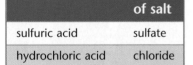 **Write word and symbol equations for the reaction between hydrochloric acid and potassium hydroxide.**

Name of acid	Name of salt
sulfuric acid	sulfate
hydrochloric acid	chloride
nitric acid	nitrate

All acids in solution in water contain hydrogen ions, H^+. All alkalis in solution in water contain hydroxide ions, OH^-. When an acid is neutralised by an alkali, these two ions react to form water.

$$H^+ + OH^- \rightarrow H_2O$$

More about bases

Metal oxides and metal hydroxides are bases, and will neutralise acids. For example:

$$H_2SO_4 \quad + \quad CuO \quad \rightarrow \quad CuSO_4 \quad + \quad H_2O$$
sulfuric acid + copper(II) oxide → copper(II) sulfate + water

$$2HCl \quad + \quad Cu(OH)_2 \quad \rightarrow \quad CuCl_2 \quad + \quad 2H_2O$$
hydrochloric acid + copper(II) hydroxide → copper(II) chloride + water

e Write word and symbol equations for the reaction between nitric acid and copper(II) oxide.

f (i) What salt is produced when magnesium hydroxide neutralises sulfuric acid?
  (ii) Write a balanced symbol equation for the reaction.

Ammonia, NH_3, is a base. When ammonia gas is bubbled into an acid a neutralisation reaction takes place.

$$NH_3 \quad + \quad HNO_3 \quad \rightarrow \quad NH_4NO_3$$
ammonia + nitric acid → ammonium nitrate

g Write word and symbol equations for the reaction between sulfuric acid and ammonia.

Acids can also be neutralised by carbonates. In this reaction as well as a salt and water, carbon dioxide gas is made. For example:

$$2HCl \quad + \quad CaCO_3 \quad \rightarrow \quad CaCl_2 \quad + \quad CO_2 \quad + \quad H_2O$$
hydrochloric acid + calcium carbonate → calcium chloride + carbon dioxide + water

h Write word and symbol equations for the reaction between sulfuric acid and sodium carbonate.

▲ *Calcium carbonate and hydrochloric acid reacting together*

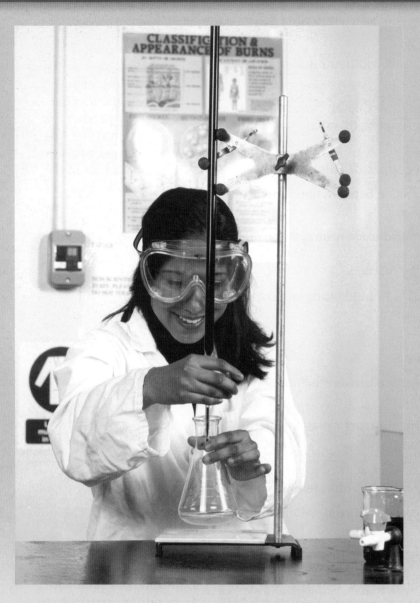

An acid test

Manjit works for a company that makes vinegar. She is a laboratory technician.

She measures the concentration of ethanoic acid in samples of vinegar.

For each sample she:
- accurately measures a volume of the vinegar sample
- adds a few drops of phenolphthalein indicator
- sets up a burette containing sodium hydroxide of known concentration
- adds sodium hydroxide from the burette into the vinegar
- swirls the liquid to make sure it is well mixed
- stops adding sodium hydroxide when the indicator changes to a pink colour
- notes down the volume of sodium hydroxide added.

Manjit uses phenolphthalein indicator. This gives a very clear colour change from colourless when the solution is acidic to pink when the solution is neutral.

She repeats the test until she has two results that are within $0.2\,cm^3$ of each other. She then takes the average of these results.

From the volume of vinegar used and the volume of sodium hydroxide added, Manjit can work out the concentration of vinegar in the sample.

Questions

1. Suggest why the company wants to know the concentration of ethanoic acid in its vinegar.

2. Why does Manjit use phenolphthalein instead of Universal Indicator?

3. Why does she stop adding sodium hydroxide when the liquid turns pink?

4. Why do you think she repeats her experiments until the results are in close agreement?

Disappearing act

▲ *Forest devastated by fire*

In this item you will find out

● why mass is conserved during chemical reactions

● how to work out the masses of reactants and products in a reaction

● how to work out percentage yield for a reaction

Every summer fires devastate large areas of forest.

Very little is left of the trees that once stood in the forest. Just a few charred stumps and some ash remain. What has happened to the wood in the trees that burned? Where have the many tons of mass gone?

Apart from water, most of the mass in the trees is made of carbon compounds. Only small amounts of other substances are present, for example, compounds of metallic elements. When the carbon compounds in the trees burn they produce carbon dioxide. This goes into the atmosphere, together with the water, which evaporates.

 Suggest why when trees burn some of the mass remains as ash.

None of the mass from the trees has been lost. The air has gained exactly the mass that has gone from the forest.

This idea can be demonstrated using a candle. Candle wax is a hydrocarbon. As a candle burns it gets smaller. The candle wax seems to disappear. The hydrogen in the hydrocarbon reacts with oxygen in the air to make water. In the hot flame, this water is formed as a vapour. Carbon in the hydrocarbon also reacts with oxygen, forming carbon dioxide. The water vapour and carbon dioxide go into the air.

In the apparatus on the right, the water and carbon dioxide are absorbed by soda lime (a mixture of sodium hydroxide and calcium hydroxide) in the tube. The mass of both the candle and the tube of soda lime are measured before and after the experiment. It is found that the soda lime gains more mass than that lost by the candle. The extra mass comes from oxygen in the air that has combined with carbon and hydrogen in the wax hydrocarbons to form carbon dioxide and water.

In a chemical reaction the mass of products is always the same as the mass of reactants.

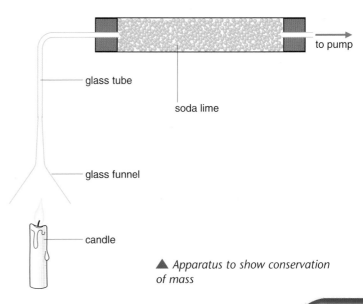
▲ *Apparatus to show conservation of mass*

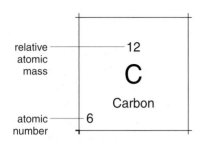

relative atomic mass — 12

C

Carbon

atomic number — 6

Relative formula mass

In the Periodic Table both the atomic number (proton number) and the **relative atomic mass** (RAM) are shown for each element as shown on the left.

Relative atomic masses are a way of comparing the masses of one atom of each element, using a scale of one atom of the isotope carbon-12 having 12 units of mass.

On this scale an atom of magnesium has a relative atomic mass (RAM) of 24, and an atom of hydrogen has a RAM of 1. This means that an atom of magnesium has the same mass as two atoms of carbon, or 24 atoms of hydrogen. This is shown in the diagram below.

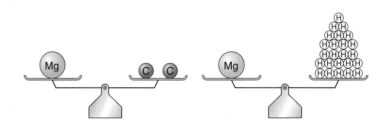

Amazing fact

Atoms are very small. One gram of magnesium contains 25 000 000 000 000 000 000 000 atoms.

The formula of a compound tells us which atoms are joined together, and how many there are of each. We can use the relative atomic masses shown in the Periodic Table to work out the **relative formula mass** (RFM) of a compound. For example:

$H = 1$ $O = 16$ $H_2O = (2 \times 1) + 16 = 18$

The relative formula mass of water is 18.

Sometimes a formula includes symbols in brackets. When the RAMs of the symbols in brackets have been added together, they are multiplied by the number following the brackets.

For example, calcium hydroxide, $Ca(OH)_2$, has two hydroxide groups joined to one calcium atom.

$Ca = 40$ $O = 16$ $H = 1$ $Ca(OH)_2 = 40 + [2 \times (16 + 1)] = 40 + 34 = 74$

The relative formula mass of calcium hydroxide is 74.

 Work out the relative formula mass for each of the following compounds.

   CaO CO_2 Na_2O $MgCl_2$ $CaSO_4$ $Mg(OH)_2$

Mass of reactants and products

During a chemical reaction reactants are changed into products.

reactants $\rightarrow$ products
$2Mg + O_2 \rightarrow 2MgO$

A reaction involves a rearrangement of atoms into new compounds. No atoms are gained or lost, so the total mass of the reactants is exactly the same as the total mass of the products.

We can work out how much product is produced from a specific mass of reactant, or how much reactant is needed to make a certain mass of product. For this we use relative formula masses but with g, kg or tonnes as the units.

For example, how much magnesium oxide is made when 6.0 g magnesium burns in an excess (more than enough to react) of oxygen?

$2Mg + O_2 \rightarrow 2MgO$

$2 \times 24 = 48$ g magnesium produces $2 \times (24 + 16) = 80$ g magnesium oxide

so 6 g magnesium produces $80 \times \dfrac{6}{48} = 10$ g

c What mass of magnesium oxide is produced when 16 g of magnesium is burned in excess oxygen?

d What mass of magnesium must be burned in excess oxygen to produce 16 g of magnesium oxide?

Yield

Yield describes how much product has been collected. We can use relative formula masses to work out the maximum mass of product that can be made from the masses of the reactants used. This is called the **predicted yield**.

If we collect the product and weigh it, the mass we have is called the **actual yield**.

During the experiment some of the product is usually lost, so the actual yield is less than the predicted yield. We can compare predicted yield and actual yield by working out the **percentage yield**.

$$\text{percentage yield} = \frac{\text{actual yield}}{\text{predicted yield}} \times 100$$

▲ Magnesium burning in a gas jar of oxygen

For example:

In an experiment 11.5 g of sodium is reacted with an excess of chlorine.

The mass of sodium chloride made is 23.4 g. What is the percentage yield?

$2Na + Cl_2 \rightarrow 2NaCl$

$2 \times 23 = 46$ g sodium produces $2 \times (23 + 35.5) = 117$ g sodium chloride

so 11.5 g sodium produces $117 \times \dfrac{11.5}{46} = 29.25$ g sodium chloride

$$\text{percentage yield} = \frac{23.4}{29.5} \times 100 = 80\%$$

e In another experiment 4.60 g sodium is reacted with an excess of chlorine. The mass of sodium chloride collected is 9.72 g. What is the percentage yield?

Keep on trucking

Bill drives a truck at a limestone quarry.

The quarrymen use explosives to blast the limestone from the quarry. A crane loads large boulders of limestone onto Bill's truck. Each truckload contains 15 tonnes of limestone. Bill drives across the quarry and tips this load into the crusher.

When the limestone is crushed, the smaller pieces of limestone are heated in a rotating furnace. Limestone is made of calcium carbonate. When heated, this decomposes to form quicklime, calcium oxide.

$$CaCO_3 \rightarrow CaO + CO_2$$
calcium carbonate → calcium oxide + carbon dioxide

A measured amount of water is added to this quicklime to produce slaked lime, calcium hydroxide.

$$CaO + H_2O \rightarrow Ca(OH)_2$$
calcium oxide + water → calcium hydroxide

Bill's friend Stan is in charge of the production of calcium oxide and calcium hydroxide at the quarry. Part of his job is to work out the yield of these products.

Questions

1 Work out the maximum mass of calcium oxide that could be made from each load of 15 tonnes of limestone that Bill tips into the crusher. For your calculation assume that limestone is pure calcium carbonate. This is the predicted yield.

2 The predicted yield is less than 15 tonnes. Where do you think the rest of this mass goes?

3 Stan says that the actual yield of calcium oxide from each truckload of limestone is 5.2 tonnes. Suggest why the actual yield for this reaction is less than the predicted yield.

4 Work out the percentage yield for the reaction.

5 What is the maximum mass of calcium hydroxide that could be made from 5.2 tonnes of calcium oxide?

6 The reaction produces calcium hydroxide with a percentage yield of 79%. What mass of calcium hydroxide is produced from each truckload of limestone?

Food for plants

In this item you will find out

● how fertilisers can supply the minerals needed by plants for their growth

● how fertilisers can be made

● some problems caused by using fertilisers

Have you ever seen a polluted river like the one in the photograph on the right? Dead fish float on the surface and the water has a very unpleasant smell.

Lots of chemicals can pollute rivers. One cause of pollution is the overuse of fertilisers. Farmers use fertilisers to increase crop yield. They replace **essential elements** that have been removed from the soil by the previous crop. They can also provide extra essential elements to help the crop to grow better. One of the main elements provided by fertilisers is nitrogen. This gets incorporated into plant protein and so increases growth.

But overuse of nitrogen-containing fertilisers can cause a type of pollution called **eutrophication**. This happens in several stages.

• rain water dissolves fertiliser and the solution runs off from fields into rivers
• the concentration of nitrate or phosphate in the river water increases
• microscopic water plants called algae use these nutrients to grow at a very fast rate, causing an **algal bloom**
• the dense growth of algae blocks sunlight from reaching water plants
• water plants die from lack of sunlight, and the algae also die as nutrients are used up
• bacteria feed on the dead plants and algae, and multiply rapidly, using up oxygen in the water
• without oxygen, fish and other water animals die.

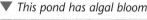
▼ This pond has algal bloom

a Why do the water plants die when sunlight is blocked by algae?

Most farmers are very careful to apply only the correct amount of fertiliser. They also check the weather forecast before spreading fertiliser, to make sure that there will not be heavy rain.

b Suggest why farmers need to check the weather forecast before spreading fertiliser.

Nutrients and plant growth

Plants need a number of chemical elements to grow well. These essential elements are contained in compounds called minerals. Plants get minerals from the soil. When crops are grown and harvested, the soil loses these minerals.

Unless the minerals are put back into the soil by adding fertilisers, future crops will not grow well. Fertilisers also provide extra essential elements, such as nitrogen, phosphorus and potassium, to help plant growth.

Plants take in water through their roots. Minerals are dissolved in this water. The minerals in fertilisers must be in compounds that dissolve (are soluble) in water. Plants can then take in the solution through their roots. You can see this in the diagram below.

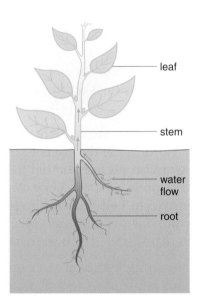

leaf

stem

water flow

root

 How do minerals get to the leaves?

Plants use the nitrogen in fertiliser to make protein. When a fertiliser is used to provide more nitrogen, the plants grow faster and bigger. This increases the yield from the crop.

Ammonium nitrate, NH_4NO_3, is a good fertiliser because it contains a lot of nitrogen and is very soluble in water.

The uptake of minerals by a plant is also affected by soil conditions. If the soil is too acidic or too alkaline, plants may not take up as much of a mineral. Farmers may test a sample of soil using Universal Indicator before applying fertiliser.

 Suggest what farmers could do if the soil is too acidic?

Fertiliser calculations

The relative formula mass of ammonium nitrate can be worked out from the relative atomic masses of the elements.

relative atomic masses: N = 14   H = 1   O = 16

relative formula mass of $NH_4NO_3 = (2 \times 14) + (4 \times 1) + (3 \times 16) = 80$

The percentage nitrogen in ammonium nitrate can then be calculated.

percentage nitrogen $= 100 \times \dfrac{28}{80} = 35\%$

Ammonium nitrate contains a high proportion of nitrogen. A small amount of this fertiliser gives plants a lot of this essential element.

 e **What is the percentage of nitrogen in the fertiliser sodium nitrate, $NaNO_3$?**

Making a fertiliser

A fertiliser can be made by a neutralisation reaction. An acid and an alkali react together to make a salt. For example:

NH_3 + HNO_3 → NH_4NO_3
ammonia + nitric acid → ammonium nitrate

The correct quantities of the acid and the alkali must be mixed. To do this, accurate volume measurements have to be made using a pipette and burette.

 f **Suggest why accurate measurement of the amounts of acid and alkali is important.**

The salt solution is evaporated to a smaller volume, then left to cool until solid crystals of the salt form. These crystals are separated from the remaining solution by filtration.

By using different acids and alkalis, different fertiliser compounds can be made.

Examiner's tip

Lime, calcium hydroxide, is often spread on fields to neutralise acidity, but it is not a fertiliser. Ammonium nitrate is a fertiliser because it supplies nitrogen for plant growth.

▲ Fertiliser bags

Acid	Alkali	Fertiliser
nitric acid	ammonia	ammonium nitrate
sulfuric acid	ammonia	ammonium sulfate
phosphoric acid	ammonia	ammonium phosphate
nitric acid	potassium hydroxide	potassium nitrate

These salts can then be mixed to make a fertiliser that will provide plants with nitrogen, phosphate and potassium. This is often referred to as an NPK fertiliser.

Keywords

algal bloom • essential element • eutrophication

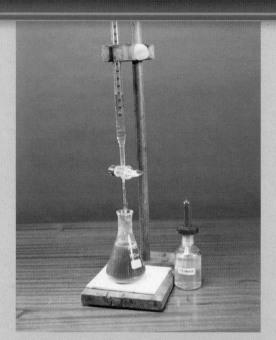

▲ *Apparatus used for titration*

▲ *Crystals are separated by filtration*

Making potassium nitrate

Chris works in the laboratory of a chemical company. He makes a small quantity of potassium nitrate to test its use as a fertiliser.

He follows a procedure called a titration to make a solution of potassium nitrate.

He repeats this titration to get a second solution. He then makes crystals from the second solution.

Chris fills a burette with dilute potassium hydroxide solution.

He then uses a pipette to measure out a volume of dilute nitric acid into a conical flask.

To this nitric acid he adds a few drops of phenolphthalein indicator – this is colourless in an acidic solution but pink in a neutral solution. To the mixture in the conical flask he gradually adds potassium hydroxide solution from the burette.

Chris stops adding the potassium hydroxide when the indicator changes from colourless to pink, showing that all of the acid has reacted with the alkali. He notes down the volume of potassium hydroxide added from the burette, and throws away this first pink solution.

Then Chris measures a fresh sample of dilute nitric acid (the same volume as before) into a clean conical flask, but this time he does not add any phenolphthalein indicator. He adds to this nitric acid the same volume of potassium hydroxide from the burette as he used the first time.

He uses heat to evaporate some of this second solution so that the volume is reduced then he leaves the solution to cool and form crystals.

Finally, Chris separates the crystals from the remaining solution by filtration and leaves the potassium nitrate crystals to dry.

Questions

1. Write a symbol equation for the reaction Chris is using.

2. Why does Chris need to use an indicator?

3. Phenolphthalein changes from colourless in acid to pink when neutral. Why does this give a clearer indication of when enough alkali has been added than Universal Indicator?

4. Why does Chris not make crystals of potassium nitrate from the first solution he makes?

5. Why do you think he reduces the volume of the second solution by evaporation to make the crystals?

Reversible reactions

▲ *Farmers used to plough using horses instead of tractors*

In this item you will find out

- how ammonia is made using the Haber Process

- how conditions used for the process affect the cost of the product

- how we use the ammonia that is produced

For centuries farmers used manure and crop rotation (growing a different crop each year) to give their crops enough nitrogen for them to grow well. Simpler methods of agriculture were used than today. When the population of Europe was small, enough food could be grown this way.

During the nineteenth century the population in Europe increased at a fast rate.

To provide the nitrogen needed to grow enough food, guano (bird droppings) was imported from Chile and Peru. However, by the beginning of the twentieth century these supplies were used up.

a Suggest why guano could no longer supply enough nitrogen for crops grown in the twentieth century?

The famous scientist Sir William Crookes warned that the exhaustion of these nitrogen-rich guano deposits would lead to worldwide starvation if no alternative could be found.

In 1908, the German chemist Fritz Haber found a way to combine nitrogen and hydrogen to make ammonia.

Ammonia made by this process is used to make nitric acid, which is used to make fertilisers (such as ammonium nitrate) and explosives. Ammonia is also used in household cleaning products.

b Explain how Fritz Haber's discovery solved the problem of food supply in Europe.

During the First World War, Fritz Haber's process supplied the materials needed to make munitions such as bombs. He also devised and manufactured poison gases, which he described as 'a higher form of killing'.

In recognition of his work, Fritz Haber was awarded the Nobel Prize for chemistry in 1918. At the presentation ceremony other scientists refused to shake his hand.

Thanks to Fritz Haber's discovery, it is now possible to grow more than enough crops to feed the population in the developed countries.

▼ *Fritz Haber*

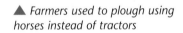

Amazing fact

China now uses more synthetic fertiliser than any other country – over 40 million tons in 2004.

The Haber Process

In the Haber Process, ammonia is made from nitrogen and hydrogen.

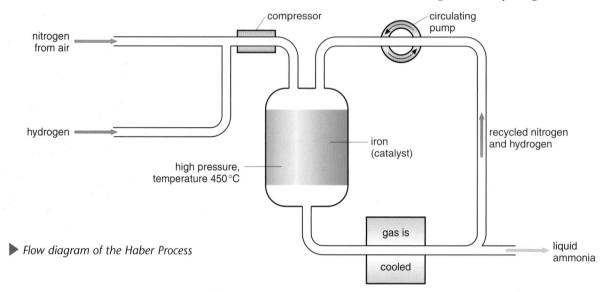

▶ *Flow diagram of the Haber Process*

Nitrogen gas is extracted from the air, and hydrogen is obtained from natural gas or the cracking of fractions from the distillation of crude oil.

c **The air contains about 78% nitrogen and is free. But nitrogen for the Haber Process is an expensive raw material. Suggest why.**

Nitrogen and hydrogen are reacted together under carefully controlled conditions:

- a temperature of about 450 °C
- a high pressure
- an iron catalyst

Using these conditions about 15% of the nitrogen and hydrogen are converted into ammonia as they pass through the reaction vessel.

$$N_2 \quad + \quad 3H_2 \quad \rightleftharpoons \quad 2NH_3$$
$$\text{nitrogen} + \text{hydrogen} \rightleftharpoons \text{ammonia}$$

This is a **reversible reaction**. It can go in either direction. As ammonia is formed it breaks down into nitrogen and hydrogen. This means that the reaction mixture always contains unreacted nitrogen and hydrogen. For this reason not all of the nitrogen and hydrogen form ammonia.

d **Why does the mixture of gases leaving the reaction vessel contain only 15% ammonia?**

> **Examiner's tip**
>
> In a reversible reaction there will always be some of each of the reactants present as well as the products.

Why certain conditions are used

So why does the Haber Process use a certain temperature and pressure, and a catalyst?

A high pressure encourages the formation of ammonia from nitrogen and hydrogen – the higher the pressure, the higher the yield of ammonia.

A high temperature encourages the reaction that decomposes ammonia into nitrogen and hydrogen. So the yield of ammonia decreases as the temperature increases. But, the higher the temperature, the faster the rate of reaction. This means that although the yield of ammonia is lower, it is produced more quickly. A compromise temperature of about 450 °C is used. This gives a reasonable yield with a fast enough rate of reaction.

An iron catalyst is used in the process. This speeds up the reaction. The catalyst alters the rate of reaction, but does not change the yield.

▲ A chemical factory

Manufacturing costs

The higher the pressure used in a reaction, the thicker the walls of the reaction vessel must be. This makes the manufacturing plant more expensive to construct. Also, the higher the temperature the higher the energy cost. However, a faster reaction makes more chemical in the same time and so reduces the cost.

Catalysts speed up the rate of a reaction. Although a catalyst costs money, a chemical can be made in a shorter time, saving fuel costs. When unreacted chemicals are recycled back into the reaction vessel, this reduces the cost of expensive raw materials. The chemicals can be passed through the reaction chamber several times which means that none is wasted.

The reaction process can be **automated**. This means that computers can be used to monitor and adjust the conditions, such as temperature and pressure, and the flow of chemicals. This reduces the number of people involved and so reduces the wages bill. It also enables the conditions to be controlled more accurately.

e Computers are used to control conditions in the Haber Process. Explain the advantages of using them.

Chemical economics

To compete with other companies, a factory that makes a chemical product must do so as cheaply as possible.

The rate of the reaction used must be high enough to make a sufficient quantity of the chemical product each day. To achieve this, for most processes a high temperature is used. For most reactions a catalyst is also used to speed up the rate of formation of product.

Optimum conditions are a compromise to produce a good enough yield at a fast enough rate, and so make the chemical at the lowest possible cost.

Sometimes a low yield is acceptable if unused reactants can be recycled back into the reaction vessel. This means that expensive raw materials are not wasted.

Keywords

automated • reversible reaction

Building a Haber Process factory

Dr Jones works for a company that is going to build a new factory to make ammonia from nitrogen and hydrogen using the Haber Process.

$$N_2 \quad + \quad 3H_2 \quad \rightleftharpoons \quad 2NH_3$$

nitrogen + hydrogen $\rightleftharpoons$ ammonia

He must decide on the conditions that will be used in the reaction vessel of the new factory, so that it can be built using the correct materials and design.

He looks at this graph showing the effect of temperature and pressure on the yield of ammonia in the Haber Process using an iron catalyst.

From this data Dr Jones decides that the new factory will use an iron catalyst and will operate at 450 °C and 175 atmospheres pressure.

Dr Smith tells Dr Jones about a new catalyst that can be used for the Haber Process. He shows Dr Jones some experimental data about the new catalyst.

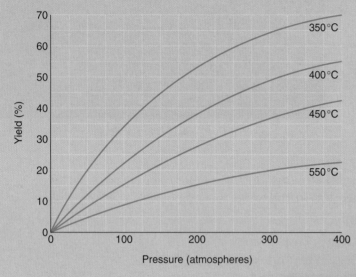

	Iron catalyst	New catalyst
Rate of ammonia formation (kg per min)	433	748
Cost of catalyst (£)	3800	12 600
Lifetime of catalyst (year)	12	4

Dr Smith says that they should use the new catalyst in their Haber Process factory.

Questions

1 What does the graph show about the relationship between percentage yield of ammonia and temperature?

2 What does the graph show about the relationship between the percentage yield of ammonia and pressure?

3 What yield of ammonia will be obtained in the new factory using the conditions proposed by Dr Jones?

4 Suggest why the new catalyst proposed by Dr Smith may be a good option for the new factory.

5 Dr Jones decides not to use the new catalyst. Suggest why he made this decision.

Whiter than white

In this item you will find out

- what goes into washing powders and washing-up liquids

- how these products clean

- how dry-cleaning works

Some clothes have a label that says 'Dry-clean only'. If you wash these clothes in a washing machine they will be damaged. Often they shrink, even if washed at low temperature. Sometimes clothes have stains that are very difficult to remove in a washing machine. Greasy stains such as lipstick or butter may still be visible after the clothes have been washed.

▲ Grease can be very difficult to wash out of clothes

These clothes are taken to a **dry-cleaning** company. Workers at the dry-cleaning company do not wash the clothes in water. They use an organic solvent. This is a compound obtained by the distillation of crude oil.

 a The solvents used in dry-cleaning are volatile (evaporate easily) and toxic. Suggest what precautions the workers at a dry-cleaning company should take.

Water is the most widely used solvent but it will not dissolve all substances. Some substances that are not soluble in water will dissolve in an organic solvent.

Water molecules have small positive and negative charges. This means that they will easily attract and dissolve other substances that also have positive and negative charges. However, they will not attract molecules that have no charge.

▲ A dry-cleaners

Oil and grease contain compounds with molecules that do not have any charge. Molecules of these compounds are not attracted to the charges on water molecules, but intermolecular forces of attraction are formed between the uncharged oil or grease molecules and the uncharged molecules of an organic solvent.

So, the organic solvents used in dry-cleaning dissolve oily and greasy stains that are difficult to remove in a washing machine. These solvents do not damage the fabric of the clothes. They are also quick to evaporate.

 b Why do you think it is important that the solvents used in dry-cleaning evaporate quickly?

Soap or not?

Washing powders are complex mixtures of ingredients. They are designed to get clothes clean even using water at temperatures as low as 30°C. This saves energy. It also avoids damaging some delicate fabrics, which would otherwise have to be dry-cleaned.

Each of the chemicals in a washing powder has a different job to do. The active **detergent** is the chemical that does the cleaning. Many of these detergents are made by the neutralisation of acids and alkalis.

The detergent in some washing powders is soap but most washing powders contain a synthetic detergent – also called a soapless detergent. Synthetic detergents clean better but soap is less damaging to delicate fabrics.

Synthetic detergents are designed to wash at low temperatures. This means that less energy is used to heat up the water. Also delicate fabrics are less likely to be damaged if washed at a low temperature. At a high temperature the dye in some clothing may 'run' as it is dissolved into the water, and the clothing may shrink.

Amazing fact

Evidence of ancient washing soap was found at Sapo Hill in Rome, where the ashes containing the fat of sacrificial animals was used as a soap.

Detergent molecules

Detergent molecules have a charged hydrophilic (water-loving) head and an uncharged hydrophobic (water-hating) tail. The tails of the detergent molecules are attracted to and stick into the greasy dirt. The heads of the detergent molecules are attracted to charged water molecules.

The force of this attraction between the heads and water molecules pulls the dirt off the clothes. The detergent molecules then surround the dirt. This keeps the dirt suspended in the water so that it doesn't go back onto the clothes.

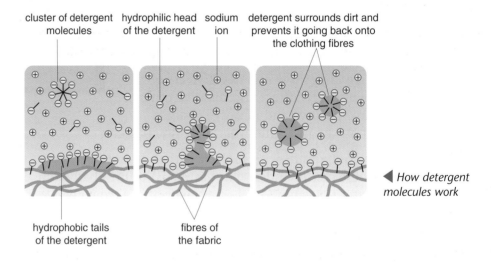

How detergent molecules work

c Why must a detergent have an uncharged tail and a charged head?

Making soap and synthetic detergents

Soap is made by the neutralisation of fatty acids from animal fats or vegetable oils with an alkali such as sodium hydroxide. Fatty acids have long chains of carbon and hydrogen atoms which form the hydrophobic end of the detergent. In fats and oils the fatty acids are joined to glycerol in a complex molecule called a triglyceride. When the triglyceride reacts with sodium hydroxide, the sodium salt of the fatty acid is formed. This is soap and the reaction is called saponification. The charged end of the sodium salt is the hydrophilic end of the molecule.

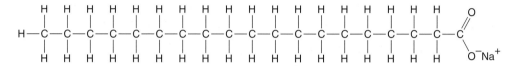

▲ *A soap molecule*

▲ *Making soap*

Synthetic detergents are made by the neutralisation of a synthetic acid that has a long hydrocarbon chain with an alkali such as sodium hydroxide. The result is a molecule similar to soap, but with much more powerful detergent properties.

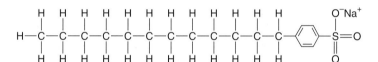

◀ *A synthetic detergent molecule*

d **What do the structural formulae of the soap and synthetic detergents have in common?**

More ingredients

In many places the tap water is hard because it contains dissolved calcium and magnesium salts. This means that it is difficult to get a lather with soap. Hard water also forms a scum with soap. Washing powders contain chemicals that soften the water. This stops clothes being covered with scum. It also means that you can use less detergent to get the clothes clean.

Some coloured stains are difficult to remove from clothes. Bleach takes the colour out of these stains so that they cannot be seen.

Optical brighteners are chemicals that give white clothes a very bright 'whiter than white' appearance. They reflect the light from the clothes to our eyes.

Food stains on clothes are broken down by enzymes. These are biological catalysts that speed up the reactions that break down some stains. They will only work in a low temperature wash, for example at 40°C. Enzymes are proteins and are destroyed at high temperatures.

e **Suggest why it may be an advantage to leave dirty clothing to soak for a while in a solution of washing powder containing enzymes, before beginning the wash cycle of the washing machine.**

Which washes whiter?

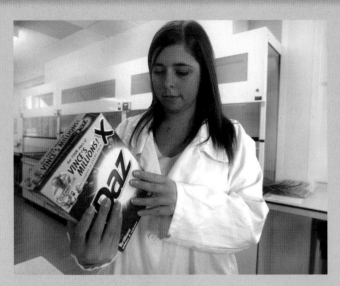

Anita works for a company that makes washing powders. The company employs scientists to develop new and better washing powders. When a new product has been developed it needs to be tested to see if it is truly better than those already sold.

Anita's job is to test new washing powders to see if they are better than the washing powders that the company has made for some time.

She tests a washing powder containing a new synthetic detergent. For comparison she also tests a washing powder containing an old synthetic detergent and another containing soap flakes.

Anita takes 11 similar pieces of white cotton cloth. She stains 10 of these pieces using the same mixture of dirt and grease.

She dissolves the two washing powders and the soap flakes in water at different temperatures, and places one of the dirty cloths in each solution – putting the clean cloth and the remaining dirty cloth to one side.

She stirs each cloth in its solution. She leaves the cloths for 30 minutes. She then stirs again. Then she rinses and dries each cloth.

Anita scores how well each piece of cloth has been cleaned on a scale of 1 (very dirty) to 10 (very clean).

Her results are shown in the table.

Washing powder	Washing temperature (°C)		
	30	60	90
containing soap	3	5	7
containing 'old' synthetic detergent	6	9	10
containing 'new' synthetic detergent	8	9	10

Questions

1 Anita did not put dirt onto one piece of cloth, and put this and one dirty cloth to one side. Suggest why.

2 What do the results show about the effectiveness of soap and synthetic detergents in removing dirt from the cotton cloth?

3 In what way is the new synthetic detergent better than the old one?

4 Why may this experiment not simulate what happens in a washing machine?

5 What do the results show about the effect of temperature on the cleaning action of soap and synthetic detergents?

6 Suggest an explanation for this effect of temperature on cleaning action.

Making drugs

In this item you will find out

- about using batch or continuous processes to make chemicals

- about the cost of research and development of new medicines

- the differences in the production of bulk and speciality chemicals

In the late 1950s and early 1960s, pregnant women across the world were prescribed a new remedy for morning sickness. At the time nobody had any idea how this would affect the lives of their unborn children. Around ten thousand babies were born with disabilities as a result of their mothers taking the drug thalidomide. Just under half of those have survived, including 456 of them in the UK.

Though the first child afflicted by thalidomide damage was born on 25 December 1956, it took about four and a half years before doctors suspected that thalidomide was causing these deformities. Thalidomide was withdrawn in the UK in 1961.

a Suggest why it took about four and a half years before doctors suspected that thalidomide was causing disabilities.

Two things are clear about the testing of thalidomide. First, thalidomide was never tested on pregnant animals before it was used in humans. Second, after thalidomide had been withdrawn, it was tested on pregnant mice, rats, hamsters, rabbits, macaques, marmosets, baboons and rhesus monkeys, and the same terrible effects were found.

At that time there was no legal requirement to test new drugs on pregnant animals before they were given to humans. If it had been tested in this way the disaster could have been avoided.

In the middle of the last century we did not know enough to prevent thalidomide being used by pregnant women. Today, laws on drug testing are much stricter. If thalidomide had been developed in the twenty-first century, rigorous testing on animals, including pregnant animals, would have been required, and this would have prevented the tragedy.

b Why is it unlikely that a similar tragedy will occur in the future?

▲ Thalidomide can cause babies to be born with disabilities

Development costs

Developing a new medicine or **pharmaceutical drug** is a long and costly process. It may take 15 years and cost over £300 million pounds to develop a new drug. The flow chart shows the steps in the development of a new drug.

▼ How a new drug is developed

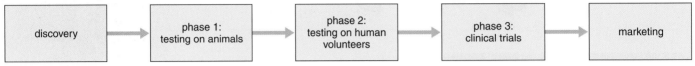

discovery → phase 1: testing on animals → phase 2: testing on human volunteers → phase 3: clinical trials → marketing

Thousands of new chemical compounds are made and tested to find one new product. When a promising chemical compound is found it has to be tested. This involves testing on animals and then on volunteers. Finally clinical tests are used to find out how effective it is at curing patients and to make sure that are no serious side effects.

When the drug is proved to be effective, it has to have legal approval before it is sold.

Finally it can be marketed. This involves advertising and supplying the drug to hospitals and doctors.

c Why do you think so few of the compounds tested are marketed as new drugs?

Production costs

The development of the drug is not the only expense that the drug company has. The company also has to meet very high costs during manufacture of the drug.

It takes a lot of people to make the new drug. Some of the processes involved cannot be automated, and many require highly skilled workers. Paying the wages of all these employees costs the company a lot of money.

The raw materials needed to extract or make the drug have to be purchased. Many of these raw materials are rare and expensive. To get some of the required materials from plant sources, costly extraction processes are required.

The manufacturing process for a drug uses a lot of energy. The company has to pay for the electricity, gas or oil used in manufacture.

Extracting chemicals

Many drugs are extracted from plants. This process follows several stages.

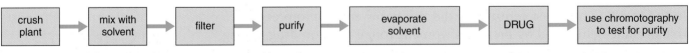

crush plant → mix with solvent → filter → purify → evaporate solvent → DRUG → use chromotography to test for purity

▲ Extracting a drug from a plant

Firstly the plant material is crushed. This breaks the tough cell walls in the plant and releases the chemicals contained in the plant cells. Most of the chemicals extracted from plants are not soluble in water so a suitable organic solvent is mixed with the crushed plant material to dissolve the chemicals. Solid plant material is then removed from the mixture by filtration.

The organic solvent dissolves other chemicals as well as the required drug so the drug must now be purified by removing it from the other chemicals. This is done by mixing the solution with another solvent that will dissolve the drug but not the other chemicals. This solvent is then evaporated off to leave the pure drug.

To make sure that the drug is pure it is tested using **chromatography**. This helps to identify both the drug and any impurities that may still be present.

 d Drugs extracted from plants are tested for purity using chromatography. Suggest how this will show whether or not the drug is pure.

Development decisions

Several factors have to be considered by a pharmaceutical company before making the decision whether or not to make a new drug:

- in terms of time and labour, what the cost of research and development for the new drug will be
- how long it will take to meet legal requirements, including testing, before the drug can be sold
- how much demand there will be for the new product
- how long it will take for profits from sale of the drug to repay the investment made by the company.

 e Pharmaceutical companies are some of the richest in the world. Suggest how they make such large profits when the expense of developing new drugs is so high.

▲ These medicines are made from speciality chemicals

Batch and continuous processes

The chemical industry can produce products using two types of process: **batch process** or **continuous process**.

The Haber Process for the manufacture of ammonia is an example of a continuous process. Nitrogen and hydrogen are passed into the reaction vessel. Here they react to make ammonia. The ammonia gas is condensed into a liquid and collected as it is produced. This process can continue for 24 hours a day until the plant has to be closed down for maintenance.

▲ Ammonia is a bulk chemical

Like other chemicals made by continuous processes, ammonia is used in the manufacture of many other products. Because they are so widely used, very large quantities of these chemicals are made. They are called bulk chemicals.

Many medicines and pharmaceutical drugs are produced by a batch process. Measured amounts of raw materials are mixed and processed to produce the drug. This happens only when a new supply is required. These chemicals are not made continually. Also, much smaller quantities of these chemicals are made. They are called speciality chemicals or fine chemicals.

 f Bulk chemicals are much cheaper to buy than speciality chemicals. Suggest why.

▲ St John's Wort

St John's Wort

St John's Wort, sometimes called the 'Sunshine herb', is a bushy perennial plant with numerous star-shaped yellow flowers. It is native to many parts of the world, including Europe and the United States, and has been used as a herbal remedy for about two thousand years.

St John's Wort is used by many people to treat mild depression, as an alternative to prescribed drugs such as Prozac (fluoxetine). Research shows that it is not the whole plant but an ingredient called hypericin that has anti-depressant activity.

Paul runs a small natural and herbal medicine company. One of the products his company sells is St John's Wort. Paul sells packets containing the dried stems and leaves of the plant.

Over the past year Paul's sales of this product have increased by 300%.

Paul has developed a process to extract the active ingredient, hypericin, from the stems and leaves of St John's Wort.

He sells this extract in tablets at a much higher price than the dried plant.

Paul produces small quantities of the extract by a batch process. This requires the work of several people for a whole day. The process uses standard equipment that Paul has in his factory.

Another way to produce the extract uses a continuous process. This involves the purchase of new, and very expensive, machinery. When this machinery is running, it requires only one person to look after the process.

Both processes require the plant St John's Wort as raw material. Paul can negotiate with his supplier to buy the plant in larger quantities at a lower price.

Questions

1 Describe an advantage and a disadvantage of Paul using a batch process to produce the extract from St John's Wort?

2 Describe an advantage and a disadvantage of Paul using a continuous process to produce the extract from St John's Wort?

3 Suggest what other costs Paul may have before his extract can be sold to the public?

4 What other information do you think Paul should obtain to help him decide which process to use to make this extract?

It's a small world

In this item you will find out

- about the three forms of carbon: diamond, graphite and fullerene

- about the properties and uses of these forms of carbon

- how fullerene has been used to create a miniature chemical world – nanochemistry

How is a pencil like a diamond ring?

They both contain carbon. The pencil 'lead' is made from graphite. The gemstone in the ring is diamond. Graphite and diamond are different forms (**allotropes**) of carbon. They contain only carbon atoms but these are arranged in different ways.

This gives these two types of carbon some different properties which you can see in the table below.

Diamond is lustrous and colourless, making it ideal for use in jewellery. The fiery appearance of a diamond is caused by the separation of white light into the colours of the spectrum as it passes through the stone. This makes diamond the most sought-after gemstone.

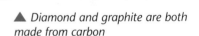 ▲ Diamond and graphite are both made from carbon

 a **Both diamond and graphite are lustrous. Why do you think only diamond is used as a gemstone?**

Diamond is also the hardest natural substance. Diamond can be cut only with another diamond, and is very resistant to wear. It is an excellent material for the cutting edges of industrial tools.

The properties and uses of graphite are quite different. Since graphite conducts electricity and has a high melting point, it is used as an electrode in electrolysis reactions. The graphite is used to pass an electric current through the molten material or solution to be electrolysed. An example is the manufacture of aluminium.

The softness and black colour of graphite make it useful for pencil 'lead'. The slipperiness of graphite means it is a good lubricator. It is used as an additive to oils and greases.

 b **Diamond is much more expensive than graphite. Suggest why.**

Diamond	Graphite
colourless and transparent	black and opaque
very hard	soft and slippery
very high melting point	high melting point
does not conduct electricity	conducts electricity
lustrous with a brilliant shine	lustrous

Diamond

The differences in properties shown by diamond and graphite are caused by the different ways that the carbon atoms are arranged in the two allotropes.

In diamond, each carbon atom is joined to four others by strong covalent bonds. To separate the atoms these covalent bonds need to be broken. This requires a very large amount of energy. This explains why diamond is so hard and has such a high melting point.

The structure of diamond contains no ions or free electrons. There are no mobile charged particles to carry an electric current, so diamond does not conduct electricity.

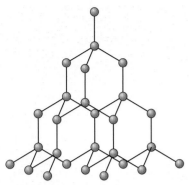

▲ How carbon atoms are arranged in diamond

Graphite

In graphite the carbon atoms are arranged in layers.

Within each layer the atoms are joined by strong covalent bonds. The large amount of energy needed to break these bonds means that graphite has a high melting point. The layers are held together by much weaker forces. They can easily slide across each other. This makes graphite soft and slippery.

The electrons between the layers of graphite are **delocalised**. This means that these electrons can move along in the space between the layers, carrying an electric current. So, graphite can conduct electricity.

strong covalent bond

weak bond between layers

▲ The layers of carbon atoms in graphite

Buckminsterfullerene

A third allotrope of carbon, buckminsterfullerene, was discovered in 1985. Each molecule of this allotrope is made up of 60 carbon atoms joined to each other in the shape of a ball. These are known as 'Bucky balls'. Buckminsterfullerene has the formula C_{60}.

Since this first discovery, other **fullerenes** have been made with different numbers of carbon atoms in each ball. The number of atoms ranges from 32 to 600.

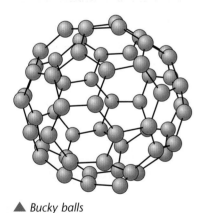

▲ Bucky balls

Nanotubes

Fullerenes can be joined together to make tube shapes called **nanotubes**. This has led to a whole new area of development called nanotechnology.

▶ How carbon atoms are arranged in a nanotube

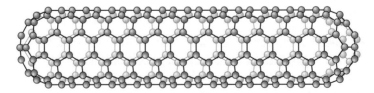

Nanotubes are very strong and can conduct electricity. They have a number of uses as:

- semiconductors in electrical circuits
- industrial catalysts
- a reinforcement for the graphite in tennis racquets.

Catalyst atoms or molecules can be attached to the outside of nanotubes. This allows a wider variety of substances to be used as catalysts. Even though the nanotubes are so small, they have a very large surface area. This gives a very large area of contact for the catalyst. The nanotubes can be separated from liquid products, allowing re-use of the catalyst.

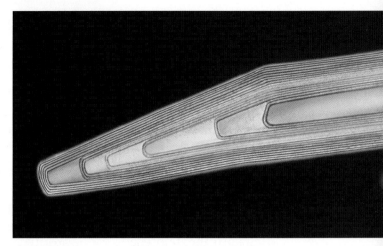

▲ *Electron micrograph of carbon nanotube fibres*

Nanoparticles

The discovery of nanotubes has created a new area of science called nanochemistry. Normally, chemistry works with materials on a large scale. Nanochemistry uses materials on a very small scale. It works with materials at the atomic level, with particles of incredibly small size, called **nanoparticles**.

These nanoparticles have different properties from 'bulk' chemicals. The electrical conductivity of single-walled nanotubes is similar to that of metals. This is because their unique structure means electrons can freely pass along a material made from nanotubes. They are the only known molecules that can electronically act as a true metallic conductor. By spacing and controlling the size of the nanotubes they can behave as semiconductors, similar to silicon.

Caging molecules

It is possible to use fullerene nanotubes as 'cages' in which to trap other molecules. Just a few molecules can fit inside or be attached to the outside of a nanotube.

In the future, nanotubes containing drugs for the treatment of diseases such as cancer may be injected into the bloodstream. They will deliver the drugs straight to the tumour and not release them elsewhere in the body. This means that less of the drugs will be needed and there will be less damage to other cells in the body.

 It is thought that drugs carried in fullerenes will be more effective in treating cancer tumours, and that they will have fewer side effects than those injected directly into the bloodstream. Suggest why.

Making molecules

It may ultimately be possible to use nanoparticles as miniature factories, producing chemical products. This **molecular manufacturing** could be achieved by nanoparticles assembling a product molecule by molecule, each nanoparticle bringing a different part, perhaps just a few atoms, to be precisely positioned in the assembly of a complete molecule. This is called **positional chemistry**.

Another possibility is to start with a larger structure, and remove part of it bit by bit until it has nanoscale features.

Keywords
allotrope • delocalised • fullerene • molecular manufacturing • nanoparticle • nanotube • positional chemistry

Nanoparticles may cause brain damage

Nanotechnology – the science of incredibly small particles – may pose a real threat to human health, scientists have warned. Research shows that nanoparticles, the ultra fine powders produced by the nanotechnology industry, can build up in the brain if they are inhaled. Because the particles are so fine, they could remain in the atmosphere for some time. We could take them in with every breath, while being unaware of the danger.

In a study carried out on rats, researchers found that once the rats inhaled tiny carbon nanoparticles, the particles not only accumulated in the lungs but also found their way to parts of the brain. Although the rats appeared to be unaffected by the particles, scientists believe they could ultimately lead to brain damage.

Nanoparticles are among the most common materials to come out of the new science, being used in everything from sun block to plastic car bumpers.

Only small quantities of nanoparticles are currently produced in Britain. But it is a growing industry which is expected to be worth billions within a decade.

Scientists fear that the more companies start producing nanoparticles, the greater the risk that these particles may get into the atmosphere where they could

be inhaled. Some nanoparticles are already widespread in the air we breathe, largely due to the burning of fossil fuels and vehicle exhaust fumes. In a busy street, each breath we take contains around 25 million nanoparticles. Scientists already suspect that nanoparticles from diesel fumes contribute to heart disease, asthma and other respiratory diseases.

They caution that this finding does not warrant a ban on the use of nanotechnology, but say we should be very careful when producing new nanoparticles. Further research is needed to find out if these tiny particles are likely to pose a big threat.

Questions

1 Why are we unaware of breathing in nanoparticles?

2 What discovery from the research on rats has worried scientists?

3 Nanotechnology is a very new science, yet scientists say that we have been breathing in nanoparticles for years. Explain this apparent contradiction.

4 Explain why scientists do not think that a ban on the use of nanotechnology is justified at the moment.

Water, water everywhere

In this item you will find out

- which chemicals may pollute our water
- about the processes used in the purification of water
- about ways of testing for some substances that may be dissolved in water

Water is essential to all living things. Without water we cannot survive for more than a few days. Not only must we have water to drink, but that water must not contain chemicals or microbes that may harm us. The water coming out of your taps at home may come from a river, lake, reservoir or aquifer.

Tap water is not pure. It contains many dissolved chemicals. These include salts that dissolved as the water passed over rocks. These are harmless to us. Water may also contain pollutants, such as:

- nitrate residues – these get into the water when rain dissolves and washes fertiliser from fields into rivers and lakes
- lead compounds – these can dissolve into water from lead pipes in very old houses
- pesticide residues – if farmers spray a pesticide too near rivers or lakes, some may drift over, or be washed by rain, into the water.

a **The water pipes in some old houses are made of lead. Why should these pipes be replaced with new ones made of copper or plastic?**

In many of the developing nations, people get their water directly from rivers or lakes, without any purification. Often this water is contaminated with sewage and contains disease-causing microbes. Aid agencies such as Oxfam are working to make clean water available to these people.

Not only is water essential for use in our homes but it is also a material vital to industry.

Water is used as:

- a cheap raw material in some manufacturing processes
- a coolant to prevent many industrial processes from overheating
- a solvent.

b **TV adverts are often used in a campaign to persuade people in the United Kingdom to use less water. This country has a high rainfall. Suggest why it is important for us to conserve water?**

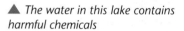
▲ *The water in this lake contains harmful chemicals*

▼ *Clean water is very important*

Is it fit to drink?

When water is pumped from a lake, reservoir or river it contains a number of materials dissolved or suspended in it. These may include:

- dissolved salts and minerals
- microbes
- pollutants
- insoluble materials.

During water purification, those materials we do not wish to remain in the water supplied to our homes are removed.

 Which of the substances in the list above would make the water unsafe to drink?

Water purification

Water from most sources contains small insoluble solid particles. The first job in the purification of water is to remove these suspended solids. Water is first passed into a **sedimentation** tank. Here the larger solid materials suspended in the water are allowed to settle. These include sand and soil particles.

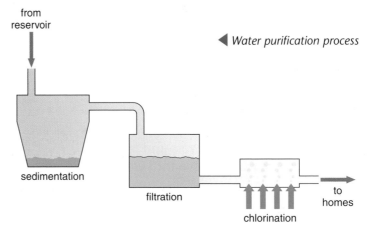

◀ *Water purification process*

Next, water goes through **filtration**. It is passed through a filter made of layers of grit, coarse sand and fine sand. This traps finer suspended materials consisting of very small and light particles such as clay. These particles are too small and light to settle out in the sedimentation tank.

Finally the water undergoes **chlorination**. A very small quantity of chlorine gas is dissolved in the water. This kills microbes that might otherwise cause disease.

 Chlorine is a very poisonous element. Suggest why it is not harmful to us when we drink chlorinated water?

The purification process does not remove all impurities from water. A number of dissolved chemicals remain. Soluble salts of calcium and magnesium cause water hardness. This is not harmful to anyone drinking the water but does cause damage to the heating elements in kettles and washing machines. Other chemicals dissolved in the water may include nitrates, pesticides, herbicides and metal salts. Some of these are poisonous. Though they are present only in very low concentrations, they may have an adverse effect on health.

Distilling seawater

In some countries, seawater is distilled to obtain drinking water. A little over 3% of the mass of seawater is dissolved salts, mainly sodium chloride. When seawater is distilled, these salts are left behind.

On a small scale, distillation can be used to provide enough water for use on long sea journeys in small yachts. On a large scale, the distillation process uses a lot of energy. The product is pure water, which has no taste.

 Suggest why distillation of seawater is used to make large quantities of fresh water only in places where water cannot be obtained from other sources.

Testing water

Water can be tested to identify some of the chemicals dissolved in it. These tests involve **precipitation** reactions. In these reactions, dissolved chemicals react to make an insoluble product. This is suspended in the solution to form a precipitate, making the mixture appear cloudy.

To test for sulfate ions, barium chloride solution is added. For example, with sodium sulfate:

$$Na_2SO_4 \quad + \quad BaCl_2 \quad \rightarrow \quad BaSO_4 \quad + \quad 2NaCl$$
sodium sulfate + barium chloride → barium sulfate + sodium chloride

Barium sulfate is insoluble in water and forms a white precipitate. This shows that there is a sulfate dissolved in the water. In a similar way, silver nitrate solution can be used to test for halide ions: chloride, bromide and iodide. Each of these ions forms an insoluble silver salt, which is precipitated out. Each halide forms a precipitate with a different colour.

▲ Seawater is turned into drinking water here

Halide	Chloride	Bromide	Iodide
Name of precipitate	silver chloride	silver bromide	silver iodide
Colour of precipitate	white	cream	yellow

For example, with sodium halides:

$$NaCl \quad + \quad AgNO_3 \quad \rightarrow \quad AgCl \quad + \quad NaNO_3$$
sodium chloride + silver nitrate → silver chloride + sodium nitrate

$$NaBr \quad + \quad AgNO_3 \quad \rightarrow \quad AgBr \quad + \quad NaNO_3$$
sodium bromide + silver nitrate → silver bromide + sodium nitrate

$$NaI \quad + \quad AgNO_3 \quad \rightarrow \quad AgI \quad + \quad NaNO_3$$
sodium iodide + silver nitrate → silver iodide + sodium nitrate

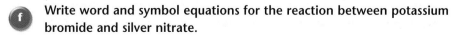 Write word and symbol equations for the reaction between potassium bromide and silver nitrate.

Examiner's tip

A precipitate is formed only when the product of a reaction is insoluble in water. Soluble products do not form precipitates.

Keywords

chlorination • filtration • precipitation • sedimentation

141

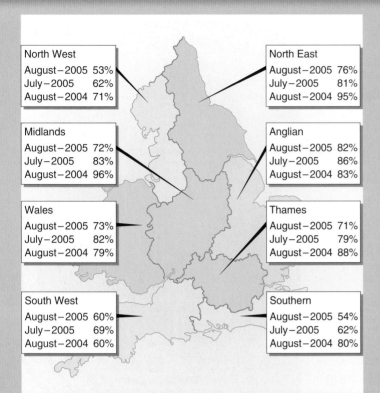

North West
August – 2005   53%
July – 2005   62%
August – 2004   71%

North East
August – 2005   76%
July – 2005   81%
August – 2004   95%

Midlands
August – 2005   72%
July – 2005   83%
August – 2004   96%

Anglian
August – 2005   82%
July – 2005   86%
August – 2004   83%

Wales
August – 2005   73%
July – 2005   82%
August – 2004   79%

Thames
August – 2005   71%
July – 2005   79%
August – 2004   88%

South West
August – 2005   60%
July – 2005   69%
August – 2004   60%

Southern
August – 2005   54%
July – 2005   62%
August – 2004   80%

Monitoring water pollution

Dr White works for a water supply company. His company takes water from reservoirs, then purifies it and supplies it to customers in industry and in private houses.

Although the United Kingdom has a high annual rainfall, most of this rain falls during the winter. This fills up the reservoirs so that they give a good supply of water during the summer. If winter rainfall is a lot less than usual, the reservoirs are not filled, and water supplies may become very low during the summer.

When water levels are very low, water supply companies have to reduce demand. They can do this by banning the use of hosepipes for watering gardens and washing cars. They can also advise people of ways to reduce the amount of water they use at home, such as taking showers instead of baths and reducing the amount of water used each time a toilet is flushed.

The water supply companies monitor reservoir levels in their areas during the year. Part of Dr White's job is to predict whether there is likely to be a shortage of water supply in his area during the next summer. He works in the Southern region, which has the highest population density in England and Wales.

Dr White looks at the map above showing reservoir levels in the year from August 2004 to August 2005.

The map shows how full the reservoirs in each area were at three times: in August 2004 after high demand during the summer, in July 2005 when they still contained most of the water from winter rain, and again in August 2005.

Questions

1 The figures for Wales show that reservoir levels rose and then fell during this year. Suggest why this happened.

2 In none of the regions were reservoirs very near to 100% full during this year. What does this suggest about the amount or rain that fell during the winter of 2004–2005?

3 How is the pattern of reservoir levels in most of the other regions different from that in Wales? Suggest a reason for this difference.

4 Dr White looks at a long-term weather forecast for the winter of 2005–2006. This suggests that rainfall will be less than average. Suggest and explain the most likely prediction that Dr White makes for water supplies in his region during the summer of 2006.

5 Suggest what advice Dr White's water supply company will give to its domestic consumers during the summer of 2006.

C4a

1 An acid is slowly added to a solution of a base. The word equation for the reaction that takes place is:

acid + base → salt + water

a What is the term used to describe a base that is soluble in water? [1]

b Explain why the pH changes during this reaction. [1]

c Write a word equation for the reaction between an acid and a carbonate. [2]

2 When an acid is added to a base a salt is produced.

Copy and complete this table – fill in the empty boxes to show which salt is produced.

acid	base	salt
sulfuric acid	sodium hydroxide	
hydrochloric acid	magnesium oxide	
nitric acid	potassium carbonate	

3 a Which ions are always present in an acidic solution? [1]

b Which ions are always present in an alkaline solution? [1]

c Write a symbol equation to show the neutralisation reaction between these two ions. [2]

4 Copper(II) oxide is added to sulfuric acid. The word equation for this reaction is:

copper(II) + sulfuric acid → copper(II) + water
oxide   sulfate

Write a symbol equation for this reaction. [3]

5 Write word and symbol equations for the following neutralisation reactions.

a sulfuric acid and potassium hydroxide [2]

b hydrochloric acid and ammonia [2]

c nitric acid and calcium carbonate [2]

C4b

1 When calcium carbonate is heated it decomposes to form calcium oxide and carbon dioxide. 100 g of calcium decomposes to give 56 g of calcium oxide.

a What mass of calcium oxide is made when 10 g calcium oxide decomposes? [1]

b Write a word equation for the reaction. [2]

2 A student adds 5.6 g calcium oxide to some hydrochloric acid.

She evaporates some water from the solution, leaves the solution to form crystals of calcium chloride, filters off the crystals and then leaves them to dry.

She uses relative atomic masses to work out that the predicted yield of calcium chloride for this experiment is 11.1 g.

She finds that the mass of calcium chloride she has made is 8.0 g

a What is the percentage yield for her experiment? [2]

b Suggest two reasons why she did not get 100% yield. [2]

3 For any chemical reaction, the total mass of reactants is the same as the total mass of products.

Explain why. [2]

4 Copper(II) carbonate decomposes when heated.

$$CuCO_3 \rightarrow CuO + CO_2$$

3.1 g of copper(II) carbonate is completely decomposed by heating.

a What mass of copper(II) oxide is formed? [3]

b What mass of carbon dioxide is given off? [3]
(Relative atomic masses: C,12; Cu, 64; O,16.)

5 When aluminium is heated in chlorine, 6.0 g of aluminium chloride is made, according to this equation.

$$2Al + 3Cl_2 \rightarrow 2AlCl_3$$

What mass of aluminium reacted to make this aluminium chloride?
(Relative atomic masses: Al, 27; Cl, 35.5.) [3]

C4c

1 The compounds used in fertilisers are soluble in water.

Explain why this is important. [2]

2 The fertiliser potassium nitrate can be made by a neutralisation reaction between an acid and an alkali.

Name the acid and alkali. [2]

3 If the same type of crop is grown in the same field for several years, the yield falls.

If fertiliser is applied to this field each year, the yield does not fall.

Explain why. [3]

4 Describe the process of eutrophication. [6]

5 Ammonium nitrate, NH_4NO_3, and ammonium sulfate, $(NH_4)_2SO_4$ are popular fertilisers.

Calculate the percentage of nitrogen by mass in each. (Relative atomic masses: H, 1; N, 14; O, 16; S, 32.) [4]

6 A scientist studies the effect of nitrate pollution on the growth of algae to give an algal bloom.

He adds different amounts of ammonium nitrate to equal volume samples of the same river water.

After five days he measures the amount of light that can pass through the water, compared with a control.

His results are shown in the table.

Mass of ammonium nitrate added (g)	Percentage of light passing through (%)
0	100
1.0	88
2.0	64
3.0	41
4.0	25
5.0	18

a Describe the correlation shown in this data. [1]
b What is the connection between the percentage of light passing through the solution and the growth of algae? [2]
c What additional information is needed to decide whether ammonium nitrate is the cause of algal bloom? [1]

C4d

1 a State two conditions used in the Haber Process to give a good yield of ammonia in a short reaction time. [2]
b Describe how each of these affects the rate and yield of the ammonia produced. [2]

2 Explain why ammonia is important in relation to world food production. [4]

3 Explain how temperature and pressure conditions used in the Haber Process affect the cost of production of ammonia. [2]

4 Explain how temperature and pressure conditions used in the Haber Process are a compromise to produce ammonia at the cheapest cost. [4]

5 For many years iron has been used as a catalyst in the Haber Process.

A new catalyst is being tested. Here is a comparison of iron and the new catalyst.

	Iron	New catalyst
Cost of Catalyst	cheap	expensive
Percentage conversion to ammonia	15	25
Pressure and temperature used	pressure 100–140 atmospheres temperature 400–700°C	pressure 80–100 atmospheres temperature 300–400°C
Replacement interval	5 years	still unknown

Describe two advantages and two disadvantages of using the new catalyst instead of iron. [4]

C4e

1 Describe the function of the following ingredients in a washing powder:

a active detergent [2]
b water softener [2]

2 Some clothes are cleaned by a dry-cleaning process.

a How is this process different from using a washing powder? [1]
b What are the reasons for using this process instead of a washing powder? [2]

3 Describe the essential features of a molecule which functions as a detergent. [2]

4 Describe how a detergent molecule:

a removes dirt from clothing during the washing process [2]
b prevents dirt from going back onto clothing during the washing process. [2]

5 Sam uses a washing powder that contains enzymes.

The instructions on the packet say that she should wash clothing at 40°C.

a What may happen to the enzymes in the washing powder if she washes the clothing at a higher temperature? [2]
b What other advantages are there for washing clothing at a low temperature? [2]

C4f

1 Making and developing a new pharmaceutical drug is usually much more expensive than producing a bulk chemical such as ammonia.

Describe three factors that make the drug so much more expensive. [3]

2 Describe the processes used in the extraction of chemicals from plant sources. [5]

3 It may take several years for a new pharmaceutical drug to move from first synthesis in a laboratory to marketing to the public.

Explain why this takes so long. [2]

4 Pharmaceutical companies carry out extensive market research to get information about the attitude of members of the public to a new product.

Market research is expensive. Why do the companies spend this money? [2]

5 A pharmaceutical company has developed a new drug.

The managing director of the company is given this data about the drug.

Cost of development (£)	120 000 000
Expected annual sales (kg)	15 000
Selling price (£/kg)	2 700
Cost of production by batch process (£/kg)	1 700
Cost of production by continuous process (£/kg)	700

a How long will it take before the company gets back the cost of developing the new drug:

  i using a batch process [2]
  ii using a continuous process? [2]
 b The managing director decides to use a batch process.
   Suggest why he made this decision. [2]

6 The drug fluoxetine is used to treat depression. Its development and testing took many years, and its side effects are well known. Some people drink tea made using leaves of the plant St John's Wort to treat depression. This is a herbal remedy which has not received the testing that is required by law for any new drug.

What are the advantages and disadvantages of using St. John's Wort to treat depression instead of fluoxetine?

C4g

1 Diamond and graphite are allotropes of carbon.

Use the properties of diamond and graphite to explain the following facts.

a Diamond is used in cutting tools. [2]
b Graphite is used to make pencil leads. [2]

2 Buckminsterfullerene is another allotrope of carbon. It can be used to make nanotubes.

Describe three uses for nanotubes. [3]

3 Use ideas about bonding to explain why diamond does not conduct electricity but graphite does. [4]

4 Explain how nanotubes can be used to increase the effectiveness of catalysts. [2]

5 Fullerenes can be used to 'cage' other molecules.

a Explain what is meant by this statement. [1]
b What advantage do caged molecules have in the treatment of diseases using drugs? [3]

6 Silicon can behave as a semi-conductor. Now silicon 'chips' are used in numerous devices from computers to washing machines. Nanotubes can also be made to act as semi-conductors.

Suggest what advantage nanotubes may have over silicon chips, and predict the effect their use may have on future computer design.

C4h

1 Describe two ways that pollutants can get into water sources in the United Kingdom. [2]

2 Write a word equation for the reaction of potassium sulfate with barium chloride. [2]

3 Water purification involves three processes: sedimentation, filtration and chlorination.

Explain why each of these processes is carried out. [3]

4 Explain why the purification carried out on the water that is supplied to our taps cannot guarantee that it is harmless to drink. [3]

5 Silver nitrate solution is used to test for the presence of halide ions in water.

Write symbol equations for the reactions that take place when silver nitrate solution is added to water containing the following halide ions.

a potassium chloride [2]
b sodium iodide [2]
c magnesium bromide [3]

- You will have seen how chemists use raw materials to make new substances that are useful to us in many different ways. Plastics, drugs and medicines, fertilisers, foodstuffs, textiles and fuels are just some of them.

- We can compare numbers of particles by measuring mass. This type of calculation can be used to interpret the results obtained from an important analytical technique called titration.

- Electricity can be used to make new substances from raw materials. We can predict what will be produced by different substances in different conditions. Many reactions exist as equilibria. Changing the conditions affects this type of reaction and industrial chemists use these ideas to manipulate reactions to make them economically viable.

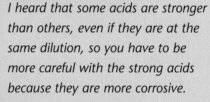

I heard that if you add enough water to an acid you can make it so dilute that it becomes harmless.

I heard that some acids are stronger than others, even if they are at the same dilution, so you have to be more careful with the strong acids because they are more corrosive.

I think you are both right. It all depends what you do with the acid. We can safely eat some acidic substances like lemon juice, but you wouldn't want to do that with some other acids like hydrochloric acid!

What you need to know

- How elements are extracted from raw materials.
- The common reactions and properties of acids and alkalis.
- How an electric current can split up some liquids.

The secrets of formulae

In this item you will find out

- how to use equations to predict the mass of substances produced in a chemical reaction

- how to work out the formula of a substance

- how to calculate the amounts of materials used and produced in reactions

▲ We can identify chemicals by their formulae

Chemists study changes in properties and look for patterns of behaviour when substances react. When we use chemical reactions to make useful materials, it is important that we know how much of each material will be involved. If we do not use exactly the right amounts it can be very wasteful. Chemical formulae tell us how much of each element there is in a particular compound.

You should remember that the relative atomic mass of an element is the average mass of an atom of the element compared to the mass of 1/12th of an atom of carbon-12.

Using relative atomic masses we can calculate the relative **molar masses** of different substances:

formula	O_2	CO_2	H_2O
formula mass	$16 \times 2 = 32$	$12 + (16 \times 2) = 44$	$(1 \times 2) + 16 = 18$

This equation shows the reaction between carbon and oxygen:

carbon + oxygen → carbon dioxide

$C(s)$ + $O_2(g)$ → $CO_2(g)$

▲ The mass of a carbon atom is 12 times the mass of a hydrogen atom

We can use these relative **formula masses** to work out the mass of oxygen needed to completely oxidise 24 kg of carbon and the mass of carbon dioxide produced.

This tells us that 12 g carbon will combine with 32 g oxygen to give us 44 g carbon dioxide. Doubling the amounts involved tells us that 24 g carbon will combine with 64 g oxygen to give us 88 g carbon dioxide. If we substitute g with kg, you can see that 24 kg carbon will require 64 kg oxygen to be completely oxidised to 88 kg carbon dioxide.

a What mass of carbon could be burned in 6.4 g of oxygen?

b What is the minimum mass of oxygen required to form 440 g of carbon dioxide?

MOLAR MASS

Counting atoms

Knowing formula masses allows us to 'count' particles. This is important if we want to measure out the right amounts of 'ingredients' needed, for example to prepare a medicine.

When a bank cashier wants to count out £10 worth of 5p coins they will do it by weighing out the correct amount rather than actually counting them. In a similar way chemists do not count out individual atoms, they measure out a certain number of atoms by measuring their mass. Since the atoms are very small, the numbers are very large. To make the numbers manageable we use the idea of **moles**.

A mole is a very large number. That number is 6×10^{23} and is called Avogadro's number. This is the number of atoms present in exactly 12 g of carbon-12.

We can calculate the number of moles of atoms in a sample of atoms using the equation:

$$\text{number of moles} = \frac{\text{mass (g)}}{\text{relative atomic mass}}$$

This can be rearranged to give:

$$\text{mass (g)} = \text{number of moles} \times \text{relative atomic mass}$$

Finding formulae

If we measure the mass changes that take place when one element combines with another, we can find out the formula of the compound formed.

The **empirical formula** is the simplest formula for a compound. When burning magnesium ribbon in oxygen in a crucible, its mass will increase as oxygen combines with the magnesium.

If the crucible is weighed before and after the reaction the result might be:

mass of empty crucible	= 20.00 g (1)
mass of crucible + magnesium	= 21.20 g (2)
mass of crucible + magnesium oxide	= 22.00 g (3)
mass of magnesium (2) – (1)	= 1.20 g
mass of oxygen combined (3) – (2)	= 0.80 g

▲ Mass measurement helps to find formulae

c What are the empirical formulae of the compounds formed by the combination of:
- 24g carbon and 8g hydrogen?
- 41.4g lead and 3.2g oxygen?

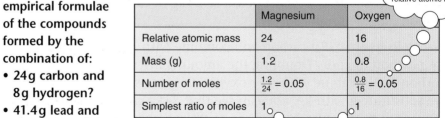

calculate number of moles using $\frac{\text{mass}}{\text{relative atomic mass}}$

	Magnesium	Oxygen
Relative atomic mass	24	16
Mass (g)	1.2	0.8
Number of moles	$\frac{1.2}{24} = 0.05$	$\frac{0.8}{16} = 0.05$
Simplest ratio of moles	1	1

the simplest ratio of moles gives the empirical formula of the compound, so the empirical formula is MgO

The empirical formula MgO can give the **percentage composition by mass** of magnesium and oxygen in magnesium oxide:

formula mass MgO = 24 + 16 = 40

percentage by mass of O = (16/40) × 100 = 40%

percentage by mass of Mg = (24/40) × 100 = 60%

The percentages by mass of each element can be used to give the empirical formula of a compound.

For example, an oxide of carbon contains 27.3% carbon and 72.7% oxygen by mass.

So, in 100 g of compound there will be 27.3 g carbon and 72.7 g oxygen (relative atomic masses: C = 12, O = 16).

The number of moles of carbon is 27.3/12 = 2.27. The number of moles of oxygen is 72.7/16 = 4.54. The ratio of moles of carbon to oxygen is 2.27 : 4.54.

This ratio can be simplified by dividing both numbers by 2.27 to give the ratio 1 : 2. The result shows the simplest ratio of atoms, in this case one carbon to two oxygen atoms. The simplest formula is CO_2.

 d **What is the empirical formula of a compound with the following percentage masses: 40% carbon, 6.7% hydrogen and 53% oxygen? (Relative atomic masses: C=12, O=16 , H=1)**

Productivity

We can use formulae to work out how much of a useful material can be extracted from a raw material. Iron(III) oxide Fe_2O_3 is one of the raw materials used for the production of iron in the blast furnace. A scientist took a 32 g sample of the oxide for analysis. How many moles was this?

formula mass   (56 × 2) + (16 × 3)   = 160

number of moles $\dfrac{32}{160}$ = 0.2 moles

What mass of iron should the sample produce? The formula Fe_2O_3 shows that one mole of iron oxide contains two moles of metallic iron.

So in this case, 0.2 moles of iron oxide will produce (0.2 × 2) = 0.4 moles of metallic iron. This has a mass of 0.4 × 56 = 22.4 g.

What mass of oxygen would need to be removed?

Since the original mass was 32 g and the final mass was 22.4 g, the mass of oxygen lost would be 32.0 – 22.4 = 9.6 g.

 e **Copper(II) oxide has the formula CuO. What mass of copper could you obtain from 40 g of this compound? (Relative atomic masses: Cu=64, O=16)**

> **Keywords**
>
> empirical formula • formula mass • molar mass • mole • percentage composition by mass

▲ *Global warming is becoming more widespread*

▲ *Alcohol is a green alternative to petrol*

Alcoholic alternative

Fears about the impact of global warming are making the search for alternative fuels increasingly urgent. Three students, Anjali, Ian and Emily are discussing the alternatives.

Glucose can be fermented to produce ethanol:

$$C_6H_{12}O_6 \rightarrow 2C_2H_5OH + 2CO_2$$
glucose   ethanol   carbon dioxide

This reaction is already being used in some parts of the world to produce ethanol as an alternative to petrol as a fuel for cars. Sugar crops are fermented to produce the alcohol.

Emily suggests that ethanol is a less effective fuel than petrol because it releases less energy. The energy released by 1 mole of ethanol is 1367 kJ whereas 1 mole of petrol (octane) releases 5470 kJ.

Anjali says the effectiveness of a fuel should be measured by calculating the energy it releases per gram of fuel burned, and that the higher percentage of carbon in the octane suggests that it will be more polluting than ethanol. She also claims that when 1 g of ethanol is burned it releases much less carbon dioxide than when 1 g of octane is burned.

Ian suggests that in order to make the comparison really fair they should calculate the number of moles of carbon dioxide produced per kJ of energy released. The equations for the complete combustion of both fuels are given below:

$$C_2H_5OH + 3O_2 \rightarrow 2CO_2 + 3H_2O$$
$$C_8H_{18} + 12.5O_2 \rightarrow 8CO_2 + 9H_2O$$

Questions

(Relative atomic masses C=12, O=16, H=1)

1 Calculate the mass of 1 mole of each of the two different fuels, ethanol and octane, that may be used to power cars.

2 Use your answer to **1** to calculate the energy released per gram of fuel burned.

3 What mass of each fuel needs to be burned in order to release 1 kJ of energy?

4 Use your answer to **3** to calculate the number of moles of carbon dioxide released by each fuel for each kJ of energy.

5 Calculate the percentage by mass of carbon in each fuel.

6 Which fuel is the better? Justify your choice.

Making new substances with electricity

In this item you will find out

- about the electrolysis of molten and aqueous salts

- how to calculate the mass changes when copper(II) sulfate solution is electrolysed

- how to write equations for the changes during electrolysis

▲ Electrolysis can split up molten compounds and solutions

Electrolysis relies upon ions becoming free to move about. This happens when the substance is in solution or when it is molten. When an electric current is applied, the positive ions move to the **negative electrode** (cathode), and the negative ions towards the **positive electrode** (anode).

At the electrodes ions are discharged. This involves loss or gain of electrons. Electrons flow through the wire from the positive electrode to the negative electrode.

Some possible electrolytes:

Ionic substance	Positive ions present	Negative ions present
aluminium oxide	aluminium, Al^{3+}	oxide, O^{2-}
lead(II) bromide	lead, Pb^{2+}	bromide, Br^-
potassium nitrate	potassium, K^+	nitrate, NO_3^-

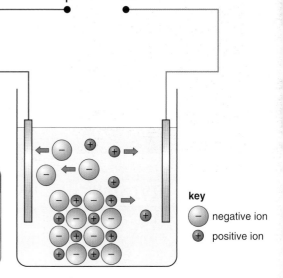

key
- — negative ion
+ positive ion

▲ Electrolysis can happen when ions are free to migrate

The products of electrolysis depend upon the material used for the electrodes. Inert or unreactive electrodes (for example, graphite or platinum) will remain unchanged. At the positive electrode, electrons are removed from negative ions. At the negative electrode, electrons are donated to positive ions. If the electrolyte is a simple molten salt containing just two elements, it will split into its two constituent elements.

 a What elements will be produced if graphite electrodes are used to electrolyse molten lead bromide?

If the electrolyte is an aqueous solution (a solute dissolved in water), different products might be obtained. Hydrogen and oxygen gases may be produced from the water instead. If the electrodes are not inert, it is also possible for them to react.

Amazing fact

Electrolysis can be used to remove unwanted hair by creating localised damage to the cells that cause hair growth.

Meltdown

A compound that is made up of only two elements is known as a binary compound. The electrolysis of an ionic binary compound with inert electrodes will produce the metal at the negative electrode and the non-metal at the positive electrode. The electrode reactions can be shown as two half equations. For example:

Molten electrolyte	At the negative electrode	At the positive electrode
lead(II) bromide ($PbBr_2$)	$Pb^{2+} + 2e^- \rightarrow Pb$	$2Br^- \rightarrow Br_2 + 2e^-$
aluminium oxide (Al_2O_3)	$Al^{3+} + 3e^- \rightarrow Al$	$2O^{2-} \rightarrow O_2 + 4e^-$
lead(II) iodide (PbI_2)	$Pb^{2+} + 2e^- \rightarrow Pb$	$2I^- \rightarrow I_2 + 2e^-$
potassium chloride (KCl)	$K^+ + e^- \rightarrow K$	$2Cl^- \rightarrow Cl_2 + 2e^-$

b The main compound in bauxite is aluminium oxide. When molten bauxite is electrolysed, aluminium is produced at the negative electrode. What will be produced at the positive electrode?

Water dividing

You can electrolyse aqueous potassium sulfate and aqueous potassium nitrate with inert electrodes. Pure water contains hydrogen, $H^+(aq)$, and hydroxide, $OH^-(aq)$, ions. These are always present in aqueous solutions.

The ions that come from the solute may be more easily or less easily displaced than the ions that come from the water. This is what determines whether or not hydrogen and oxygen are displaced when an aqueous solution is electrolysed.

▲ Electrolysis often produces gases

c What ions are always present in pure water?

d Which of these ions would be attracted to the negative electrode?

The reaction at the negative electrode can be written:

$2H^+$ $+$ $2e^-$ $\rightarrow$ H_2

hydrogen ions + electrons $\rightarrow$ hydrogen molecules

The potassium ions stay in solution.

The reaction at the positive electrode can be written as:

$4OH^- \rightarrow O_2 + 2H_2O + 4e^-$

The sulfate and nitrate ions stay in solution.

e Write a word equation for the reaction that takes place at the positive electrode.

WATER DIVIDING

Amazing fact

Pure water is a very poor conductor. It is dissolved ions that make water conductive.

Copper transfer

If copper electrodes are used to electrolyse a solution of copper sulfate, the positive copper electrode dissolves, and copper metal is deposited on the negative electrode.

At the negative electrode:

$$Cu^{2+} + 2e^- \rightarrow Cu$$

At the positive electrode:

$$Cu \rightarrow Cu^{2+} + 2e^-$$

The mass of copper lost by the positive electrode is equal to the mass of copper gained by the negative electrode.

▲ Electrolysing copper sulfate with copper electrodes

Masses of metal

The amount of copper deposited is proportional to the total charge passed (**charge transfer**) through it. The total charge passed can be calculated, knowing the current and the time. The total charge passed is the current multiplied by the time in seconds and is measured in coulombs. This is represented by the equation:

> charge = current × time
>
> $Q = It$

For example, if 0.96 g of copper is deposited by a 0.5 A current running for 100 minutes, how much copper is deposited by one coulomb?

The total charge is:

$Q = It$

$Q = 0.5\,A \times 60 \times 100\,s$

$Q = 3000$ coulombs

So, 0.96 g copper is deposited by 3000 coulombs

$\dfrac{0.96g}{3000} = 0.00032\,g$ copper is deposited by one coulomb

f If a current of 0.25 A ran for 100 minutes what mass of copper would be deposited?

g If a current of 0.75 A ran for 1 hour what mass of copper would be deposited?

Examiner's tip

Like many calculations this requires you to use the idea of proportionality. You can write 'equations' to show this.

Keywords

charge transfer • negative electrode • positive electrode

All that glistens

Electroplating uses an electric current to deposit a thin layer of metal on the surface of a metal object. This process is used to apply a thin layer of chromium metal to many metal objects in order either to enhance their appearance (decorative plating) or to improve wear resistance (hard plating).

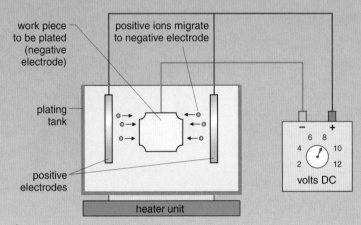

work piece to be plated (negative electrode)

positive ions migrate to negative electrode

plating tank

positive electrodes

heater unit

volts DC

▲ *A typical electroplating bath*

▲ *Electroplating gives a decorative finish*

Decorative chromium plating usually requires at least two layers of plating; a layer of nickel and a layer of chromium. High quality plating requires a minimum of two layers of nickel. The layer of nickel helps to prevent corrosion.

Hard chromium plating can be applied to objects such as cylinder rods, piston rings and rollers. This involves a much thicker coat of chromium than for decorative plating. The object is placed in a bath of liquid electrolyte and is connected to a low voltage direct current supply. The object acts as the negative electrode.

Metal ions in the solution are attracted to the metal object where they are converted to atoms and are deposited on the object's surface. Varying the current will change the rate at which the metal is deposited. The longer the object remains in the bath with a given current, the thicker the layer of metal formed.

Questions

1 What are the two main reasons for electroplating a metal object?

2 Why is a layer of nickel applied to an object before it is chromium plated?

3 The object to be plated is used as one of the electrodes in the electrolysis tank. Which one?

4 Suggest two ways in which the decorative chromium plating process could be adapted in order to achieve hard chromium plating.

5 Hard chrome plating is sometimes called engineering chrome plating. Why do you think this is?

Now concentrate

▲ 'One lump' gives a convenient measure of concentration

In this item you will find out

- how to measure the concentrations of different solutions

- why it is important to be able to measure and control concentrations

- about the measurements used for recommended daily allowances of different types of food

▲ Squash is diluted 'to taste'

If you take sugar in your tea or coffee you might ask for one or two lumps or one or two teaspoonfuls. You would never think to ask for sugar in grams or moles per dm^3 ($1\,dm^3 = 1000\,cm^3$) and yet your request does suggest a particular concentration.

We deal with concentrations every day. When we make a glass of squash we dilute the concentrate by adding a volume of water to suit our taste.

With tea or squash, accuracy is not important as sweetness is a matter of taste. The more concentrated a solution, the more crowded its particles are. But there are situations where accurate concentrations are important. For example, the accurate **dilution** of baby milk 'formula' powder is vital to ensure it is sufficiently nutritious yet still digestible.

▲ Formula milk needs accurate dilution

The incorrect dilution of car windscreen wash could cause freezing up. Windscreen wash can be diluted with water. The table below shows what the dilution should be in different seasons and temperatures.

	Percentage (by volume) of windscreen wash	Minimum temperature before fluid freezes (°C)
autumn/summer	10	−2
mild winter	25	−5
winter	50	−9
severe winter	100	−26

▲ Windscreen wash fluid needs to be diluted correctly

a What might happen if a car owner dilutes the screen wash to 25% rather than 50% in the middle of winter?

b In the summer the owner decides to dilute $500\,cm^3$ of 50% mixture to make it 10%. How should she do this?

Amazing fact

Normally, sweetened soft drinks contain about nine teaspoons of sugar per $350\,cm^3$ can.

Salt of the Earth

Sea water contains dissolved salts. Each year almost 3 billion tonnes of salts enter the sea as a result of volcanic activity on the seabed and weathering of rocks by rainfall. Although the concentration of salts (salinity) is different in different parts of the world, the salinity of normal sea water is 35 g per 1000 cm^3. Since 1 dm^3 = 1000 cm^3 this can be expressed as 35 g per dm^3. If we had 5 dm^3 of sea water, we can calculate that the mass of dissolved salts in this volume is:

5 × 35 = 175 g

Amazing fact

The salinity of the oceans has remained virtually constant for the last 15 billion years.

c What mass of salts will be dissolved in 200 cm^3 of sea water?

d Salt can be obtained from sea water by evaporation. How many dm^3 of normal sea water would you need to evaporate in order to obtain 700 g of salt?

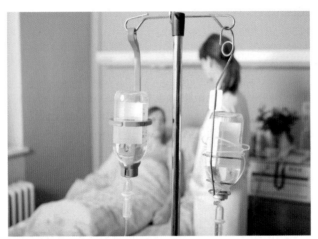

▲ *Accurate dilution can be vitally important*

Healthy hearts

Heart arrhythmia is a common but potentially life threatening condition where the heart beats in an irregular fashion. One possible treatment that a doctor might prescribe would be an intravenous drip of a solution of magnesium sulfate.

It is important that the solution administered in this treatment is accurately diluted. A normal dose might be 10 mmol per 100 cm^3 (1 mmol = 0.001 moles).

How would you make up such a solution? Since 10 mmol is the same as 0.01 moles, the normal dose is 0.01 moles per 100 cm^3 solution. This is the same as 0.1 moles per 1000 cm^3 solution.

The formula of magnesium sulfate is $MgSO_4$ (relative atomic masses Mg = 24, S = 32, O = 16).

The mass of 1 mole of magnesium sulfate is 24 + 32 + (16 × 4) = 120 g.

So the mass of 0.1 moles of $MgSO_4$ is 120 × 0.1 = 12.0 g.

e The normal dose of magnesium sulfate for heart arrhythmia is 0.1 moles per 1000 cm^3 of solution. What is this in mol/dm^3?

f The instructions above would give 0.5 dm^3 of solution. How many cm^3 is this?

Conversions

Rather than express the concentration of a solution in moles per dm^3 (mol/dm^3) it can be given in grams per dm^3. You can use the formula:

mass = number of moles × molar mass

In this case the magnesium sulfate has a concentration of $0.1 × 120 = 12\,g$ in $1\,dm^3$.

 g If a salt (NaCl) solution has a concentration of $0.5\,mol/dm^3$ what is its concentration in g per dm^3? (Relative atomic masses Na = 23, Cl = 35.5)

Normal saline

Phil wears contact lenses. Each night before going to bed he removes his lenses and leaves them to soak in normal saline. Normal saline is 0.9% by mass sodium chloride solution. Phil usually buys his normal saline from the chemist. On occasions he has run out of this solution. His friend tells him that in an emergency like this, approximately normal saline can be made using a teaspoon ($5\,g$) of salt in a pint ($570\,cm^3$) of water. Is Phil's friend right?

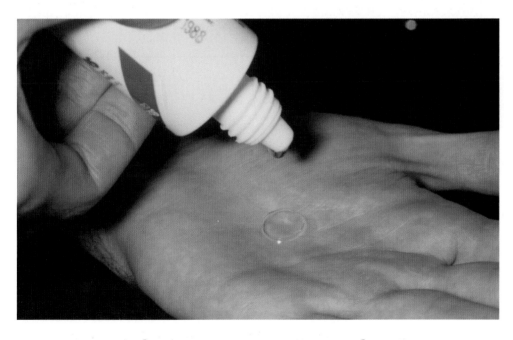

◀ Contact lenses are kept in normal saline solution

$5\,g$ of salt in $570\,cm^3$ of water = $5/570\,g$ of salt in $1\,cm^3$ of water

So $(5/570) × 100 = 0.88\,g$ salt in $100\,cm^3$ of water

Percentage by mass is $0.88\,g$ in $100\,g$ = 0.88%

So, Phil's friend appears to be correct.

h What is the concentration in mol/dm^3 of normal saline solution?

i Saturated sodium chloride solution has a concentration of $0.542\,mol/100\,g$. How does this compare with the concentration of sodium chloride in normal saline?

Salty states

▲ *People in southern Italy often bake fish whole in a bed of salt*

Nutritional information per 100g serving	
Sodium	1.1g

▲ *1.1g of sodium, but how much salt is that?*

The average western diet is too high in sodium. In the USA, average sodium intake in the daily diet is 4000–5000mg. In the UK, dietary sodium intake averages 3500mg daily.

The USA sodium recommended daily allowance (RDA) of less than 2400mg is higher than the UK recommended nutritional intake (RNI) whose upper limit for sodium is 1600mg.

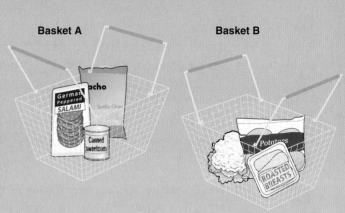

▲ *The sodium content of foods varies enormously*

Excess sodium intake is linked to high blood pressure, heart disease, fluid retention (oedema) and kidney stones.

It is not easy to predict total sodium consumption by knowing the amount of added salt in any food. Sodium may be also contained in other ingredients used to make the food. Some foods also have a natural sodium content that must be taken into account. So although the sodium content can give an idea of the amount of salt in a food, it will not necessarily be an accurate value. The table shows the amount of sodium in a 100g sample of various foods.

Foods	Concentration of sodium (mg/100g)
tomato soup, dry	3100
smoked salmon	1880
salami	1800
cornflakes	1100
tortilla chips	850
potato chips	850
chicken, meat only, roasted	64
haddock	87
potatoes, boiled, in skin	5
cabbage, green	20
cauliflower	19
sweetcorn (canned)	300

Questions

(Relative atomic masses Na=23, Cl=35.5)

1 If all the sodium in cornflakes is due to added salt, calculate what mass of salt there is in a 100g serving of cornflakes.

2 Show by calculation that the sodium content of table salt (sodium chloride) is 39,300mg per 100g serving.

3 A teaspoonful of salt has a mass of 5g. What proportion of the US RDA for sodium does this represent?

4 How does the RNI for sodium in the UK compare with a teaspoonful of salt?

5 Look at the two supermarket baskets. Imagine two meals, one made up using 100g of each of the three foods in basket A, the other made up using 100g of each of the three foods in basket B. How much sodium would there be in each meal?

6 What advice would you give a patient who had been told by their doctor that they had to significantly reduce the sodium in their diet?

A measure of strength

In this item you will find out

- how indicators can be used to monitor the pH changes during neutralisation reactions

- how titration can be used to achieve complete neutralisation

- how titration can be used to determine the concentration of an acid or alkali

▲ We can use titration to compare the vitamin C content of different fruits

Titration is a very useful technique that allows scientists to measure the amount of a substance present in a sample of a solution. For example, we can use a titration technique to compare the amount of vitamin C present in different fruits.

As alkali is added to acid, the acid is slowly neutralised and its pH value increases slowly at first. At the end of the reaction all the acid is neutralised and the pH value increases rapidly.

Acids will neutralise alkalis to produce a solution of a salt. The general reaction is written as:

acid + alkali → salt + water

If the salt is soluble, the reaction needs to be performed accurately in order to achieve neutralisation. Titration is used to measure precisely what volume of acid is required to neutralise a given volume of alkali.

When an acid is added to an alkali, or an alkali to an acid, changes in pH take place. The changes can be monitored using a pH meter or by adding a few drops of an acid/base indicator. Acid/base indicators will have one colour when in acidic solution and another colour when in alkaline conditions. Different indicators will change colour at different pH values. A pH meter will give a reading of 7 when the solution is neutral. For titration it is best to use an indicator that changes suddenly at the neutral point. The choice of indicator will be different according to the type of acid and alkali used.

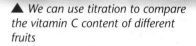

▲ Rich sources of vitamin C

Amazing fact

Titration results show that rosehip contains approximately 40 times as much vitamin C as lemon juice.

a When an alkali is neutralised by adding an acid, what happens to the pH value:
(i) when a small amount of acid is added?
(ii) as the neutral point of the titration is approached?

b How would you use a pH meter to tell when a solution had been neutralised?

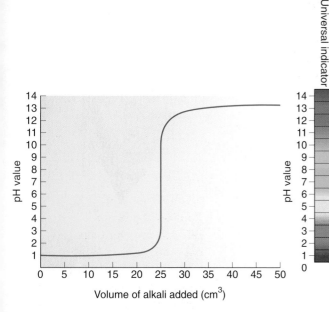

▲ *A titration curve for adding an alkali to an acid*

Titration curves

A pH titration curve shows how the pH of the solution changes when an acid is added to an alkali or when an alkali is added to an acid. Many titration curves have a section at the end point where the pH changes very rapidly.

The pH curve in the diagram shows the pH values and indicator colours obtained when 0.1 mol/dm^3 alkali is added to 25 cm^3 0.1 mol/dm^3 acid.

Use the pH curve to answer the following:

c What volume of alkali needs to be added to give a pH of 3?

d What pH would result from the addition of 20 cm^3 of alkali?

e What volume of alkali is required to neutralise the acid?

The graph obtained when you add acid to alkali is shown in the diagram below.

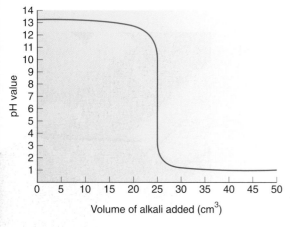

▲ *A titration curve for adding an acid to an alkali*

More about indicators

Universal indicators are mixtures of two or more different acid/base indicators and are known as **mixed indicators**. Their colours depend on pH values, so they will give a continuous colour change at the neutralisation point. This makes it difficult to use them in titration.

A **single indicator** such as **phenolphthalein** is much more useful since it will give a sudden change in colour (colourless to pink) at the neutralisation point.

Unknown acids

Some students do an experiment to find the concentration of three unknown laboratory acids. They use titration to find the volume of 0.1 mol/dm^3 alkali needed to neutralise 25.0 cm^3 of each acid. The table shows their results.

Amazing fact

Cabbage juice acts as a very effective (mixed) indicator.

	Volume of alkali required to neutralise 25 cm³ acid (cm³)		
	Acid A	Acid B	Acid C
Reading 1	12.4	50.1	5.1
Reading 2	12.6	49.9	5.0
Reading 3	12.5	31.0	4.9
Average reading	12.5	50.0	5.0

It is important to repeat titration readings until a consistent result is obtained. An average value is then calculated. The results in the table can be used to calculate the concentration of each of the acids A, B and C. Note reading 3 for acid B is very different to readings 1 and 2, and should be discarded as it is an anomalous result. The titration should be repeated to get a result close to the first two.

Acid A is hydrochloric acid. An average of 12.5 cm³ alkali is needed to neutralise it. We can use the equation below to calculate the number of moles of alkali used:

number of moles = concentration in mol/dm³ × volume in dm³

In this case:

concentration = 0.1 mol/dm³; volume = 0.0125 dm³

So the number of moles of alkali used is:

0.1 × 0.0125 = 0.00125

The equation for the reaction is:

$NaOH + HCl \rightarrow NaCl + H_2O$

So, the number of moles of hydrogen ions H⁺ in 25 cm³ of solution is equal to the number of moles of hydroxide ions (i.e. 0.00125).

We can rearrange the equation to calculate the concentration:

concentration in mol/dm³ = moles/volume in dm³

The concentration of H⁺(aq) in acid A is 0.00125/0.025 = 0.05 mol/dm³

f Calculate the concentration of H⁺ in acids B and C.

g Acid B is sulfuric acid (H_2SO_4). What is its concentration?

In a pickle

Because of its acidity, vinegar is used to preserve foods by pickling them.

If you were titrating 25 cm³ vinegar with 0.1 mol/dm³ alkali you could predict the volume of alkali needed as follows:

To find the number of moles of in 25 cm³ (= 0.025 dm³) vinegar, you use this equation:

number of moles = concentration in mol/dm³ × volume in dm³

0.83 × 0.025 = 0.021 moles

To convert this into the volume of alkali needed, you need to use the equation:

$$\text{volume in dm}^3 = \frac{\text{moles}}{\text{concentration in mol/dm}^3}$$

So the volume of alkali needed is:

$\frac{0.021}{0.1}$ = 0.21 dm³ which is the same as 210 cm³.

▲ Most vinegar contains 5 g ethanoic acid in 100 g solution; this is approximately equal to 0.83 mol/dm³

Measuring the acidity of wines

▲ It is important to measure the acidity of wine

Wine is produced by the fermentation of the sugars in grapes. As well as sugars, other substances must be present in order to keep the pH at a value between 3 and 4. This pH is required in order for fermentation to work well.

Malic acid and tartaric acid are the two main acids in grapes. Grapes grown in a warm climate have a low acid level, which is almost all due to tartaric acid. Grapes grown in colder climates tend to have more malic acid in them. If a wine has too much malic acid, it can taste harsh, but in small amounts it gives the wine a 'fresh' flavour.

A finished wine should have a pH value between 2.8 and 3.8. At pH values higher than that, the wine spoils more easily and may taste flat. The colour of a wine is better when the pH is low.

The total acidity of a wine can be determined by titrating the wine with sodium hydroxide solution. Ethanoic acid and some other organic acids contribute to the acidity of wines. Too much ethanoic acid gives poor wine with a vinegary taste and smell. It can be detected at concentrations of $0.6\,g/dm^3$ or less.

Ethanoic acid (CH_3CO_2H) is produced when ethanol is oxidised by bacteria. The determination of this sort of acidity is very important in the quality control of wines. A value of more than $0.5\,g/dm^3$ reduces the quality of the wine.

Questions

1 What sort of conditions (acidic or alkaline) are necessary for fermentation to work well?

2 How does climate affect the acid content of grapes?

3 What effect does a decrease in the acidity of a wine have upon its quality?

4 How does an increase in acidity help the taste of a wine?

5 How can the total acidity of a wine be determined?

6 Why might the use of an indicator be problematic with some wines?

7 Which acid gives wine a vinegary taste and smell?

Monitoring gases

- about reactions that release gases

- how to measure and calculate the volumes of gases involved in a reaction

Many chemical reactions, such as the fizzing in water of indigestion tablets, involve gases. In some cases gases are reactants, in others they are products. Sometimes it is important not only to be able to measure the volumes of the gases involved, but also to predict how much of a particular gas might be produced.

▲ *These tablets dissolve and give off gas when added to water*

If you measure the volume of gas produced at regular intervals you can get an idea of the progress and the rate of the reaction. You can use a variety of measuring techniques to measure the volume of gas produced or used up in a reaction. These are shown in the diagram.

- **Diagram A:** Where an insoluble gas is produced you can measure the volume using an inverted burette in a bowl of water. Reactions that produce hydrogen can be monitored in this way.

- **Diagram B:** Alternatively, a gas syringe can be connected to a reaction flask. This method can be used to collect any gas.

- **Diagram C:** Where a gas is absorbed, a pair of linked gas syringes allows a measured volume of gas to be passed to and fro across a solid reactant.

- **Diagram D:** It is also possible to follow some reactions involving gases by placing the reaction vessel on an accurate balance so as to monitor the mass of gas evolved. This method is best for more dense gases like carbon dioxide.

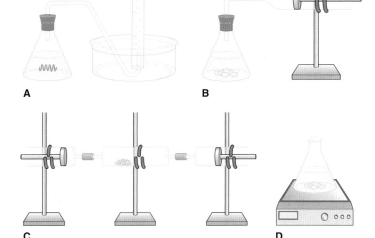

A   **B**

C   **D**

▲ *Gas reactions can be monitored in many ways*

a What sort of gases cannot be collected by bubbling through water?

b Carbon dioxide is slightly soluble in water. Which method would be most suitable to monitor a reaction that produces carbon dioxide?

Amazing fact

When heated strongly, just 10 g of calcium carbonate will produce 2 400 cm^3 of carbon dioxide gas.

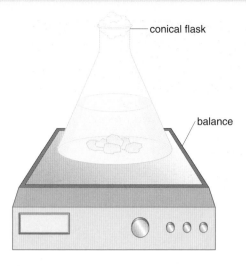

conical flask

balance

▲ *Monitoring the mass*

Losing your marbles!

Marble chips react with dilute hydrochloric acid. They dissolve and give off carbon dioxide gas. The mass of the reactants can be monitored as shown in the diagram.

The equation is:

$$CaCO_3(s) + 2HCl(aq) \rightarrow CaCl_2(aq) + H_2O + CO_2(g)$$

calcium carbonate + hydrochloric acid →
                    calcium chloride + water + carbon dioxide

First rate

The volume of carbon dioxide given off provides a method of monitoring the rate of the reaction.

▼ *Monitoring the volume*

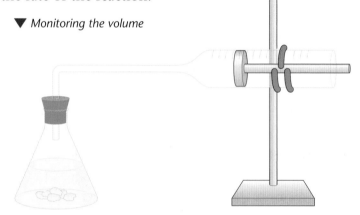

Time (s)	Volume of gas produced (cm^3)	Marble chips left?
50	288	✔
100	420	✔
150	504	✔
200	528	✔
250	540	✔
300	540	✔

The reaction stops when one reactant has been used up. A graph showing the mass or volume of reactants against time will level off at this point. The table shows the volume of gas produced and the presence of marble chips at 50 second time intervals.

The results can be plotted as shown in the diagram on the left.

▼ *Graph to show the rate of production of carbon dioxide*

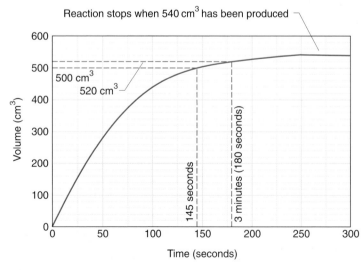

As the acid gets used up, the rate decreases and the slope becomes less steep until the reaction stops when $540\,cm^3$ gas has been produced. Marble chips are still present and so are 'in excess'. The acid was used up and is the **limiting reactant**. Changing the volume or concentration of the acid would change the volume of gas produced proportionally.

Other deductions from the graph include:

- the volume of gas produced after 3 minutes was approximately $520\,cm^3$
- the time taken for $500\,cm^3$ to be produced was 145 seconds.

c **What would you see in the flask at the end of the reaction if the marble chips were the limiting reactant?**

The table shows the volumes of carbon dioxide produced with different starting quantities.

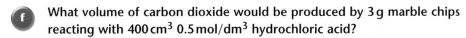

Reaction	Mass of marble chips (g)	Volume of 0.5 mol/dm³ HCl (cm³)	Volume of carbon dioxide produced (cm³)
A	10 (excess)	25	150
B	10 (excess)	50	300
C	1	400 (excess)	240
D	5	400 (excess)	1200

d Identify the limiting reactant in each of the reactions A to C.

e What volume of carbon dioxide would be produced by 10 g marble chips reacting with 25 cm³ of 0.1 mol/dm³ hydrochloric acid?

f What volume of carbon dioxide would be produced by 3 g marble chips reacting with 400 cm³ 0.5 mol/dm³ hydrochloric acid?

You can see from these data that the volume of gas produced will be proportional to the amount of limiting reactant available.

Know your moles

The mass of marble chips and the volume and concentration of the acid allow us to identify the limiting reagent and the volume of gas.

(*Note:* 1 mole of any gas at room temperature and pressure has a volume of 24 dm³.)

Reacting 10 g marble chips and 25 cm³ 0.5 mol/dm³ hydrochloric acid gives:

$$CaCO_3 + 2HCl \rightarrow CaCl_2 + H_2O + CO_2$$

molar mass of $CaCO_3$: $40 + 12 + (3 \times 16) = 100$ g

number of moles in 10 g $CaCO_3 = \dfrac{10}{100} = 0.1$

number of moles HCl $= \dfrac{0.5}{(1000)} \times 25 = 0.0125$

From the equation above, the ratio of moles of $CaCO_3$: HCl is 1 : 2. So, the number of moles of hydrochloric acid required to react completely with 0.1 moles of calcium carbonate is 0.2. Since only 0.0125 moles of acid are available, the calcium carbonate is in excess in this reaction.

If 0.0125 moles of acid react, the number of moles of calcium carbonate used will be 0.0125/2 = 0.00625. The number of moles of carbon dioxide is equal to the number of moles of calcium carbonate, that is 0.00625. Then, knowing the volume of one mole of any gas, the volume of gas produced is 0.00625 × 24 = 0.150 dm³.

For gases at 25 °C and atmospheric pressure:

volume (in dm³) = number of moles × 24

number of moles = volume (in dm³)/24

g What mass of marble chips would need to react with hydrochloric acid to produce 48 dm³ carbon dioxide?

Keywords

limiting reactant

Houston, we have a problem

▲ Apollo 13 *was made up of two modules; the command and the lunar modules*

In April 1970, the *Apollo 13* space craft was on route to the Moon. Only 56 hours into the mission, the immortal words 'Houston, we have a problem' signalled the beginning of an extraordinary drama.

With the spacecraft damaged by explosion and compromised life support systems, the proposed Moon landing mission had quickly become a battle for survival. *Apollo 13* had to orbit the Moon and use its gravity to send the craft hurtling back towards Earth.

Part of the rescue plan required the astronauts to move from the crippled command module into the lunar module. Although the oxygen supply in the lunar module was adequate to support the astronauts in their return to Earth, another problem loomed. Normally, onboard lithium hydroxide (LiOH) canisters absorbed exhaled carbon dioxide (CO_2) from the air, but since the lunar module was intended to support two men for two days (not three men for four days) the canisters onboard the lunar module were being overwhelmed by rising carbon dioxide levels.

The command module had more than enough spare LiOH canisters onboard, but these did not fit into the holes intended for the lunar module's canisters. Thanks to the extraordinary level-headed ingenuity of the ground team at Mission Control in Houston, the three astronauts were brought back safely to Earth. Using only components and materials they knew to be available in the lunar module, they improvised a design for removing excess carbon dioxide that made use of the wrong shaped canisters.

Questions

(Relative atomic masses Li = 7, Na = 23, K = 39)

1 The reaction between lithium hydroxide and carbon dioxide produces lithium carbonate (Li_2CO_3) and water. Write a balanced symbol equation for this reaction.

2 What mass of lithium hydroxide is required to absorb 1 mole of carbon dioxide?

3 An average man will produce approximately $550\,dm^3$ of carbon dioxide per day. What is the minimum mass of lithium hydroxide that the lunar module should have?

4 How much extra lithium hydroxide did they need to make the lunar module habitable for the entire mission?

5 Sodium hydroxide and potassium hydroxide are equally effective at absorbing carbon dioxide. Why do you think lithium hydroxide was favoured for the Apollo

A question of balance

In this item you will find out

- about chemical equilibria

- how chemists alter conditions in order to change the position of equilibria

- why equlibria are important industrially

Why do the bubbles in a bottle of fizzy drink only appear when the bottle is opened?

Why is there a warning on a bottle of domestic bleach as shown in the photograph below?

a Suggest what the 'other products' referred to on the bleach bottle might be?

▲ Disturbing an equilibrium

Although they involve very different chemistry, both the bubbles leaving the bottle of fizzy drink and the chlorine gas released from bleach are reversible changes where the rate of the **forward reaction** and **backward reactions** are equal and so exist in a state of equilibrium.

Many chemical systems are in **equilibrium**. When the conditions are changed in any way, the equilibrium is disrupted and its position moves.

A number of chemical reactions can be **reversed** quite easily. An example of this is the reaction that happens when blue copper(II) sulfate crystals are heated. The heat causes the water contained in the blue crystals to be removed leaving anhydrous copper sulfate, a white powder. The reverse reaction happens when water is added to the white powder:

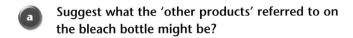

blue copper(II) sulfate + heat ⇌ white copper(II) sulfate + water

b Blue copper(II) sulfate has the formula $CuSO_4.5H_2O$. Try to write a balanced symbol equation for the reversible reaction when it is heated.

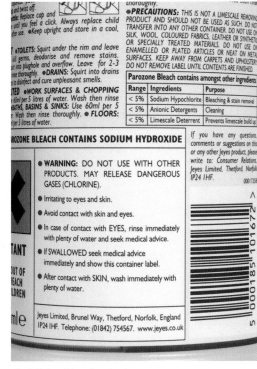

▲ Mixing bleaches is dangerous

Backwards and forwards

Equilibrium happens when the forward and backward reactions of a reversible change take place at the same time and at the same rate. Since both reactions are happening simultaneously, no overall change can be seen.

One example of an equilibrium might be where a boy is walking down an 'up' escalator, or up a 'down' escalator. So long as the boy walks at the same speed as the escalator, he will remain in the same place (in equilibrium). If either the boy or the escalator change speed, the boy will move up or down accordingly. When their speeds become equal again, equilibrium will be established in a 'new position'.

Fizzy equilibrium

You will probably know that the bubbles in a fizzy drink are carbon dioxide gas. If you have ever used a Sodastream™ machine you might know that the 'fizziness' is a result of carbon dioxide gas being pumped at high pressure into the space at the top of the bottle.

Under pressure, the gas dissolves into the drink. This is the forward reaction. Carbon dioxide will react with the water in the drink to produce a weak acid called carbonic acid.

$$CO_2 + H_2O \rightarrow H_2CO_3$$

c In what way do you think the acidity of fizzy water compares with still water?

d Write the balanced symbol equation for the backward reaction.

At first, the concentration of carbonic acid is low and so the backward reaction is slow.

$$CO_2 + H_2O \rightleftharpoons H_2CO_3$$

As the gas dissolves, the concentration of carbonic acid increases and the rate of the backward reaction increases, until both reactions are happening at the same rate and equilibrium is established. When the top is on the fizzy drink bottle, the equilibrium is maintained in the bottle and no change can be seen inside it.

The equation for this is:

$$CO_2 + H_2O \rightleftharpoons H_2CO_3$$

Removing the bottle top releases the carbon dioxide, which is under high pressure. This disturbs the equilibrium. The removal of carbon dioxide from above the liquid means that the rate of the forward reaction rapidly decreases so that the backward reaction is much faster for a while:

$$CO_2 + H_2O \rightleftharpoons H_2CO_3$$

▲ Pumping the carbon dioxide in

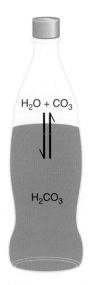

▲ The system in equilibrium

▲ Equilibrium disturbed!

This continues until the concentration of carbonic acid has decreased so much that the rate of the forward reaction once again becomes equal to the rate of the backward reaction:

$$CO_2 + H_2O \rightleftharpoons H_2CO_3$$

When this happens the fizzy drink has gone 'flat'; the equilibrium is now between carbon dioxide in the atmosphere and the carbonic acid in the drink. The carbon dioxide has left the drink and we say that the equilibrium has 'moved to the left'.

e Suggest why putting the bottle lid back on quickly after pouring a drink helps to keep it fizzy.

f Carbon dioxide is in the atmosphere. Can you use this fact to help explain why rainwater is naturally acidic?

Changes in concentration of reactants or products will change the equilibrium position. The possible changes and their effects are summarised below:

If the concentration of		The equilibrium position will move to the
one of the reactants is	increased	right →
	decreased	left ←
one of the products is	increased	left ←
	decreased	right →

Bleach alert

The active ingredient in many types of bleach is a substance called sodium chlorate. It is made by reacting chlorine gas (Cl_2) with an alkali such as sodium hydroxide solution (NaOH) at room temperature. An equilibrium is set up:

$$Cl_2 + NaOH \rightleftharpoons NaClO + Cl^- + H^+$$

         sodium chlorate

g What are the three elements combined in sodium chlorate?

h In which direction would the equilibrium above have to move in order to release chlorine gas?

i What ions could you add which would cause the equilibrium to move this way?

j Why do you think mixing bleach with 'other products' might release chlorine?

Examiner's tip

An equilibrium will shift in order to compensate for any change which has been applied to it.

MAINTAINING EQUILIBRIUM

Keywords

backward reaction • equilibrium • forward reaction • reversible reaction

Industrial compromises

Ideas about equilibrium reactions are used by industrial chemists to help them make their manufacturing processes profitable.

Sulfuric acid is a very important chemical as it is used as a starting material for a wide range of other manufacturing processes. It is made by a three-stage process known as the Contact process.

First, sulfur is burned in air to form sulfur dioxide:

(reaction 1) $S + O_2 \rightarrow SO_2$

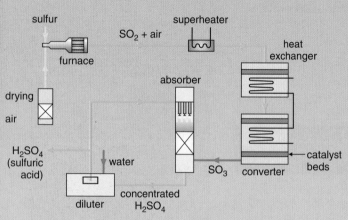

The three-stage process for sulfuric acid production

The sulfur dioxide is then oxidised further by reaction with more oxygen:

(reaction 2) $2SO_2 + O_2 \rightleftharpoons 2SO_3 + \text{heat}$

The sulfur trioxide is then combined with water:

(reaction 3) $SO_3 + H_2O \rightarrow H_2SO_4$

A temperature of 450 °C is used for reaction 2. Although a lower temperature would shift the equilibrium to the right, it would also reduce the rate of the reaction. 450 °C is a compromise between rate and yield.

A catalyst of vanadium(II) oxide (V_2O_5) is used to help speed up the reaction. The catalyst has no effect on the position of the equilibrium.

A high yield of sulfur trioxide is obtained at atmospheric pressure. This is more economic as building high pressure vessels is very expensive.

You have seen how the Haber process is used to produce ammonia. The percentage yield of this process is also affected by pressure and temperature, as shown in the graph.

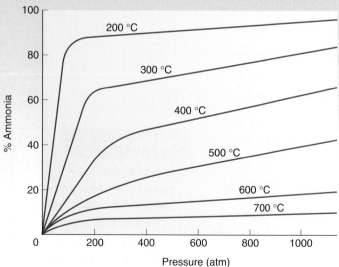

Graph of yield vs pressure at a range of temperatures for the Haber process

Questions

1 Reaction 2 in the Contact process is represented as an equilibrium. Does this reaction give out or take in heat?

2 What effect would raising the temperature of reaction 2 have upon this equilibrium?

3 What effect does an increase in pressure have upon the yield obtained from the Haber process?

4 Given your answer to **3**, what effect would high pressure have upon the equilibrium in reaction 2 of the Contact process?

5 What effect does high temperature have upon the yield of ammonia?

6 In both the Haber and the Contact processes a relatively high temperature is used. Explain why.

7 Explain why a catalyst is used in both these reactions.

The acid test

▲ Acids you can taste

We have known about acids for thousands of years. Wine that is left open to the air quickly develops a sour taste. We now know that this is the result of the formation of ethanoic acid (the acid in vinegar). Lemon juice, vinegar and vitamin C are all acidic substances. They all taste sour (although this is not an appropriate way to test any substance in the laboratory).

Acids will dissolve the more reactive metals, and are generally corrosive.

The table below gives the names and formulae of some common aqueous acids.

Name of acid	Strong or weak acid	Formula	Ions present
hydrochloric	strong	HCl	H^+, Cl^-
sulfuric	strong	H_2SO_4	$2H^+$, SO_4^{2-}
nitric	strong	HNO_3	H^+, NO_3^-
ethanoic	weak	CH_3CO_2H	H^+, $CH_3CO_2^-$

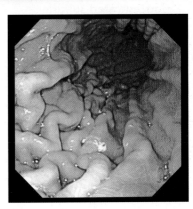

▲ Stomach secretions are more acidic than laboratory acid

a Looking at the list of ions present in each of the acids, which is the ion that is present in all the acids?

b Which of the acids listed produces the largest number of these ions when in solution?

DANGER Acid

Wear personal protective equipment

▲ Acids are corrosive

Amazing fact

When they are stimulated, special cells in your stomach lining secrete hydrochloric acid at a pH value of less than 1.

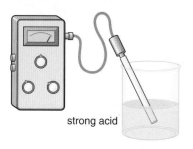

▲ Strong acids conduct better than weak acids

A test of strength

All acids contain replaceable hydrogen atoms. When dissolved in water these hydrogen atoms can become aqueous ions. It is these H^+ ions that give acids their properties.

Hydrochloric and ethanoic acids both have just one replaceable hydrogen atom in each molecule of acid, but ethanoic acid is known as a weak acid while hydrochloric acid is a strong acid.

Conductivity measurements can help us to explain the difference between strong and weak acids. The greater the concentration of free ions in a solution, the higher its conductivity will be. A strong acid will conduct better than a weak acid of the same concentration. This is shown in the diagram.

Although the concentration (the number of moles dissolved in $1\,dm^3$) of the two acids is the same, hydrochloric acid ionises more completely, so more ions are in solution and the conductivity is higher. Bubbles of hydrogen gas are produced at the negative electrode in both acids. This is because hydrogen ions attracted to the negative electrode receive electrons and become hydrogen molecules:

$$2H^+ + 2e^- \rightarrow H_2$$

c Why will a strong acid conduct an electric current better than a weak acid?

Amazing fact

Concentrated sulfuric acid 'needs' water so much that it will violently dehydrate sugar turning it black and causing it to steam vigorously.

pH and acidity

A similar comparison can be made using the pH scale. You will recall that any substance whose pH value is less than 7 can be classified as acidic.

Universal indicator can be used to measure the pH of the acid. pH gives a measure of the hydrogen ion concentration in a solution. The higher the hydrogen ion concentration, the lower the pH.

It is clear from these comparisons that although there is the same amount of acid initially, the ethanoic acid actually produces fewer hydrogen ions.

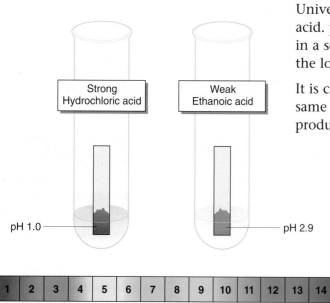

Strong Hydrochloric acid

Weak Ethanoic acid

pH 1.0

pH 2.9

1	2	3	4	5	6	7	8	9	10	11	12	13	14

▲ You can use universal indicator to measure the pH of an acid

Different rates

The effect of a different concentration of hydrogen ions can be seen when a strip of magnesium is placed in each of the two acids. The metal will dissolve much more quickly in the strong (hydrochloric) acid than in the weak (ethanoic) acid. A higher concentration of $H^+(aq)$ ions gives more collisions per second between metal and acid and a faster rate of reaction in the hydrochloric acid.

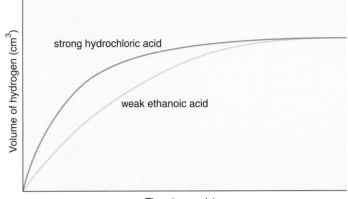

▲ *Same amount of acid – different rate*

d Why does the magnesium dissolve more quickly in the hydrochloric acid than in the ethanoic acid?

Both graphs level off at the same final volume of hydrogen because although it is released more slowly by the ethanoic acid, there is the same total number of replaceable hydrogen atoms in each acid.

A two way street

The reason ethanoic acid releases its hydrogen ions more slowly than hydrochloric acid has to do with equilibrium. The hydrochloric acid is formed when hydrogen chloride dissolves in water. When this happens, all the hydrogen and chlorine atoms split up to form aqueous ions:

$$HCl + water \rightarrow H^+ + Cl^-$$

This reaction is fast and goes to completion; all the hydrogen atoms in the hydrogen chloride become aqueous hydrogen ions in water. We say that the hydrogen chloride has ionised completely.

When a weak acid like ethanoic acid dissolves, only some of its molecules will ionise. The ionisation is reversible and so an equilibrium is set up:

$$CH_3CO_2H \rightleftharpoons CH_3CO_2^- + H^+$$

This incomplete ionisation explains why weak acids have fewer free hydrogen ions available to collide with the other reactants and so weak acids will react less vigorously than strong acids.

▲ *Weak acids will remove limescale*

The relatively gentle action of weak acids explains why they are more often used as **descaling** agents. These are products used to remove limescale from kitchen and bathroom surfaces, fittings and appliances.

e Why do you think strong acids might cause difficulties if used as descalers?

Keywords
conductivity • descaler • strong acid • weak acid

Acid rain

▲ *Acid rain can kill*

Atmospheric carbon dioxide exists in equilibrium with rainwater in which it forms carbonic acid:

$$CO_2 \qquad + H_2O \rightleftharpoons \quad H_2CO_3$$

carbon dioxide + water $\rightleftharpoons$ carbonic acid

Carbonic acid then partially ionises:

$$H_2CO_3 \rightleftharpoons H^+ + HCO_3^-$$

The hydrogen ions (H^+) give natural rainwater a pH value of 5.6.

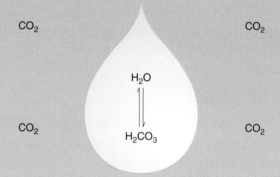

▲ *Carbon dioxide in the atmosphere makes rainwater naturally acidic*

Acid deposition happens when acidic pollutants from the atmosphere are deposited on the Earth's surface. The main pollutants involved are sulfur dioxide and nitrogen oxides which are formed when fossil fuels are burned. These pollutants can be transported thousands of miles in the atmosphere.

The sulfur and nitrogen oxides can dissolve directly in rain drops to form solutions of sulfuric acid (H_2SO_4) and nitric acid (HNO_3). These acids can dissolve and ionise completely. This makes the rainwater so acidic that when it falls to the ground it can damage plant and animal life as well as artificial structures.

Dry deposition processes take place where sulfur dioxide and nitrogen oxides are absorbed onto the surface of solid materials. It is not until these materials come into contact with water that the absorbed gases dissolve to form acidic solutions which can then cause damage.

Questions

1 What is the usual pH value of rainwater?

2 What are the main acidic pollutants formed by the burning of fossil fuels?

3 Which acids are produced in rainwater as a result of these pollutants?

4 What sort of acids (strong or weak) are the acids in your answer to 3?

5 Why does dry deposition on its own not cause acid damage?

Producing precipitates

In this item you will find out

- about precipitation reactions

- how precipitation reactions can be useful

- how to construct ionic equations to describe precipitation reactions

▲ *Some ionic solutions react when mixed*

Compounds formed between metals and non-metals contain ions. When these ions are held in an ionic crystal they occupy fixed positions relative to one another. When dissolved in solution or when molten, the ions become free to move. Because of this, when two ionic solutions are mixed, the ions from each solution can mix easily. As a result extremely fast reactions can sometimes take place.

Ionic compounds are often but not always soluble in water. The approximate solubility of a number of ionic compounds is listed in the table below.

Positive ions	Negative ions			
	carbonate CO_3^{2-}	sulfate SO_4^{2-}	chloride Cl^-	nitrate NO_3^-
potassium K^+	✔	✔	✔	✔
silver Ag^+	✗	✗	✗	✔
calcium Ca^{2+}	✗	sp	✔	✔
barium Ba^{2+}	✗	✗	✔	✔
sodium Na^+	✔	✔	✔	✔
lead Pb^{2+}	✗	✗	✗	✔

Key: ✔ = soluble; ✗ = insoluble; **sp** = sparingly (slightly) soluble

a What can you say about the solubility of lead compounds compared with others?

b All the compounds of two of the metals shown are soluble in water. Which metals are these?

c Which negative ions produce a soluble compound regardless of the positive ions with which they are combined?

When two solutions are mixed, the products of the mixing of ions may or may not be soluble. If one of the products is insoluble it will appear as a solid **precipitate**.

Amazing fact

Insoluble precipitates of silver bromide are used as the basis for photographic film.

Which solution?

Hydrochloric acid will release bubbles of carbon dioxide gas from a solution containing a carbonate. This allows us to test a solution to see if it is a carbonate. The differing solubilities of ionic compounds allow us to use certain solutions of them to test for the presence of other ions.

You can test for sulfate by adding a few drops of acidified barium nitrate solution; a white precipitate indicates sulfate. A word equation can be written for the reaction with sodium sulfate, for example:

barium nitrate + sodium sulfate → barium sulfate + sodium nitrate

The insoluble white precipitate is barium sulfate. The sodium nitrate remains in solution.

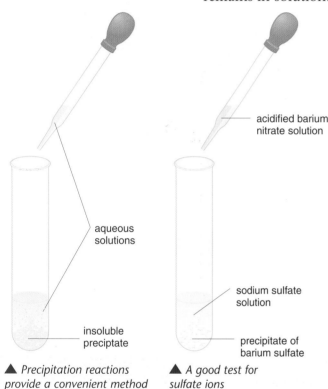

▲ Precipitation reactions provide a convenient method for testing for ions

▲ A good test for sulfate ions

Now consider the ions involved in the reaction. The symbol equation for this reaction is:

$$Ba(NO_3)_2 + Na_2SO_4 → BaSO_4 + 2NaNO_3$$

In reactions like this two types of ions are removed from solution and change state, Ba^{2+} and SO_4^{2-}. Two types of ions remain in solution and are unchanged as a result of the reaction, Na^+ and NO_3^-. The unchanged ions are known as **spectator ions**. **Ionic equations** leave out the spectator ions showing only those ions which have changed as a result of the reaction.

The ionic equation is:

$$Ba^{2+} + SO_4^{2-} → BaSO_4$$

To test for chloride ions, add a few drops of acidified silver nitrate solution to a sample of the unknown solution; a white precipitate indicates chloride. A bromide will give a cream coloured precipitate and an iodide a yellow precipitate. The same results are obtained with lead(II) nitrate solution.

Negative ion	Colour of precipitate obtained with lead or silver nitrate solution
chloride	white
bromide	cream
iodide	yellow

d Write a word equation for the two reactions which would prove that sodium chloride solution contains chloride ions.

e Write a symbol equation for both reactions.

f Write an ionic equation for both reactions.

Precipitating a pigment

Chrome yellow is a yellow pigment that can be made in the laboratory by a simple precipitation process. The laboratory instructions are shown in the diagram.

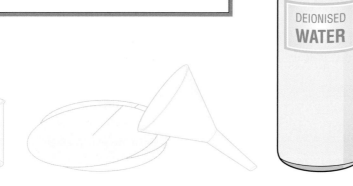

Lead compounds are all toxic

1. Dissolve 5.1g lead(II) nitrate solid in 30cm^3 deionised water.
2. Dissolve 3.0g potassium chromate solid in 30cm^3 deionised water.
3. Mix the two solutions carefully together in a large beaker.
4. Filter the resultant mixture to separate the precipitate.
5. Wash the precipitate carefully with deionised water.
6. Dry the precipitate.

DEIONISED **WATER**

▲ *How to prepare a sample of precipitate*

Steps 1 and 2 produce two solutions, the first one is lead nitrate, the second potassium chromate. In step 3 the two solutions are mixed to produce a precipitate of lead(II) chromate ($PbCrO_4$).

g Write an ionic equation for this reaction.

h Which ions are the spectator ions?

i Although once popular in pigments, lead compounds are now not usually used in paints and dyestuffs. Why do you think this is?

Lead(II) chromate is the pigment in the paint used to produce yellow lines on roads.

Keywords

ionic equation • precipitate
• spectator ion

Barium meals

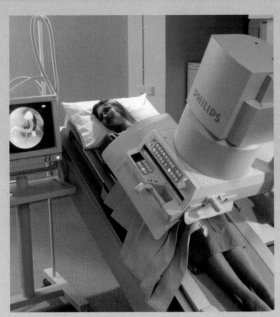

▲ *A barium meal helps to show up the digestive system in X-rays*

Doctors use X-rays to investigate internal organs that are otherwise impossible to see. In some parts of the body, such as the digestive system, the X-rays can pass through almost unaffected, and the X-ray image obtained has poor contrast and is of little medical use. A barium sulfate 'meal' is often given to a patient needing an investigation of their digestive system. Since X-rays are absorbed by barium sulfate this meal helps to show up the digestive system in the X-ray images.

A simple suspension of barium sulfate in water is unpleasant to 'eat' and can settle out and form sediments rather too quickly. It is important that the barium sulfate used is chemically pure as the common impurity barium carbonate is extremely poisonous. Other factors that must be considered are:

- particle size: if the particles of barium sulfate are too large they tend not to stay in suspension but settle out (form a sediment)
- non-ionic medium: if the medium (liquid) in which the barium sulfate is suspended contains ions, it can form charges on the barium sulfate particles causing them to group together and form a sediment more easily
- pH of the solution: the ideal barium sulfate suspension has a pH value of 5.3. If the solution is more acidic sedimentation happens readily
- taste: grinding the barium sulfate to make it fine reduces the chalky taste of the barium sulfate/water suspension. Many commercial preparations contain a flavouring agent to further disguise the unpleasant taste.

Questions

1 Explain why barium meals are given to patients before having an X-ray of their digestive system.

2 What are the drawbacks of using a simple barium sulfate/water suspension?

3 Why is the usual impurity found in barium sulfate such a hazard?

4 The particle size of the barium sulfate needs to be very small. Explain why.

5 What problems are caused by the formation of charges on the barium sulfate particles?

6 What happens if the pH value of the barium sulfate solution falls much below 5.3?

7 What two methods can be used to improve the taste of the barium meal?

C5a

Use the following relative atomic masses to answer the questions that follow: C=12, O=16, Cu=64, H=1, S=32.

1 What is the molar mass of:

a carbon monoxide, CO? [1]
b sulfuric acid, H_2SO_4? [1]
c copper(II) oxide, CuO? [1]
d water, H_2O? [1]
e copper(II) hydroxide, $Cu(OH)_2$ [1]

2 When heated in air, copper metal will combine with oxygen to form copper(II) oxide. The equation for the reaction is: $2Cu + O_2 \rightarrow 2CuO$

In one reaction, 128 g copper reacted completely to produce 160 g copper oxide.

a What mass of oxygen must have combined with the copper? [1]
b What mass of copper oxide would be produced by the complete oxidation of:
• 1.0 g copper? [1]
• 5 kg copper? [1]

3 Complete the following sentences using words from the list. You can use each word once, twice or not at all.

chemical ratio simplest approximate
percentage formula composition

a The formula of a compound gives the____ of one type of atom to another. [1]
b The empirical formula gives the ____ of one type of atom to another. [1]
c The empirical formula of a compound can be deduced from its ____ . [1]

4 Calculate the number of moles of atoms in:

a 5 g hydrogen [1]
b 16 g sulfur [1]
c 1.6 g oxygen [1]
d 128 g copper. [1]

5 Calculate the number of moles of molecules in:

a 980 g sulfuric acid, H_2SO_4 [1]
b 90 g water, H_2O [1]
c 3.2 g methane, CH_4 [1]

6 A compound is made up of the following percentages by mass: 52% carbon, 13% hydrogen, 35% oxygen.

a Use this information to calculate the empirical formula for the compound. [2]
b The formula mass of the compound is 46. What is its molecular formula? [1]

C5b

1 Use the words from the list to complete the passage below:

electrolyte ions dissolved melted

Electrolysis is the process that takes place when an electric current is passed though an __(1)__. This is a substance containing positive and negative __(2)__ which have become free to move because the ionic compound they were in has either been __(3)__ in water or __(4)__. [4]

2 The apparatus below can be used to electrolyse aqueous solutions.

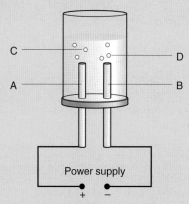

Power supply
+ −

a What is the part labelled A? [1]
b What is the part labelled B? [1]
c If the electrolyte is potassium sulfate solution, what gas is produced at C? [1]
d If the electrolyte is potassium nitrate solution, what gas is produced at D? [1]
e Given an equation for the change taking place at D.

3 When molten aluminium oxide is electrolysed, aluminium is produced at the negative electrode and oxygen is produced at the positive electrode.

a Write an equation for the reaction at the positive electrode. [1]
b Write an equation for the reaction at the negative electrode. [1]

4 When molten lead bromide is electrolysed using a current of 5 A for 60 minutes, approximately 19.5 g of lead is deposited.

a At which electrode is the lead produced? [1]
b What will be produced at the other electrode? [1]
c If the current used was 10 amps rather than 5.0 amps, what mass of lead would be produced? [1]
d What mass of lead would be produced if a current of 30 amps was used for 10 minutes? [1]

C5c

Volume can be measured in a number of different ways. Chemists use cm^3 and dm^3.

1 Convert the following into dm^3:

    a $2500\,cm^3$ [1]   **b** $100\,cm^3$ [1]   **c** $24\,000\,cm^3$ [1]

2 Convert the following into cm^3:

    a $36\,dm^3$ [1]   **b** $0.25\,dm^3$ [1] **c** $5.2\,dm^3$ [1]

3 Concentration can be measured in g/dm^3 or mol/dm^3.

    Molar masses: Na=23, Cl=35.5, N=14, O=16, H=1

    Convert the following to mol/dm^3:

    a $58.5\,g$ sodium chloride (NaCl) dissolved in $1\,dm^3$ solution [1]

    b $17.0\,g$ sodium nitrate ($NaNO_3$) dissolved in $1\,dm^3$ solution [1]

    c $7.3\,g$ hydrogen chloride dissolved in $100\,cm^3$ solution. [1]

4 Convert the following to g/dm^3:

    a $0.1\,mol/dm^3$ nitric acid (HNO_3) [1]

    b $3.0\,mol/dm^3$ sodium chloride (NaCl) [1]

    c $10.0\,mol/dm^3$ sodium nitrate ($NaNO_3$). [1]

5 Calculate the total number of moles of:

    a nitric acid in $25\,cm^3$ $0.1\,mol/dm^3$ nitric acid (HNO_3) [1]

    b ions in $55\,cm^3$ of $3.0\,mol/dm^3$ sodium chloride (NaCl). [1]

6 What volume of $10.0\,mol/dm^3$ sodium nitrate ($NaNO_3$) would you need in order to have 3 moles of sodium nitrate? [2]

C5d

1 The diagram below shows the change in pH that takes place when an alkali is added to an acid. Universal indicator was used to monitor the reaction.

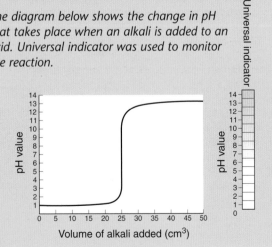

Volume of alkali added (cm^3)

a What volume of alkali is needed to neutralise this acid? [1]

b What is the pH of the acid before any alkali has been added? [1]

c What is the pH of the solution obtained after $30\,cm^3$ alkali has been added? [1]

d What colour will the indicator be after $23\,cm^3$ alkali has been added? [1]

e Why is this mixed indicator not very good for finding the end point for this titration? [1]

2 The table below shows the results obtained when two different samples of battery acid were titrated to find their strength.

	Acid from battery 1	Acid from battery 2
First reading (cm^3)	12.4	7.8
Second reading (cm^3)	12.5	8.0
Third reading (cm^3)	12.6	
Average (cm^3)	12.5	7.9

a Why is it necessary to take more than one reading for each acid? [1]

b In which battery is the acid stronger? [1]

c What would you expect the third reading for the acid from battery 2 to be? [1]

3 Hydrochloric acid is neutralised by sodium hydroxide solution. The equation for the reaction is:

$$HCl + NaOH \rightarrow NaCl + H_2O$$

An average of $20\,cm^3$ $0.1\,mol/dm^3$ sodium hydroxide solution was required to neutralise $10\,cm^3$ hydrochloric acid.

a How many moles of sodium hydroxide was used? [1]

b What was the concentration of the hydrochloric acid? [1]

c What volume of $0.1\,mol/dm^3$ sodium hydroxide would be required to neutralise $50\,cm^3$ of this acid? [1]

C5e

1 Hydrogen gas is produced when magnesium metal dissolves in hydrochloric acid:

$$Mg + 2HCl \rightarrow MgCl_2 + H_2$$

Two students decided to investigate the effect that changing the amount of magnesium had upon the volume of hydrogen gas produced.

a Sketch a diagram of the apparatus that could be used to do this investigation. [2]

b The students' results are shown in the table:

Mass of magnesium (g)	Volume of gas (cm³)
0.1	100
0.3	300
0.5	500

   (i) How does the volume of hydrogen depend upon the mass of magnesium used? [1]

   (ii) Which reactant, acid or magnesium, is the limiting reactant in this reaction? [1]

c What volume of gas would be produced by:
   (i) 0.2 g magnesium? [1]
   (ii) 0.4 g magnesium? [1]

d What is the minimum amount of $1.0\,mol/dm^3$ hydrochloric acid that could have been used in this investigation? (Molar mass Mg=24) [2]

2 Use the results in the table and the fact that 1 mole of any gas at 25 °C and atmospheric pressure has a volume of $24\,dm^3$ to calculate the number of moles of gas produced by:

a 0.3 g magnesium [1]
b 0.2 g magnesium. [1]

3 If acid was in excess, what volume of hydrogen would be produced by 2.4 g magnesium? [2]

C5f

1 Describe the key features of a chemical equilibrium. [2]

2 Explain what changes will alter the position of a chemical equilibrium. [2]

3 This question is about the reaction between nitrogen and hydrogen to make the gas ammonia:

     iron catalyst
$$N_2 + 3H_2 \rightleftharpoons 2NH_3 + heat$$

The reaction is in equilibrium.

a What effect will an increase in pressure have upon the position of this equilibrium? [1]
b How will an increase in pressure affect the yield of ammonia? [1]
c How will an increase in temperature affect the yield of ammonia? [1]
d What effect will the catalyst have upon the equilibrium? [1]

C5g

1 What ion is released by all acids when in water? [1]

2 Explain the difference between a strong acid and a weak acid. [2]

3 Write equations to compare the behaviour of hydrogen chloride and ethanoic acid when each is added to water. [2]

4 Use your answer to **2** to help to explain why reactions of hydrochloric acid are faster than those of ethanoic acid. [2]

C5h

1 Write word equations for the reactions that take place between:

a silver nitrate solution and sodium chloride solution [1]
b barium nitrate solution and potassium sulfate solution [1]
c lead nitrate solution and potassium iodide solution. [1]

2 In each of the reactions in **1**, an insoluble salt will be produced.

a What is the name given to this type of reaction? [1]
b What is the general name given to the insoluble salts formed in these reactions? [1]
c Outline how you could obtain a pure sample of an insoluble salt from one of these reactions. [2]

3 Use the following information to write ionic equations for each of the reactions below.

silver Ag^+, nitrate NO_3^-, sodium Na^+, chloride Cl^-, sulfate SO_4^{2-}, iodide I^-, lead Pb^{2+}

Insoluble salts: silver chloride, barium sulfate, lead iodide.

a Silver nitrate solution and sodium chloride solution. [1]
b Barium nitrate solution and potassium sulfate solution. [1]
c Lead nitrate solution and potassium iodide solution. [1]

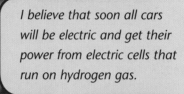

C6 Chemistry out there

I believe that soon all cars will be electric and get their power from electric cells that run on hydrogen gas.

I think it will be easier to run cars on the alcohol made from sugar cane or other crops.

I heard about someone running their car on recycled vegetable oil from a chip shop. Surely that's the most green fuel of all?

- Chemists use raw materials to make new substances. They measure and control the amounts involved in reactions and the rates at which they react.

- There are a number of ways in which we might use alternative energy sources to improve the efficiency and reduce the pollution of our transport system.

- Most people will take a type of painkiller called an analgesic at some time in their lives. There are a number of popular analgesics, each with different chemical compositions and different benefits and drawbacks.

What you need to know

- How fuels release energy when they burn.

- How one metal can displace another metal.

- How alcohols and acids behave.

Cleaner cars?

In this item you will find out

- about the reaction of hydrogen and oxygen
- how the reaction between hydrogen and oxygen can be used to provide an electric current
- about the advantages of this technology

When a sample of hydrogen and air is ignited in a test tube, it burns explosively to produce a squeaky pop. It is an exothermic reaction.

Being a gas of low density, hydrogen was once used to fill airships. In 1937, a stray spark started a fire and caused the Hindenberg disaster. Thirty-three people died as the whole airship was engulfed in flames.

▲ Hydrogen burns explosively in air

Although the hydrogen contributed significantly to the explosion and fire, there is evidence to suggest that it was the ease with which the surface skin of the airship burned that was the initial cause. Today, airships are filled with the inert noble gas helium, rather than the highly combustible hydrogen.

The word and symbol equations for the reaction between hydrogen and water are shown below:

hydrogen + oxygen → water
$$2H_2 + O_2 \rightarrow H_2O$$

This exothermic reaction gives off a lot of energy and needs careful handling if it is to be carried out safely. It is used to power space shuttles and many similar rocket systems.

▲ The destructive power of hydrogen

▲ The combustion of hydrogen provides useful power!

a Why is hydrogen burned in this way regarded as a clean fuel?

b Suggest why hydrogen is less convenient to handle than fuels like ethanol and petrol.

The challenge facing scientists has been to find a way of using this reaction to release its energy in a controllable and safe manner. One answer is the **fuel cell**.

Amazing fact

4 200 000 000 000 gallons of water would be required each year to make enough hydrogen to power the US economy.

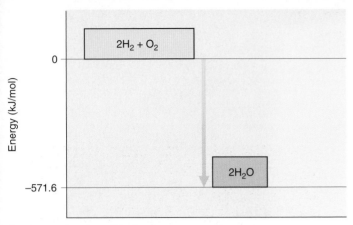

▲ *The combustion of hydrogen releases a lot of energy*

How a fuel cell works

The reaction between hydrogen and oxygen can be represented as an **energy level diagram**.

Energy level diagrams show how energy is gained or lost when a reaction takes place. The reactants are shown on the left-hand side and the products on the right. If energy is given out (an exothermic reaction), the products are shown at an energy level lower than the reactants. The reverse applies for an endothermic reaction. These diagrams can be drawn to scale so as to indicate the amount of energy released.

 Look at the diagram. What energy change takes place when 1 mole of hydrogen is burned in oxygen?

In a fuel cell like the one in the diagram below, hydrogen and oxygen react together in a controlled fashion to release energy in a useful form. The reaction is divided into two half reactions, one at each electrode. The two electrodes are separated by a membrane. Hydrogen ions (protons) can pass through the membrane but the hydrogen and oxygen gases cannot.

Examiner's tip

Although it looks complicated, it helps to remember that the overall reaction for the hydrogen fuel cell is just the combustion of hydrogen.

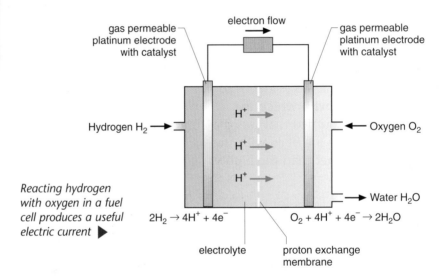

Reacting hydrogen with oxygen in a fuel cell produces a useful electric current ▶

At the hydrogen electrode, hydrogen gas is bubbled into the solution where protons (H^+) and electrons (e^-) are produced:

$$2H_2 \rightarrow 4H^+ + 4e^-$$

At the oxygen electrode, oxygen gas is bubbled in and it combines with hydrogen protons and the electrons to produce water:

$$O_2 + 4H^+ + 4e^- \rightarrow 2H_2O$$

Electrons are released by the reaction at the hydrogen electrode and are used up by the oxygen electrode. This 'pushing' and 'pulling' of electrons creates a **potential difference** between the two electrodes. This causes the electrons to travel around an external circuit from the hydrogen electrode to the oxygen electrode and do work.

Since the oxygen gains electrons, it is REDuced. The hydrogen loses electrons and is OXidised. This reaction is an example of a **redox reaction**. The equation for the overall reaction is:

$$2H_2 + O_2 \rightarrow 2H_2O$$

Clean energy?

Fuel cells provide a means of generating electrical energy as it is needed without producing pollution. This removes the need for expensive and heavy batteries. Car companies are currently very interested in fuel cells as a means to power environmentally friendly vehicles.

It is important to note that the hydrogen for fuel cells must be obtained from somewhere (probably by electrolysis) using electrical energy which will most likely have been produced in a power station fuelled by fossil fuels!

▲ Many vehicle manufacturers are developing fuel cell technology

d Suggest why a spillage of hydrogen would be less dangerous than a spillage of a fuel such as petrol.

e How could we make sure that the use of fuel cells as a means of powering vehicles is completely non-polluting?

Fuel cells are also used to provide the electrical energy for spacecraft including the *Apollo* missions. The fact that fuel cells are lightweight, compact and have no major moving parts makes them particularly suitable for this purpose. In addition hydrogen and oxygen are usually carried by spacecraft anyway.

Fuel cell advantages

Fuel cells have lots of advantages over other ways of generating electricity.
- Fuel cells are more efficient because they make energy electrochemically and do not burn fuel, fuel cells are more efficient than combustion systems.
- There are fewer stages in the process of creating electricity; fuel and oxygen are fed in, electricity comes out.
- There is a direct transfer of energy; electricity is produced on demand where and when it is needed.
- There is no pollution; the only waste product is non-polluting water.

The efficiency of an engine is measured in terms of the percentage of the energy available in the fuel that is converted to the form in which it is required. Internal combustion engines convert a lot of the energy in the fuel to heat. A typical fuel cell powered vehicle can achieve 45–60% efficiency, while a typical petrol combustion engine has an efficiency of 15–35%.

f Why are petrol engines so inefficient?

> **Amazing fact**
>
> If just 20% of cars used fuel cells, the USA could cut oil imports by 1.5 million barrels every day.

> **Keywords**
>
> energy level diagram
> • fuel cell • potential
> difference • redox reaction

Fuel cells for the future

▲ *Cleaner power for urban transportation*

FUEL CELL FANS CLAIM FANTASTIC EFFICIENCY!

Fuel cells offer a unique combination of efficiency, fuel flexibility and portability. Fuel cells could enable a move to a secure renewable energy future, based on the use of hydrogen.

Modern fuel cells using hydrocarbons, like petrol, can achieve a 40% fuel-to-electricity efficiency, while 50% has been achieved using hydrogen as the fuel. A combined fuel cell and gas turbine power supply can achieve as much as 60% efficiency. By recycling the heat generated, the overall efficiency can be higher than 85%.

Fuel cells can help us to produce vehicles that are more energy efficient. Buses powered by fuel cells are expected to be up to three times more efficient than those with conventional diesel engines.

Fuel cells are far less polluting than conventional combustion engines. Data show that in order to generate 1000 kilowatt-hours of electricity, a fuel cell power plant may create less than 28 g of pollution, while conventional combustion systems produce 11.4 kg of pollutants.

Many large lorries use auxiliary power units (APUs) to power air conditioners and accessories. It is claimed that fuel cells could reduce emissions from these units by up to 45%. Because fuel cells have few moving parts this will also reduce fuel consumption and wear and tear on the vehicle. Research shows that using fuel cells to power the APUs in lorries could save 670 million gallons of diesel fuel per year and reduce carbon dioxide emissions by 4.64 million tonnes per year. ■

Questions

1 What efficiency can be achieved using hydrocarbon fuel cells?

2 How can the overall system efficiency be improved beyond this value?

3 If diesel powered buses operate at about 20% efficiency, what is the maximum increase in efficiency that can be expected if they are converted to fuel cell technology?

4 In generating 1000 kW-hours of electricity, how much pollution would be produced by a conventional system compared with a fuel cell system?

5 How many tonnes of carbon dioxide are produced by the combustion of 670 million gallons of diesel fuel?

Potential protection?

- about reduction and oxidation reactions
- how some metals will displace others from solution
- about rusting and ways to prevent it

When a piece of magnesium burns in air a vigorous reaction takes place. The magnesium burns with a very bright white light. A white ash of magnesium oxide is produced.

The word equation for this reaction is:

magnesium + oxygen → magnesium oxide

▲ *A vigorous redox reaction*

a Write a balanced symbol equation for this reaction.

b What particles make up magnesium oxide?

Since the magnesium has had oxygen added to it, we can say it has undergone oxidation. The reverse of this process (the removal of oxygen from a compound) is known as reduction. This is an example of a redox reaction.

We make pure iron in a blast furnace from iron ore by using a reduction reaction. The iron oxide in the ore is heated with carbon and carbon monoxide from the coal in the reaction mixture. This combines with the oxygen in the iron ore to leave pure iron behind. Since oxygen is removed from the iron oxide we say that it has been reduced. The equation for this reaction is:

$$Fe_2O_3 + 3CO \rightarrow 2Fe + 3CO_2$$

The definition of oxidation and reduction can be extended to include many more reactions than those involving just the addition and removal of oxygen. Lots of reactions can be explained in terms of the loss and gain of electrons.

One redox reaction that costs society many millions of pounds each year is the oxidation of iron; also known as rusting. A lot of research goes into finding out how we can control rusting. The reactivity of iron is part, but not all, of the story. More reactive metals, such as zinc, can be used to protect iron from rusting.

▲ *Rusting costs!*

Amazing fact

Scientists think that it is the impurities or imperfections in the metal that trigger the rusting of iron.

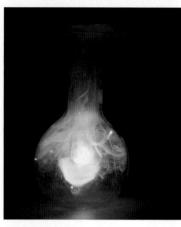

▲ *Oxidation does not always need oxygen*

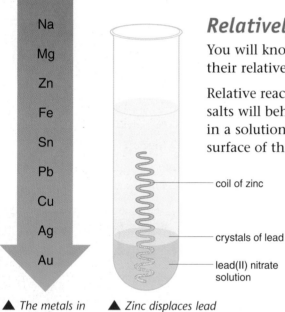

▲ *The metals in reactivity order* ▲ *Zinc displaces lead*

Give and take

A more general definition of reduction and oxidation considers the gain and loss of electrons. When a particle gains electrons it is reduced, and when it loses electrons it is oxidised. The mnemonic OILRIG is helpful in remembering this:

Oxidation **I**s **L**oss, **R**eduction **I**s **G**ain

For example, in the reaction between sodium metal and chlorine gas, sodium chloride solid is produced in a vigorous reaction:

$$Na + \tfrac{1}{2}Cl_2 \rightarrow NaCl$$

Positive sodium ions (Na^+) and negative chloride ions (Cl^-) are produced. The sodium atoms lose electrons and are oxidised. The chlorine atoms gain electrons and are reduced.

A substance that takes electrons from another substance is called an **oxidising agent**. A substance that gives electrons to another is a **reducing agent**.

Relatively reactive

You will know that the metals can be organised in a series according to their relative reactivity.

Relative reactivity helps us to explain and predict how metals and their salts will behave together. For example, when a strip of zinc metal is placed in a solution of lead(II) nitrate, little crystals of metallic lead grow on the surface of the zinc.

The equations for this are:

zinc + lead(II) nitrate → zinc nitrate + lead
$$Zn + Pb(NO_3)_2 \rightarrow Zn(NO_3)_2 + Pb$$

Zinc atoms lose electrons and become ions (they are oxidised). Lead ions gain electrons and become atoms (they are reduced). A more reactive metal will usually displace a less reactive one from solution. So zinc can also displace metallic iron from a solution of iron(II) sulfate:

$$Zn + FeSO_4 \rightarrow ZnSO_4 + Fe$$

Here zinc is again oxidised and the iron is reduced. If copper metal had been used, it would have no effect on the iron(II) sulfate solution.

c What will be produced when magnesium ribbon is placed in copper sulfate solution?

d Write word and symbol equations for this reaction.

Hydrogen displacement

Iron metal will displace hydrogen from hydrochloric acid in another redox reaction:

$$Fe + 2HCl \rightarrow FeCl_2 + H_2$$

Amazing fact

The metal caesium is so reactive that on contact with water it displaces hydrogen so violently that it explodes.

Here, the iron is oxidised and the hydrogen ions in the acid are reduced. The iron(II) ions produced are often oxidised further to iron(III) ions.

Oxidation by chlorine

Chlorine gas is a powerful oxidising agent. It takes electrons out of most materials it meets. This is why chlorine is extremely damaging to biological systems. When chlorine gas is bubbled through a solution containing iron(II) ions, chloride ions and iron(III) ions are produced:

$$2Fe^{2+} + Cl_2 \rightarrow 2Fe^{3+} + 2Cl^-$$
oxidised   reduced

Arresting rusting

Rusting is a redox reaction that takes place when iron is exposed to water and oxygen. Rust is hydrated iron oxide. The word equation for the reaction is:

iron + oxygen + water → hydrated iron(III) oxide

Iron ions are positively charged and oxide ions are negative. In rusting, iron atoms have lost electrons and have been oxidised, oxygen atoms have gained electrons and been reduced.

Since rusting requires iron to be exposed to both oxygen and water, then any method that excludes one of these substances will protect the iron from rust. Paint will keep out both air and water, but it will not work if the surface is scratched or chipped. Oil and grease will repel water and keep out air from surfaces where the paint might have worn off.

▲ Zinc is used to galvanise iron and protect it from rusting

Rust prevention

Galvanising iron involves applying a layer of zinc to its surface. While the zinc excludes air and water in the way that paint does, it has a major advantage over paint in that it continues to protect the iron, even if the zinc layer is scratched or chipped.

Because the zinc is more reactive than iron and is in electrical contact with it, it loses its electrons (it is oxidised) rather than the iron. The iron is left intact. This is called **sacrificial protection**.

Magnesium can also be used as a sacrificial metal. A piece of magnesium can be attached to a piece of iron and the magnesium will lose electrons in preference to the iron. This method is used to protect the steel hulls of ships and any steel moving parts that are below the water line. Blocks of zinc or magnesium are bolted to the appropriate parts.

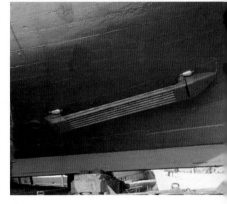

▲ A zinc block attached to the hull of a boat

 Why do you think this process is called *sacrificial* protection?

Adding a coating of tin (**tinning**) will have a similar protective effect on iron, but if the surface is scratched the iron will tend to react more easily. It is more reactive than tin so will lose electrons more easily.

Keywords

galvanising • oxidising agent • reducing agent • sacrificial protection • tinning

▲ *Galvanising gives excellent protection against corrosion*

Resisting rusting

Hot dip galvanising involves coating a steel object with a layer of molten zinc. Because high temperatures are involved, the zinc forms strong (metallic) bonds with the steel.

Although galvanising continues to protect steel even if scratched, with major damage a repair may be considered. Repeating the hot dip process is difficult and very expensive.

The advertising feature below suggests an alternative.

Endrust Zinco paint
85% zinc in a paint – as good as galvanising!!

Endrust Zinco paint is designed to provide a virtually permanent and highly effective repair for galvanised surfaces that have been damaged or worn. It will protect iron and steel even in the most hostile of environments. Unlike conventional paints, which can enable rust to creep underneath them, *Endrust Zinco* bonds so strongly with the surface of the metal that moisture simply cannot get under it. Just like conventional paints *Endrust Zinco* can be applied with a brush, roller or spray.

Unlike galvanising, no heat is needed to apply *Endrust Zinco*. This means that there is no risk of the metal distortion that galvanising can cause to thin metal sheets. A film of *Endrust Zinco* is conductive. This means that being made of zinc it will corrode sacrificially, protecting the steel underneath. Even if it is scratched, *Endrust Zinco* will carry on protecting the area around the scratch. You'll soon be painting it everywhere!

Questions

1 Why does hot dip galvanising form particularly strong bonds?

2 Why would you be unlikely to repair damaged galvanising?

3 What sort of environment is the worst for rusting?

4 In what ways is *Endrust Zinco* different to conventional paints?

5 In what way is *Endrust Zinco* similar to conventional paints?

6 What advantage does the low temperature use of *Endrust Zinco* have over hot dip galvanising?

7 How does *Endrust Zinco* carry on working even if scratched?

Future fuels?

In this item you will find out

- about the structure of alcohols

- how ethanol is made by the fermentation of glucose

- how ethanol can be made from ethene, and ethene from ethanol

▲ Ethanol is the chemical name of the alcohol that is found in drinks

The process of sugars converting into **alcohol** by **fermentation** occurs regularly in nature through contact with airborne **yeasts**. When we talk about alcohol we often mean drinks such as wine, beer and spirits. These drinks all contain an alcohol called **ethanol**.

As well as being used as a drink, ethanol (often as methylated spirits) can be used as an industrial solvent in paints, adhesives and even perfumes. Methylated spirits is made poisonous so that it cannot be drunk.

Ethanol produced by fermentation will usually contain many other compounds. These compounds give beers and wines their distinctive flavours. Sometimes very pure ethanol is needed for the production of other chemicals. A different method is needed to prepare ethanol for this purpose.

Amazing fact

Higher primates, such as chimpanzees, will eat rotting fruit to enjoy the 'high' from the alcohol in the fermenting juices.

a What is very pure ethanol often needed for?

b Methanol is toxic but is added in a very small proportion (about 5%) to pure ethanol to make methylated spirits. Why is this done?

In some parts of the world, ethanol is also being used as an alternative fuel to petrol. The fermentation of sugars from vegetable matter produces an ethanol solution that can then be distilled to produce ethanol pure enough to be burned in a car engine. Ethanol has several advantages over petrol. Its combustion is more complete, which improves efficiency and reduces pollution.

c Explain why ethanol made from vegetable material is a renewable source of energy.

d What other advantage does ethanol have as a fuel for cars?

▲ Methanol as a solvent

▲ The OH group can be found in all alcohols

What's in a name?

The word 'alcohol' actually refers to a class of organic compounds whose molecules contain a hydrocarbon chain with an OH (hydroxyl) group attached.

Like the alkanes, the alcohols are named according to the number of carbon atoms in their molecules. The table below shows the molecular formulae of methanol to pentanol.

The formula for each of these alcohols can be worked out using the general formula:

$$C_nH_{2n+1}OH$$

e What is the molecular formula of an alcohol containing six carbon atoms?

> **Amazing fact**
>
> The oldest evidence of beer is on a 6000-year-old Sumerian tablet from Mesopotamia, which shows people drinking through reed straws from a communal bowl.

Number of carbon atoms	Molecular formula	Displayed formula	Name of alcohol
1	CH_3OH	H—C—O—H (with H above and below C)	Methanol
2	C_2H_5OH	H—C—C—O—H	Ethanol
3	C_3H_7OH	H—C—C—C—O—H	Propanol
4	C_4H_9OH	H—C—C—C—C—O—H	Butanol
5	$C_5H_{11}OH$	H—C—C—C—C—C—O—H	Pentanol

This apparatus can be used to produce a sample of alcohol by the fermentation of sugar ▼

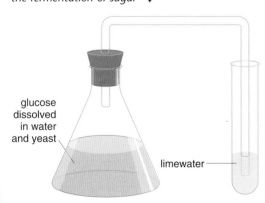

glucose dissolved in water and yeast

limewater

From sugar to alcohol

Fermentation has been used by humans for centuries to produce alcohol. A wide range of vegetable materials can act as the starting materials as long as they contain sugar or starch which can be broken down to simple sugars, such as glucose. Yeast acts on glucose in the absence of air to produce carbon dioxide gas and ethanol. The word and symbol equations for this reaction are:

glucose → carbon dioxide + ethanol
$$C_6H_{12}O_6 \rightarrow 2CO_2 + 2C_2H_5OH$$

You can make ethanol quite easily in the laboratory using the apparatus shown in the diagram.

Enzymes in yeast will, in the absence of air, break down a glucose solution to ethanol and carbon dioxide. The glucose solution is mixed with yeast and left in the apparatus in the diagram at a temperature of between 25 and 50 °C. Temperature control is important; if the enzymes are too cold they will become inactive, and if too warm their delicate structures will be affected and they will become **denatured**. The temperature at which they are most active is known as the **optimum temperature**.

It is important to keep air out of the apparatus to prevent the oxidation of ethanol to **ethanoic acid** (vinegar). The ethanol solution produced this way can then be **distilled** in order to concentrate it.

▲ Large scale fermentation needs careful temperature control

▲ Ethanol can be distilled to make it more concentrated

Just add water!

Very pure ethanol for industrial use can be made by an addition reaction between ethene and water. Ethene and steam are passed over a heated phosphoric acid catalyst. The double bond in the ethene molecules opens up and water molecules join up with them. This is called the **hydration** of ethene. The word and symbol equations for the reaction are:

ethene + water → ethanol
$C_2H_4 + H_2O → C_2H_5OH$

f Why do you think this is called an addition reaction?

g Why do you think ethanol produced in this way is so pure?

In deciding which of these two methods of ethanol production to use, the following factors would need to be considered.

Producing ethanol by fermentation:

- is simple to set up
- requires low temperatures
- produces impure ethanol that requires distillation to be purified.

Producing ethanol from ethene:

- requires high temperatures and a catalyst
- is complex to set up
- produces very pure ethanol.

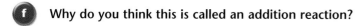

ethene   +   water   →   ethanol

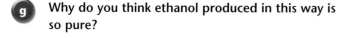
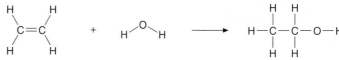

▲ Making ethanol from ethene

Keywords

alcohol • distillation • dehydration • denatured • ethanoic acid • ethanol • fermentation • hydration • optimum temperature • yeast

Dehydration of ethanol

The addition reaction shown above can be reversed by using powerful **dehydrating** conditions. Ethanol vapour is passed over a hot aluminium oxide catalyst.

The word and symbol equations for this reaction are:

ethanol → ethene + water
$C_2H_5OH → C_2H_4 + H_2O$

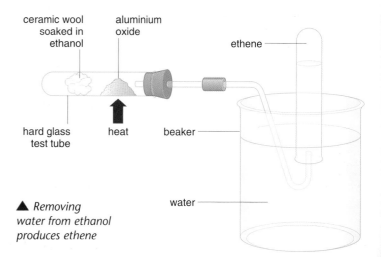

▲ Removing water from ethanol produces ethene

Henry Ford – ahead of his time

The Model T Ford was first produced in 1908. At that time its designer, Henry Ford, expected that ethanol, made from renewable biological materials, would be a major car fuel.

However, petrol, rather than ethanol, became the main fuel for transport in the early twentieth century. This was because petrol engines were easy to operate with the materials that were available for engine construction, and more oil was being discovered all the time.

But petrol had lots of disadvantages. Petrol is more difficult to store and transport than ethanol, particularly since it often has to be transported a long way from the place where it is found to where it is needed. Accidental explosions and fires are more likely. In addition, petrol needs to be extracted (refined) from crude oil, which is a mixture of many different compounds. This can be a complex and expensive process. Petrol also needs additives such as lead compounds to make it perform smoothly, and using petrol means that engines have to be low compression engines and need large cooling systems.

Even though there are environmental problems with fuels made from crude oil, they have been used as fuels for cars and lorries for the past three-quarters of a century. There are two reasons. They are cheap to use. Also, large investments made by the oil and car industries in people, technology and equipment make it difficult for a new cost-competitive industry to compete.

▲ Introduced in 1908, 15 million Model T Fords had been made by 1927

Questions

1 Why was petrol the favoured fuel in the early car industry?

2 What are the disadvantages of using petrol as a fuel for cars?

3 Why is the production of petrol suitable for use in cars more complex than the production of ethanol?

4 Why did petrol have to have lead compounds added to it?

5 What two reasons are given to explain why petrol is still the most popular fuel for today's cars?

Salt of the Earth

In this item you will find out

- how we obtain adequate supplies of salt

- why salt is an important raw material for industry

- about the electrolysis of salt

▲ *Salt can be obtained by the evaporation of sea water*

Sodium chloride is the chemical name for common **salt**. Salt is a biological necessity for human life. In ancient times trade in salt for the preservation of food was important. Salt was even valuable enough to be used as a currency in some areas. Nowadays we have other methods to preserve food and there is concern that many of us have too much salt in our diets.

Salt is extremely important for other reasons. The chemicals we can extract from salt are essential for the manufacture of a wide range of other products such as bleach and margarine.

So how do we get the elements out of sodium chloride? Both sodium and chlorine are very reactive elements. When they combine they form positively charged sodium ions and negatively charged chloride ions and release a lot of energy. So the product (sodium chloride) is stable and difficult to split up.

Water molecules are polar. This means that parts of them are slightly positively charged and others are slightly negatively charged. Water molecules are attracted to other charged particles such as other polar molecules and ions.

Amazing fact

The Latin phrase *salarium argentum* (salt money) referred to part of the payment of salt made to every Roman soldier, and the word has been carried down the ages into the English word 'salary'.

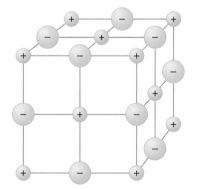

Each ion is surrounded by ions of the opposite charge. In this way, the ions are held firmly in fixed positions.

◀ *The sodium chloride lattice – melting point 801 °C*

a Because sodium chloride is an ionic lattice it will dissolve easily in water. Suggest why this is.

b Suggest why the melting point of salt is so high.

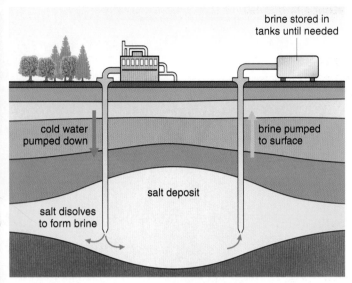

▲ Solution mining dissolves underground salt and pumps it to the surface

brine stored in tanks until needed

cold water pumped down

brine pumped to surface

salt deposit

salt disolves to form brine

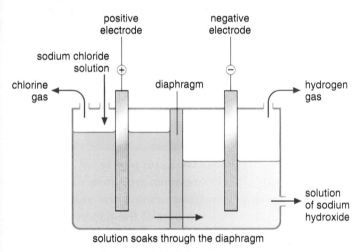

positive electrode

negative electrode

sodium chloride solution

chlorine gas

diaphragm

hydrogen gas

solution of sodium hydroxide

solution soaks through the diaphragm

▲ A cell used for the electrolysis of brine

Amazing fact

In December 1880, solution mining caused so much subsidence that the River Weaver in Cheshire flowed backwards for a week!

Mining with water?

In some parts of the UK, such as in Cheshire, vast underground deposits of **rock salt** were laid down long ago when ancient seas evaporated. Although the salt can be dug out of the ground by conventional mining methods, the high solubility of salt makes it possible to extract these deposits by **solution mining**. Water is pumped down into the deposits. The salt dissolves and the salt solution (**brine**) formed is pumped to the surface.

Taking vast amounts of salt from underground deposits has resulted in some famous examples of **subsidence**, with buildings cracking and deep holes suddenly appearing in roads and gardens.

Electrolysis of sodium chloride

Concentrated sodium chloride solution (brine) can be electrolysed to produce hydrogen and chlorine, which can be used in the industrial manufacture of a wide range of products. The ions present in sodium chloride solution are Na^+ and Cl^- from the sodium chloride, and H^+ and OH^- from the water. The sodium chloride solution is fed into an electrolysis cell like that shown in the diagram.

The electrode materials need to be chosen so that they are **inert**, i.e. they do not react with the substances being produced.

 Which positive ions are present in sodium chloride solution?

At the electrodes

Hydrogen gas is produced at the negative electrode (cathode):

$$2H^+ + 2e^- \rightarrow H_2$$

Chloride ions each lose an electron to the positive electrode (anode). The atoms produced pair up to form molecules of chlorine gas (Cl_2).

$$2Cl^- - 2e^- \rightarrow Cl_2$$

The diaphragm in the electrolysis cell is used to keep the hydrogen and chlorine separate. As hydrogen and chloride ions are converted to hydrogen and chlorine molecules, the remaining solution becomes an increasingly concentrated solution of sodium and hydroxide ions.

If a dilute solution of sodium chloride is used instead of a concentrated solution, then chlorine is not produced at the anode but hydrogen is still produced at the cathode. The hydroxide ions (OH^-) from the water are converted to oxygen gas instead:

$$4OH^- \rightarrow O_2 + 4e^- + 2H_2O$$

d Why do you think sodium atoms are not produced at the cathode in this cell even if the solution is concentrated?

In molten sodium chloride only sodium ions and chloride ions are present. If it is electrolysed, then the product at the anode is chlorine gas, but the product at the cathode is sodium metal. The reaction at the cathode is:

$$Na^+ + e^- \rightarrow Na$$

e Write an equation for the reaction at the anode.

Use your brine

The substances produced from the electrolysis of concentrated sodium chloride have a wide range of uses, as shown in the diagram. The diagram also shows how both starting materials required for the production of bleach are produced by the electrolysis of brine. Most domestic bleach contains the active ingredient sodium chlorate(I). This is produced when chlorine is dissolved in sodium hydroxide solution.

▼ *The products of the electrolysis of sodium chloride have many uses*

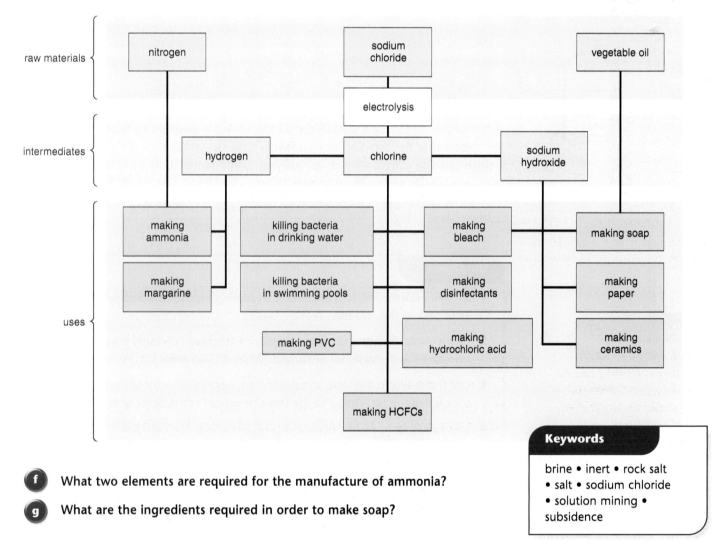

f What two elements are required for the manufacture of ammonia?

g What are the ingredients required in order to make soap?

Keywords

brine • inert • rock salt • salt • sodium chloride • solution mining • subsidence

Which bleach?

Two students, Yuko and Laura, decide to investigate which bleach is the best. They devise an experiment where they find how much iodine is produced when bleach is added to some acidified potassium iodide solution in a flask. Their teacher tells them that they can measure the amount of iodine (and the strength of the bleach) by measuring the volume of sodium thiosulfate solution they need to add to remove the iodine colour from the flask.

The girls' results are shown below. For each bleach, Laura takes readings 1 and 2, while Yuko takes readings 3 and 4.

▲ Bleaching strength can be used to determine best value in a range of bleaches

Name of bleach	Bleaching strength (Volume of sodium thiosulfate needed to remove iodine (cm^3)		
	Fresco Thick Bleach	Betterbuy Economy	Domezone
Reading 1	13.1	4.1	19.1
Reading 2	11.2	5.0	18.6
Reading 3	12.5	4.6	18.4
Reading 4	10.9	2.1	18.9
Average			

Yuko thinks that this experiment alone is not a fair test of which bleach is the best value for money. She suggests that they should take into account the volume in the bottle as well as the price. She suggests they should devise a measure which she calls the 'bleaching value':

$$\text{bleaching value} = \frac{\text{bleaching strength} \times \text{volume in bottle}}{\text{price of bottle}}$$

▲ The three types of bleach tested

Questions

1 In their experiment, it is important to make sure the comparison is a fair test. How should they do this?

2 Laura thinks that one of their results for Betterbuy Economy bleach is unreliable and should be discarded. What do you think?

3 Use the results in the table to calculate an average value for bleaching strength for each of the bleaches. Put the three bleaches in rank order of bleaching power.

4 Use Yuko's formula to calculate a bleaching value for each bleach.

5 Is Yuko right to say the first test was an unfair measure of which was the best value bleach?

6 What other factors might you consider when deciding which bleach to buy?

Our vital, delicate shield

In this item you will find out

- why the ozone layer is vital to protect life on Earth

- how the use of CFCs leads to ozone depletion

- how other substances can be used to replace CFCs

Our atmosphere not only provides us with the oxygen for life, it also provides the means for recycling carbon dioxide and the generation of our weather. In addition, the atmosphere is a vital and delicate shield. It protects us from unwelcome extraterrestrial forces and events. One example of this protection is the fact that most meteorites burn up as a result of friction in the atmosphere, well before they reach the Earth's surface.

A less obvious but equally dangerous threat is that posed by the intense, high energy short wavelength light known as **ultraviolet light**, which is one component of the light produced by the Sun. Without our atmosphere and the **ozone layer** within it, which absorbs the ultraviolet light, life on the Earth's surface would be exposed to damaging and potentially deadly levels of UV radiation.

▲ *Our protective atmosphere*

Thousands of millions of years ago, primitive organisms evolved. Once these early organisms started photosynthesising they produced oxygen (O_2) with molecules containing two atoms each (diatomic), which built up in the atmosphere. Solar radiation acted on this oxygen high in the atmosphere to produce a layer of ozone gas (O_3).

Amazing fact

If the ozone layer had not formed, life would never have emerged onto land from the protection of the seas.

a   What is meant by the word 'diatomic'?

b   What is the formula of ordinary atmospheric oxygen?

c   Atmospheric oxygen reacts with itself to form ozone when exposed to solar radiation. Try to suggest a balanced symbol equation for this reaction.

CFCs – wonder gases?

In the 1930s the DuPont Corporation was looking for compounds to use as propellants in aerosol cans, as the liquid in refrigerators and to make gas bubbles in the manufacture of foam. They wanted gases that were easily liquefied by compression, chemically inert, insoluble in water, non-flammable, inexpensive to manufacture, non-toxic and had no odour.

They found **CFCs** had most of these properties and were very enthusiastic about using them. CFCs (chlorofluorocarbons) contain carbon, chlorine and fluorine. By the mid-1970s, the use of CFCs was almost universal as aerosol propellants, refrigerants and foaming agents.

▲ CFCs were used as propellants for aerosols

Amazing fact

In 1986, the worldwide production of CFCs was about 1.25 million tonnes; that is about 250 g for each person on the Earth.

A chain reaction

Because of the very properties that make them useful, CFCs do not decompose, react or get washed out of the atmosphere in the way that many pollutants do. This means that they stay in the atmosphere for a very long time and eventually they find their way to the **stratosphere** (the layer in the atmosphere between 17 and 50 km above the Earth). The reactions that then take place can remove the CFCs, but only very slowly and at the expense of the ozone layer.

When the CFCs in the stratosphere are exposed to ultraviolet light the covalent bonds in the molecule can be split. When covalent bonds split unevenly, then this produces a positive and a negative ion. When covalent bonds split evenly, then this forms highly reactive particles called **free radicals** each with an unpaired electron.

A chlorine molecule has a shared pair of electrons between the two chlorine atoms:

Cl–Cl

When this bond breaks evenly, each fragment has a single atom with an unpaired electron. This is shown as:

• Cl

This is a chlorine free radical. The equation for the reaction between a CFC and ultraviolet light is shown below:

$CClF_3$ + ultraviolet light → $•CF_3$ + $•Cl$

Examiner's tip

Remember that a chlorine radical is just a single atom of chlorine.

Ultraviolet light splits up CFC molecules to form free radicals ▶

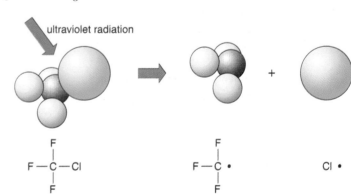

d Suggest why a chlorine free radical is so reactive.

A chlorine free radical will attack an ozone molecule, producing an oxygen molecule and another free radical. That free radical can then take part in more reactions which themselves produce more free radicals. This means that a small number of chlorine free radicals can set up lots of **chain reactions**. So the formation of chlorine atoms in the stratosphere leads to the ozone layer being depleted, which allows more ultraviolet light to reach the Earth's surface. These are the equations for the chain reaction:

$\bullet Cl + O_3 \rightarrow \bullet ClO + O_2$

$O_3 \rightarrow O + O_2$

$\bullet ClO + O \rightarrow \bullet Cl + O_2$

Adding these three equations together gives:

$2O_3 \rightarrow 3O_2$

$\bullet Cl + O_3 \rightarrow \bullet ClO + O_2$

$O_3 \rightarrow O + O_2$

$\bullet ClO + O \rightarrow \bullet Cl + O_2$

▲ A chain reaction initiated by ultraviolet light

▲ Ozone depletion; more intense ultraviolet light ages skin faster

A chain reaction will continue until a free radical meets another free radical and the chain reaction is stopped.

It has been estimated that by 1990 the total world production of CFCs had reached 15 million tonnes. It is also thought that eventually, every single molecule of these chemicals will find its way into the stratosphere. In 1975, scientists discovered the ozone damaging effect of CFCs. This led to a general acceptance that what they originally thought were 'wonder gases' should in fact now be banned altogether and alternatives should be found. Because CFCs are so stable, they are likely to remain in the atmosphere for a very long time. The damage will therefore be repaired only very slowly.

e One of the problems with CFCs is the fact that once released, they stay in the environment for a very long time. Why do you think this is?

Amazing fact

A single chlorine atom can cause the removal of as many as 100 000 molecules of ozone.

Keywords

chain reaction • CFCs • free radical • ozone layer • stratosphere • ultraviolet light

Global agreement!

The discovery of the damaging effects that CFCs have upon the ozone layer led to the signing of the Montreal Protocol in 1987. This became effective in 1989. It provides an international framework for the control of the production and consumption of CFCs.

This quickly led to an agreement among most of the major industrialised nations of the world for the complete phasing out of the production of CFCs in more-economically developed countries, including the UK, by 1996. Less-economically developed countries can continue to produce and purchase CFCs until 2010. It was felt that applying these restrictions to less economically developed countries would put their development at risk, as implementing alternative technology would be expensive.

It was clear that there would still be a need for aerosol sprays and refrigerators so simply banning CFCs was not enough; alternatives to CFCs had to be found.

Suitable alternatives are hydrofluorocarbons (HFCs), hydrochlorofluorocarbons (HCFCs) and alkanes. These molecules have hydrogen in their molecules. This makes them more reactive than CFCs and so alkanes and HFCs can be broken down by natural processes in the lower atmosphere.

Scientists have predicted that the breakdown products of these alternative compounds will not be harmful.

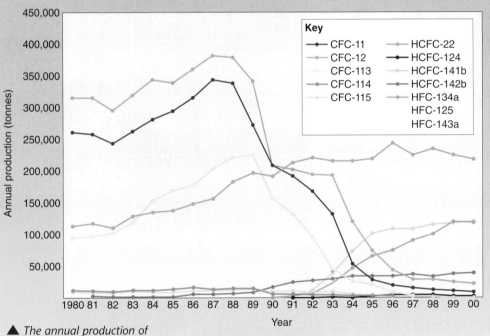

Key

CFC-11	HCFC-22
CFC-12	HCFC-124
CFC-113	HCFC-141b
CFC-114	HCFC-142b
CFC-115	HFC-134a
	HFC-125
	HFC-143a

▲ The annual production of CFCs shows some significant changes in recent years

Questions

1. Look at the graph. How effective has the global agreement been in reducing the world production of CFCs?

2. Why do you think less-economically developed countries have been allowed to continue producing CFCs?

3. What feature of HFC molecules makes them less ozone-depleting than CFCs?

4. What can you say about the annual level of production of HCFCs since 1990?

5. The production of HFCs is not considered a threat to the ozone layer. Why do you think this is?

Water problem?

In this item you will find out

- how rainwater reacts with limestone and chalk

- what hard water contains

- how to remove the hardness from water

Water is vital for life. We often take a clean water supply for granted. One way or another all our water supplies are derived from rainwater. Is rainwater pure?

You may have seen advertisements for products that help washing machines to last longer.

Soaps and detergents help us to use water to wash away dirt and grease from dishes and cutlery, from clothes and from our faces and bodies.

▲ Hard water makes it more difficult to form a lather with soap

▲ Additives can help reduce damage due to limescale formation

In some areas the drinking water supplies contain dissolved minerals that cause **water hardness**. Some of the minerals come from chalk, limestone or marble, which the water may have flowed over or through. Chalk, limestone or marble are insoluble in pure water. However, they will dissolve slowly in rainwater, producing 'hard' water.

Hardness in some water supplies causes problems in the washing process. The dissolved minerals can make it more difficult to produce a lather with soap, and this can lead to an increased consumption of soap. In some parts of the country, hot water pipes and heating elements in kettles and washing machines become clogged up as a result of the deposits of **limescale** that form when the water is heated.

a Why can hardness in water lead to us using more soap?

b How can it cause damage to heating elements in kettles and washing machines?

Amazing fact

10% of electric steam irons sold are returned within a year of being sold. 65% of these are due to problems with limescale.

▲ *Hard water dripping can create impressive formations over thousands of years*

Amazing fact

Approximately 60% of the UK population lives in a hard water area.

soap solution

lather

water sample being tested

▲ *The amount of soap solution required to produce a permanent lather gives a measure of water hardness*

Corrosive rain!

Limestone, marble and chalk are all forms of calcium carbonate. Calcium carbonate is insoluble in pure water. Other salts such as calcium sulfate occur in certain rocks, and these salts can dissolve in water.

Rainwater is not pure since carbon dioxide in the atmosphere dissolves in it to form a weak acid. This is shown in the equation below:

water + carbon dioxide → carbonic acid
$$H_2O + CO_2 → H_2CO_3$$

This explains why ordinary (unpolluted) rainwater has a pH value of 5.6. This weak acid can dissolve the calcium carbonate in rocks to form a soluble calcium hydrogencarbonate salt in water:

calcium carbonate + carbonic acid → calcium hydrogencarbonate
$$CaCO_3 + H_2CO_3 → Ca(HCO_3)_2$$

Over thousands of years this process can erode limestone to form networks of potholes and caves. Stalactites and stalagmites form very slowly when hard water continually drips in the same place and the dissolved calcium carbonate is left behind.

Temporary or permanent?

The calcium hydrogencarbonate can remain in solution in ground water and can get into our domestic water supplies. This salt causes **temporary hardness** in water. The hardness is temporary because when the water is boiled, the calcium hydrogencarbonate reaction shown above is reversed to produce insoluble calcium carbonate, carbon dioxide and water, leaving the water soft. The equation for this reaction is:

calcium hydrogencarbonate + heat →

calcium carbonate + carbon dioxide + water

This is what causes the formation of limescale on heating elements and in hot water pipes.

c What is the chemical name of solid limescale?

d Some people use boiled water to top up a steam iron. Why do you think this is sensible?

Permanent hardness is so called because it is not removed by boiling the water. It is caused by dissolved salts such as calcium sulfate.

Comparing water hardness

You can use the fact that the dissolved salts in hard water react with soap to form an insoluble scum in a simple laboratory experiment to measure the hardness of water. Soap solution is added drop by drop to three samples of water. The number of drops of soap required to produce a permanent lather is counted; the more drops that are needed, the harder the water. This experiment is shown in the diagram.

Some students carried out this experiment. The table shows their results.

Water sample	Number of drops of soap solution required to lather
domestic supply in Hampshire	33
boiled domestic supply in Hampshire	13
rainwater	1
domestic supply in Cornwall	9

e Which of the water supplies listed is the hardest?

f Can you explain the result for rainwater?

Softening water

Both temporary and permanent hardness can be removed by adding a chemical water softener. The cheapest softener is **washing soda** (sodium carbonate). When it is added to water it dissolves and reacts with the calcium ions to form calcium carbonate, which is insoluble and so precipitates out of the water.

This method is only suitable for softening water being used for laundry. Water softened this way cannot be used for drinking.

Swapping ions

It is also possible to remove both temporary and permanent hardness from water supplies by passing the water through an **ion exchange resin**. This type of water softener works by swapping sodium ions attached to the resin with the calcium ions in the hard water. This type of system is used in 'in line' water systems that can be plumbed into domestic water supplies.

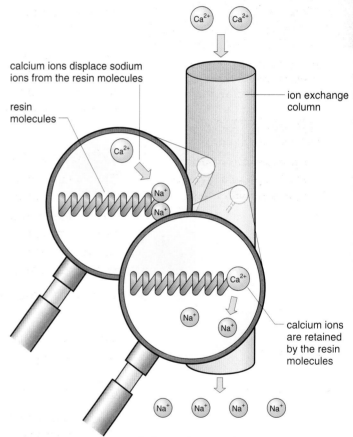

▲ Ion exchange columns can remove hardness from water

Removing limescale

You have seen how limestone will dissolve in a weak acid such as the carbonic acid in rainwater. Since limescale is chemically identical to limestone, it can be removed using a weak acid. A weak acid can be used to remove the build up of limescale in domestic appliances, such as wash basins and baths:

limescale + acid → soluble calcium salt + carbon dioxide + water

$$CaCO_3 + 2HA \rightarrow CaA_2 + CO_2 + H_2O$$

(HA = general formula for an acid)

Keywords

• ion exchange resin • limescale • permanent hardness • temporary hardness • washing soda • water hardness

Which softener?

Colin is a builder. He is working on a development of ten luxury houses in an area that is known to have hard water.

The houses range in size. Colin finds the hardness of water expressed as 'mg per dm^3' and as 'grains per gallon'. He is installing water softeners but is not sure which size of appliance to use.

The table shows how water hardness can be classified.

Classification of water	mg/dm^3	grains/gallon
soft	0–17.1	0–1
slightly hard	?	1–3.5
moderately hard	60–120	3.5–X
hard	120–180	X–10.5
very hard	180 and over	10.5 and over

▲ *Without water softeners pipes fur up in hard water areas*

He also finds the following scribbled advice from a colleague:

Tests show that water in this area has a hardness of 5 grains per gallon.

The size of water softener needed = water hardness × total demand (per week)

The total demand = 80 (average gallons per day per person) × number of people × 7 (days per week)

Colin decides to organise his calculations in a table.

Bedrooms	No. of people	Total demand	Softener needed (grains per week)
2	3	3 x 80 x 7 = 1680	5 x 1680 = 8400
3	4		
4	5		
5	6		

▲ *The capacity of water softeners is expressed in grains*

Questions

1 In the first table some of the data for 'slightly hard water' is missing. What is the range in mg/l for this water?

2 What is 1 grain/gallon equivalent to in mg/dm^3?

3 Use your answer to **2** to calculate the value of X in the first table.

4 How hard is the water in the area where Colin is building his houses?

5 Use the information in the second table to complete the calculations for the 3, 4 and 5 bedroom houses.

Fats – friends or foes?

In this item you will find out

- about the chemical composition of fats and oils

- about unsaturated fats and oils

- how natural oils are used to make soaps

We hear a lot about fat. We are often told we should not eat so much fat. We are sometimes told that we are eating the wrong kind of fat.

The advice is sometimes bewildering and often confusing. You might have wondered about the difference between a fat and an oil, or what is meant by 'high in polyunsaturates'.

All the naturally occurring oils and fats from animals and vegetables are very closely related chemically. They are all esters of a molecule called glycerol.

A fat or oil that contains only single carbon–carbon bonds is called **saturated**. Fats or oils that have at least one double bond between carbon atoms are called **unsaturated**.

When a fat or oil has one double bond between two of its carbon atoms it is known as monounsaturated. When a fat or oil has more than one carbon–carbon double bond, it is described as **polyunsaturated**.

Most animal fats tend to be more saturated than vegetable oils, which are relatively unsaturated.

▲ We consume fats and oils in many different forms

(a) What class of compounds do all fats and oils belong to?

(b) What makes a fat polyunsaturated?

Amazing fact

Health experts recommend we obtain a maximum of 30% of our calories from fat. In the USA the average diet carries 38% of its calories in fats.

▲ Bromine water is decolourised by unsaturated compounds

Healthy fats

A fat or an oil can be tested for unsaturation by the addition of bromine water. The bromine will react with the double bonds in an unsaturated fat or oil, and lose its orange/brown colour.

Saturated fats, such as animal fats and oils, present a health problem because they can contribute to the build up of cholesterol. The build up of this in the body leads to the hardening of arteries and veins, which may lead to heart problems. Reducing the amount of cholesterol and the amount of saturated fats in your diet will reduce your risk of heart disease. Unsaturated fats do not contribute to the build up of cholesterol so they are healthier. Polyunsaturated fats and oils are better for you than monounsaturated ones.

The table below gives the fat content in a typical 100 g measure of a number of foods.

Food	Cholesterol (mg)	Fat and oil content (g)		
		Saturated	Monounsaturated	Polyunsaturated
butter	219	50.5	23.4	3.0
cheese	105	21.1	9.4	0.9
beef	91	2.7	2.7	0.5
margarine	0	13.2	45.8	18.0
safflower oil	0	9.1	12.1	74.5

c Which of the foods listed in the table has the highest cholesterol content?

d Margarine can be made from safflower oil. Compare the data for safflower oil with that for margarine. In what way does the margarine differ from the safflower oil?

e Use the information in the table to suggest why margarine is thought to be better for you than butter.

▼ Adding hydrogen to unsaturated molecules makes them become saturated

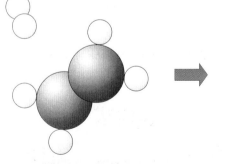
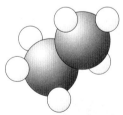

Making margarine

Saturated fats are more likely to be solids at room temperature than unsaturated ones. This fact is exploited by margarine manufacturers. Margarine is made by adding hydrogen to unsaturated oils in the presence of a catalyst. This makes the unsaturated liquid oil become more saturated and more solid. The reaction is called **hydrogenation**.

f Why is it desirable for margarine to be more solid than oil?

Keywords

glycerol • hydrogenation • hydrolysis • immiscible • polyunsaturated • saponification • saturated • soap • unsaturated

Oil and water

The expression 'they're like oil and water' is sometimes used to describe two people who just cannot get on with one another. This is because normally oil and water do not mix. They are **immiscible** liquids.

If you shake oil and water well and tiny droplets of one liquid form, the two liquids have mixed as an emulsion. Milk is an example of oil-in-water emulsion. It is formed when tiny droplets of fat are suspended in water. The oils in ordinary milk do not stay in emulsion. After a while, they separate out as a layer on the surface of the milk. The layer that forms is the 'cream'.

▲ Oil and water do not mix

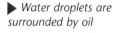 Suggest why skimmed milk is regarded as more healthy than unskimmed.

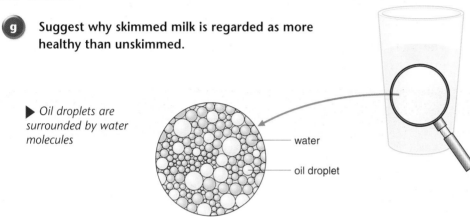

▶ Oil droplets are surrounded by water molecules

water

oil droplet

▲ Milk is an emulsion of tiny droplets of oil in water

Butter is an example of a water-in-oil emulsion. It is formed when tiny droplets of water are suspended in oil.

▶ Water droplets are surrounded by oil

water droplet

oil

Making soaps

Soap can be made commercially by splitting up natural fats and oil with a strong alkali such as sodium hydroxide. A hot sodium hydroxide solution will split up a fat or oil to form soap and glycerol; the process is called **saponification**.

▲ Butter is an emulsion of water in oil

The equation for the reaction is:

fat + sodium hydroxide → soap + glycerol

In this reaction the hydroxide ion is responsible for breaking down the fat or oil. It attacks the ester in a similar way to a water molecule. This process is a **hydrolysis** reaction.

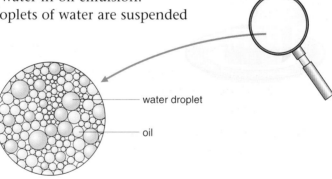

fat or oil molecule

hydroxide ions

fatty acid molecules

glycerol

▲ Sodium hydroxide will break down fats to form soaps

Oil paints

Polyunsaturated oils are much more reactive than saturated ones. This is shown by the addition reaction of these molecules with iodine and bromine. Polyunsaturated fats and oils will also react with oxygen in the atmosphere.

▲ *Oil-based paints often contain oils high in polyunsaturates*

This oxidation reaction is used to good effect in oil-based paints. The oil and pigment are left behind when the solvent has evaporated. The oil then reacts with the oxygen in the air to form a tough web of oil molecules on the surface of the paint.

To find the best oil to use in paints, chemists test different oils to see how unsaturated they are. In the laboratory they carefully measure out equal volumes of each oil. They use burettes to add iodine solution carefully into each sample of oil. The iodine colour disappears as it reacts with the carbon–carbon double bonds. They keep adding iodine solution until there is a permanent colour change. The more carbon–carbon double bonds in the oil, the more iodine the chemist needs to add. The iodine value of the oil is then calculated as the number of grams of iodine that will react with 100 g of the oil. A high iodine number indicates an oil high in polyunsaturates. The chart below gives some results:

Oil type	Fat or oil	Iodine number
animal fats	lard	47–67
fish oils	cod liver oil	135–165
vegetable oils	olive oil	80–88
	linseed oil	180–195
	tung oil	168

Questions

1 When paint is applied to a surface what happens to the solvent in the paint?

2 What reaction then causes a hard layer to form on the surface of the paint?

3 Why do you think the chemists analysing different oil samples use burettes to add iodine solution?

4 How do the chemists ensure that the comparison between the oils is fair?

5 Which two of the oils tested would be the best to use in an oil-based paint?

Easing the pain

In this item you will find out

- about common analgesics currently in use
- how analgesics have developed
- why analgesics can be dangerous

Analgesics are medicines that we often call painkillers. **Aspirin**, **paracetamol** and **ibuprofen** are the three common examples. Like all **drugs**, analgesics are externally administered chemicals that affect or change chemical reactions in your body.

If you have a headache or similar pain you may choose one of the painkillers you can buy from a chemist. In a chemist shop there are many different brands and types of analgesic. There is usually a trained pharmacist available who can give advice about which one is best and any possible side effects.

Analgesics can be taken in different forms. The photograph shows some of these different forms.

a What are the different types shown in the photograph.

b What do you think are the advantages of each type?

Some analgesics, for example aspirin, are used in a soluble form. The photograph shows a **soluble aspirin** dissolving in water.

c Suggest what advantage there is in taking a soluble aspirin rather than an ordinary aspirin tablet.

The chemicals in analgesics are called 'fine chemicals'. They have to be made very pure. Purity is important in drug production to avoid the possible toxic or corrosive side effects that might be caused by impurities from unreacted starting materials .

Making medicines, such as analgesics, is an important part of the chemical industry. These chemicals are called pharmaceuticals.

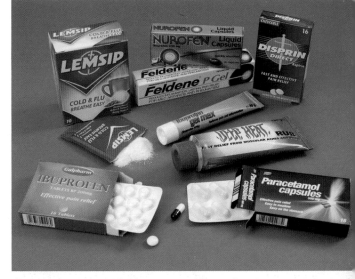
▲ Analgesics are available in many different forms

▲ Some analgesics are made easy to dissolve

Amazing fact

Every year in the UK people take 1 000 000 000 doses of analgesics.

▲ *The displayed formula of aspirin*

▲ *Extract of willow bark relieves pain*

salicylic acid   ethanoic anhydride

H⁺

2-(acetyloxy)benzoic acid   ethanoic acid

▲ *The formation of aspirin*

Aspirin

Aspirin was the first painkilling drug to be developed. Having discovered that **salicylic acid** was the chemical in willow trees that relieved pain, scientists set about producing a form of this chemical that could be used safely. Salicylic acid causes severe irritation of the mouth and stomach. A solution of salicylic acid has a pH value of approximately 3.

Aspirin is acetylsalicylic acid. The diagram shows the displayed formula of aspirin.

d Write down the names of the three chemical elements combined in aspirin.

e Count up the atoms to work out the molecular formula of aspirin.

Aspirin is manufactured by reacting ethanoic anhydride (acetic anhydride) dissolved in methylbenzene with salicylic acid. The mixture is heated to 90 °C for 20 hours. The mixture is then left to cool to room temperature and the aspirin crystallises out. The displayed formulae alongside summarises this reaction.

f Why is it necessary to purify the aspirin before it is used?

g A typical reactor vessel produces 180 kg of aspirin. How many tablets can be made from this? (1 tablet contains 300 mg of aspirin.)

Problems with aspirin

Aspirin reduces the tendency for the blood to clot. Although this can be beneficial to heart and stroke patients, an overdose can cause stomach ulcers and internal bleeding.

Aspirin should not be given to children under 16. This is because it can lead to Reye's syndrome, which is a disease that affects all organs especially the liver and the brain, and can be fatal. The normal dose of aspirin for adults is 1–3 tablets (each 300 mg of aspirin). It can be taken every 4 hours. The maximum dose of aspirin is 12 tablets per day.

h How many grams is the maximum daily dose of aspirin for an adult?

Why take aspirin?

Apart from its use as a painkiller, there are other reasons to take small doses of aspirin.

- It lowers the body temperature quickly if you have a fever.
- It thins the blood, which reduces the risk of blood clots and heart attacks.
- It has an anti-inflammatory action (it reduces inflammation).
- It protects against bowel cancer.
- It slows down senile dementia (the early loss of some brain function in older age).

Amazing fact

Americans consume over 50 million aspirin tablets every day. That is over 15 billion a year.

Soluble aspirin

In normal aspirin all of the bonds are covalent bonds. Compounds containing covalent bonds are usually insoluble or slightly soluble in water. For aspirin to work, it must dissolve in the stomach before it can get into the bloodstream.

To make aspirin work more quickly, scientists modified aspirin by reacting it with a measured quantity of sodium hydroxide to create soluble aspirin. This produces the sodium salt. This is soluble because it contains ions. The displayed formula of soluble aspirin is shown in the diagram. Soluble aspirin works faster as it dissolves very rapidly and can enter the bloodstream much more quickly than the non-soluble type.

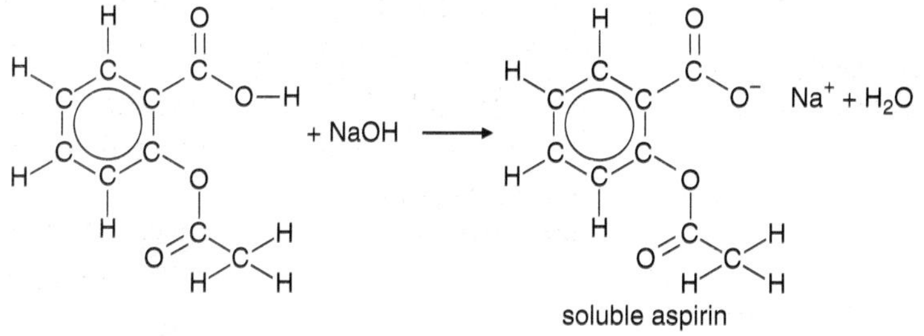

▲ *The displayed formula for soluble aspirin*

Paracetamol

Paracetamol does not have the irritant action of aspirin on the stomach. It has become one of the most commonly used analgesics in the UK. It reduces fever, but does not have the anti-inflammatory action of aspirin. It can be taken in small doses by children. It does, however, have one problem. Any overdose of paracetamol is likely to seriously damage the liver and may be fatal.

The displayed formula of paracetamol is shown in the diagram.

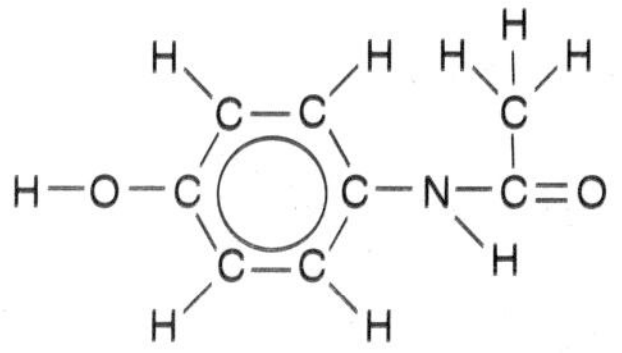

i What is the molecular formula of paracetamol?

j Identify one similarity and one difference between the displayed formulae of aspirin and paracetamol.

▲ *Displayed formula for paracetamol*

Ibuprofen

One of the most popular painkillers today is ibuprofen. Like aspirin, it is also an anti-inflammatory drug. One of the possible side effects of ibuprofen is an irritation of the gut. As with all drugs, it must be taken with care and according to the guidelines provided. The graphical formula of ibuprofen is shown in the diagram.

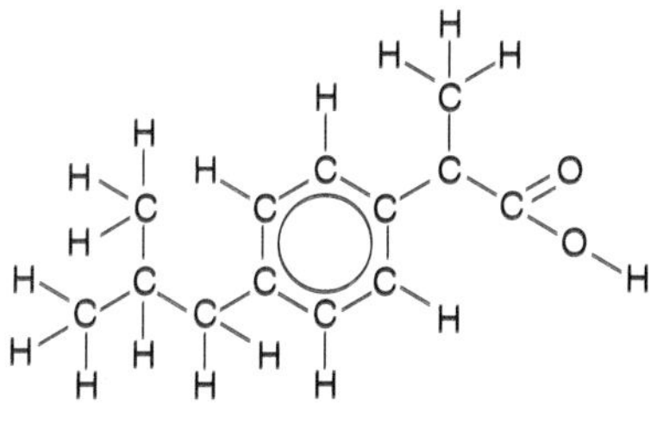

k What is the molecular formula of ibuprofen?

l Identify one similarity and one difference between the displayed formulae of aspirin and ibuprofen.

▲ *The graphical formula of ibuprofen*

Keywords

analgesic • aspirin • drug • ibuprofen • paracetamol • salicylic acid • soluble aspirin

▲ *Aspirin under the microscope*

Questions

1 What is the name of the pain relieving substance found in willow?

2 Salicylic acid was extracted from willow but had a serious drawback. What was it?

3 An extract of the wintergreen plant relieves muscle ache. What is the active ingredient?

4 What chemical change needs to be made to salicylic acid to make aspirin?

5 What advantages does aspirin have over salicylic acid?

6 What advantages does paracetamol have over aspirin?

History of analgesics

The timeline shows the history of painkillers.

c400 BC Hippocrates gives women willow leaf tea to relieve pain during childbirth.

1763 Reverend Edward Stone gives dried willow bark to people who are very ill to reduce pain. He reports his findings to the Royal Society of London. The active ingredient in willow is extracted in Italy. This is called salicin. Salicylic acid is extracted from salicin but causes great irritation to mouth and stomach.

1843 Two chemists show that methyl salicylate, extracted from the wintergreen plant, relieves muscle ache.

1853 Charles Gerhardt replaces the hydroxide group of salicylic acid to produce aspirin. This is effective at relieving pain. He does not continue because the process is too difficult.

1893 Paracetamol is discovered by accident. It does not have the side effects of aspirin.

1897 Felix Hoffman, in Germany, makes aspirin. Aspirin does not irritate the stomach as much as salicylic acid. Bayer patents the drug.

1900 Bayer produces water-soluble aspirin tablets.

1930 The patent on the drug runs out so other companies can make it.

1956 Paracetamol available on prescription.

1963 Paracetamol available without a prescription.

1969 Ibuprofen introduced as a painkilling drug after 15 years of development.

1974 Professor Elword reports that aspirin can prevent heart attacks.

1982 John Vane is awarded the Nobel Prize for Medicine for finding out how aspirin relieves pain.

1989 American scientists find that aspirin can delay senile dementia.

1995 American scientists find that aspirin can delay bowel cancer.

1999 A special award is made by the American Museum of American History in honour of the wonder drug aspirin.

C6a

1 Use words from the list to complete the following:

squeaky pop   energy   water   non-polluting

When hydrogen is burned in air a lot of ____(1)____ is released. If a hydrogen/air mixture in a test tube is ignited it can burn with a ____(2)____. The reaction is ____(3)____ as the only product is____(4)____.   [4]

2 Write a balanced symbol equation for the reaction of hydrogen with oxygen.   [2]

3 The energy change for the reaction of hydrogen with oxygen is −285 kJ/mol.

Sketch an energy level diagram to represent this information.   [3]

4 The reaction between hydrogen and oxygen can be performed in a fuel cell where a different reaction takes place at each electrode. Give the equation for the reaction at:

   a   the hydrogen electrode   [2]
   b   the oxygen electrode.   [2]

5 Explain why the reaction in **4** is regarded as an example of a redox reaction.   [3]

6 List three of the advantages that Fuel Cells powered by hydrogen have over conventional fuels.   [3]

C6b

1 Calcium metal burns brightly in oxygen gas. Give a word equation for the reaction.   [2]

2 What reactants are necessary for the formation of rust?   [2]

3 When a sample of reactive metal is put into a solution of a compound of a metal of lower reactivity, the metal of lower reactivity is displaced from the solution. Complete the three word equations below:

   a   zinc + copper sulfate → ____ + ____   [2]
   b   iron + silver nitrate → ____ + ____   [2]
   c   ____ + ____ → zinc nitrate + silver   [2]

4 Explain why the reactions in **3** are regarded as redox reactions.   [2]

5 Write symbol equations for each of the following reactions:

   a   magnesium + lead nitrate solution   [1]
   b   iron + copper sulfate solution   [1]
   c   zinc + silver nitrate solution.   [1]

6 In each of the redox reactions in **5** one of the substances is oxidised, the other is reduced. For each reaction state which substance is oxidised and which is reduced.   [3]

7 One method of rust prevention involves attaching a lump of reactive metal to the iron object to be protected.

   a   Which metals are commonly used for this purpose?   [1]

   b   Why is this method of protecting iron called 'sacrificial' protection?   [1]

   c   Why does galvanising give iron better rust protection than ordinary painting?   [1]

C6c

1 Use words from the list to complete the following:

optimum   fermentation   enzymes

A sample of ethanol can be made by the ____(1)____ of a sample of glucose in water. Yeast is added to the mixture because it contains the ____(2)____ necessary for the reaction. Care is taken to exclude air from the apparatus as this reaction only happens under these conditions. The rate of reaction is maximised by ensuring that the enzymes are at their ____(3)____ temperature.   [3]

2 Write a word equation to represent the reaction in **1**. [2]

3 How would you obtain a fairly pure sample of ethanol from the reaction mixture produced in **1**?   [1]

4 Ethanol can be dehydrated to produce ethene.

   a   Write a word equation for this reaction.   [2]
   b   The reverse reaction is used where water is added to ethene to produce ethanol. Write a word equation for this reaction.   [2]

5 Draw the displayed formula for ethanol.   [2]

6 What is the general formula for an alcohol with 'n' carbon atoms?   [2]

7 Draw the displayed formula for pentanol.   [2]

8 Which of the two methods – fermentation followed by distillation or hydration of ethene – will produce a purer sample of ethanol? Explain your answer.   [3]

9 It is claimed that ethanol made by fermentation is a much 'greener' fuel for cars than petrol.

   a   Explain why this is so.   [2]

   b   Explain why ethanol is not more widely used as a fuel for cars.   [2]

C6d

1 When a concentrated solution of sodium chloride in water is electrolysed using inert electrodes what gas is produced:

a at the positive electrode (anode)? [1]
b at the negative electrode (cathode)? [1]

2 Two of the products from the reaction in **1** can be combined to produce the chemical that often makes up household bleach. Which two substances combine to make bleach? [2]

3 The salt solution for the reaction in **1** can be obtained by a process called 'solution mining'. Explain how this works and the problems it has caused in the past. [3]

4 Give a symbol equation for the processes in **1**:

a at the anode [2]
b at the cathode. [2]

5 If molten sodium chloride is used for electrolysis what is produced:

a at the anode? [1]
b at the cathode? [1]

6 The products of the electrolysis of brine are the two gases hydrogen and chlorine.

a Give one major industrial use for the hydrogen produced in this way. [1]
b Chlorine is used to make bleach. What other products is it used for? [2]

C6e

1 What is the chemical name for CFCs? [1]

2 The action of ultraviolet radiation on CFCs in the stratosphere causes problems.

a What particles are produced from the CFCs? [1]
b What effect do these particles have upon the ozone layer? [1]
c Why is this a problem for life on the surface of the planet? [2]

3 Why do CFCs stay in the environment for so long? [2]

4 Why did people start using CFCs in the 1930s? [2]

5 Just one molecule of a CFC affects many molecules in the ozone layer.

a What sort of reaction is set up? [1]
b How is the reaction initiated? [1]
c Give equations to describe this reaction. [2]

6 Why, despite the banning of CFCs, will it take so long for the ozone layer to recover? [2]

C6f

1 Use words from the list to complete the passage below:

**temporary   sulfate   calciumhydrogencarbonate
acidic   calcium carbonate**

Rainwater is naturally ____(1)____ due to dissolved carbon dioxide. When rain falls on rocks containing chalk or limestone the ____(2)____ in these rocks reacts to form a solution of ____(3)____. It is this substance which is responsible for the ____(4)____ hardness in domestic water supplies in some parts of the UK. Permanent hardness is the result of dissolved calcium and magnesium ____(5)____ . [5]

2 Write a word equation to show the reaction between limestone (calcium carbonate), carbon dioxide and water. [2]

3 Temporary hardness is removed by boiling.

a Explain why. [1]
b Give a word equation to show this change. [2]

4 What sort of substances can be used as limescale removers? [2]

5 The action of water and carbon dioxide on the calcium carbonate in limestone produces a solution of calcium hydrogen carbonate. This reaction can be reversed by boiling the solution. Write balanced symbol equations to represent these changes. [3]

6 Ion exchange columns can be used to soften the water supply for many homes.

a Which ions need to be removed by the ion exchange column in order to soften the water? [2]
b What are these ions 'exchanged' with? [1]

7 The hardness in water can be removed by the addition of a chemical water softener such as sodium carbonate.

a How does adding sodium carbonate remove the hardness from water? [2]
b What is the disadvantage of water which has been softened in this way? [1]

C6g

1 Explain the following terms to do with fats and oils:

   a unsaturated [1]
   b saturated [1]
   c emulsion. [1]

2 Use words from the list to complete the following passage:

margarine polyunsaturates hydrogen solid

Many vegetable oils are high in ____(1)____ this means that they are liquid. If these oils are reacted with ____(2)____ they react and become more ____(3)____ and can be used as ____(4)____ for cooking and spreading. [4]

3 Soaps can be made by heating fats or oils with sodium hydroxide solution.

   a What happens to the fat or oil molecule in this reaction? [1]
   b One of the products is a soap. What is the other product in this reaction? [1]
   c What name is given to this reaction? [1]

4 Give a word equation for the reaction in **3**. [2]

5 This question is about testing for unsaturation.

   a What solution can be used to test for unsaturation in a fat or oil? [1]
   b What result does an unsaturated fat or oil give with this solution? [2]
   c Explain which part of the unsaturated molecule takes part in this reaction. [1]

6 Use words form the list to complete the following passage:

**Soap fatty acid hydrolysis reaction
saponification sodium hydroxide**

Hot _____ solution will react with an oil or fat to form _____. In this reaction the hydroxide ions attack the fat or oil molecules and break them down to form smaller _____ molecules. This is a special case of a _____ and is known as____. [5]

C6h

1 **a** What is an analgesic? [1]
   b Give the names of three common analgesics. [2]

2 The displayed formula of paracetamol is shown below.

   a What elements are present in paracetamol? [1]
   b Give the molecular formula of paracetamol. [2]
   c Why should you be careful not to exceed the recommended dose for paracetamol? [1]

3 Aspirin is often described as a 'wonder drug'.

   a List the beneficial effects of aspirin. [2]
   b What are the drawbacks with using aspirin? [1]
   c Why should children not take aspirin? [2]

4 This question is about soluble aspirin. The displayed formula is given below.

soluble aspirin

   a What is the molecular formula for this substance? [2]
   b What makes this form of aspirin soluble in water? [1]
   c How is ordinary aspirin made into soluble aspirin? [2]

5 This question is about a comparison between aspirin and ibuprofen.

Aspirin   Ibuprofen

   a Which elements are present in both compounds? [2]
   b What elements make up the hexagonal ring in both compounds? [2]

6 Use words form the list to complete the following passage:

**ethanoic anhydride analgesic
ethanoic acid cooling heating**

Although it was invented over 100 years ago, aspirin is still a very popular ____(1)____. It is made by ____(2)____salycilic acid with ____(3)____. The products of this reaction are aspirin and ____(4)____. The product is obtained from the mixture by____(5)____ so that the dissolved aspirin crystallises out. [5]

Useful data

Physical quantities and units

Physical quantity	Unit(s)
length	metre (m); kilometre (km); centimetre (cm); millimetre (mm)
mass	kilogram (kg); gram (g); milligram (mg); migrogram (µg)
time	second (s); millisecond (ms)
temperature	degrees Celsius (°C); kelvin (K)
current	ampere (A); milliampere (mA)
voltage	volt (V); millivolt (mV)
area	cm^2; m^2
volume	cm^3; dm^3; m^3; litre (l); millilitre (ml)
density	kg/m^3; g/cm^3
force	newton (N)
speed	m/s; km/h
energy	joule (J); kilojoule (kJ); megajoule (MJ)
power	watt (W); kilowatt (kW); megawatt (MW)
frequency	hertz (Hz); kilohertz (kHz)
gravitational field strength	N/kg
radioactivity	becquerel (Bq)
acceleration	m/s^2; km/h^2

Electrical symbols

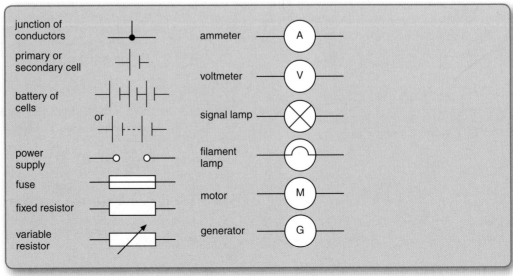

junction of conductors

primary or secondary cell

battery of cells

power supply

fuse

fixed resistor

variable resistor

ammeter

voltmeter

signal lamp

filament lamp

motor

generator

Periodic Table

Key

relative atomic mass
atomic symbol
name
atomic (proton) number

1	2												3	4	5	6	7	8
							1 **H** hydrogen 1											4 **He** helium 2
7 **Li** lithium 3	9 **Be** beryllium 4												11 **B** boron 5	12 **C** carbon 6	14 **N** nitrogen 7	16 **O** oxygen 8	19 **F** fluorine 9	20 **Ne** neon 10
23 **Na** sodium 11	24 **Mg** magnesium 12												27 **Al** aluminium 13	28 **Si** silicon 14	31 **P** phosphorous 15	32 **S** sulfur 16	35.5 **Cl** chlorine 17	40 **Ar** argon 18
39 **K** potassium 19	40 **Ca** calcium 20	45 **Sc** scandium 21	48 **Ti** titanium 22	51 **V** vanadium 23	52 **Cr** chromium 24	55 **Mn** manganese 25	56 **Fe** iron 26	59 **Co** cobalt 27	59 **Ni** nickel 28	64 **Cu** copper 29	65 **Zn** zinc 30	70 **Ga** gallium 31	73 **Ge** germanium 32	75 **As** arsenic 33	79 **Se** selenium 34	80 **Br** bromine 35	84 **Kr** krypton 36
85 **Rb** rubidium 37	88 **Sr** strontium 38	89 **Y** yttrium 39	91 **Zr** zirconium 40	93 **Nb** niobium 41	96 **Mo** molybdenum 42	[98] **Tc** technetium 43	101 **Ru** ruthenium 44	103 **Rh** rhodium 45	106 **Pd** palladium 46	108 **Ag** silver 47	112 **Cd** cadmium 48	115 **In** indium 49	119 **Sn** tin 50	122 **Sb** antimony 51	128 **Te** tellurium 52	127 **I** iodine 53	131 **Xe** xenon 54
133 **Cs** caesium 55	137 **Ba** barium 56	139 **La*** lanthanum 57	178 **Hf** hafnium 72	181 **Ta** tantalum 73	184 **W** tungsten 74	186 **Re** rhenium 75	190 **Os** osmium 76	192 **Ir** iridium 77	195 **Pt** platinum 78	197 **Au** gold 79	201 **Hg** mercury 80	204 **Tl** thallium 81	207 **Pb** lead 82	209 **Bi** bismuth 83	[209] **Po** polonium 84	[210] **At** astatine 85	[222] **Rn** radon 86
[223] **Fr** francium 87	[226] **Ra** radium 88	[227] **Ac*** actinium 89	[261] **Rf** rutherfordium 104	[262] **Db** dubnium 105	[266] **Sg** seaborgium 106	[264] **Bh** bohrium 107	[267] **Hs** hassium 108	[268] **mt** meitnerium 109	[271] **Ds** darmstadtium 110	[272] **Rg** roentgenium 111							

Elements with atomic numbers 112–116 have been reported but not fully authenticated

* The lanthanoids (atomic numbers 58–71) and the actinoids (atomic numbers 90–103) have been omitted.

Introduction to skills assessment

Work carried out by you outside an examination (called 'Skills assessment') is an important aspect of GCSE Chemistry. This will include practical work, research and report writing – all things a real chemist has to do.

For GCSE Chemistry you have a choice of the items that you submit for assessment.

1 The 'Skills assessment' that is used for Core Science:
Can-do tasks
Science in the news

2 The 'Skills assessment' that is used for Additional Science:
Research Task
Data Task
Assessment of your practical skills

Either route is worth one third of the marks available for GCSE Chemistry. So this practical assessment is very important.

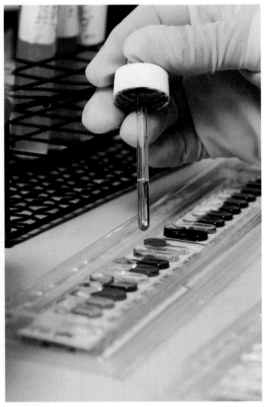

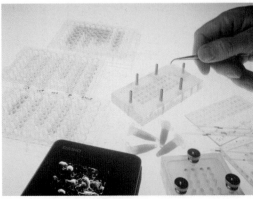

Can-do tasks

Chemistry is a practical subject and you deserve credit for being able to do practical things. 'Can-do tasks' are an opportunity for you to demonstrate some of your practical and ICT skills throughout the course.

There are 46 of these tasks throughout your GCSE Chemistry course. Some are practical and some require the use of ICT.

You can only count a maximum of eight of these tasks and these tasks are set at three levels:

Basic (worth 1 mark): These are simple tasks that you can usually complete quickly. You may have done many of these before you started the course.

Intermediate (worth 2 marks): These are slightly harder tasks that might take a little longer to do.

Advanced (worth 3 marks): These are even more difficult tasks that may take you some time to do.

A complete list of Chemistry 'Can-do tasks' is shown below.

Basic: 1 mark 'Can-do tasks'		
1 C1a	I can heat a solid substance safely.	**11** C2h I can measure the volume of a liquid using a measuring cylinder.
2 C1a	I can test for carbon dioxide.	**12** C5a I can measure the mass of a sample to the required level of precision.
3 C1c	I can test whether a substance dissolves in a solvent.	**13** C5b I can measure changes in electrode mass.
4 C1h	I can accurately measure the temperature in °C.	**14** C5c I can measure amounts of liquid to the nearest division on a measuring cylinder.
5 C1h	I can measure the mass of an object using an electronic balance.	**15** C5d I can read a burette to the nearest scale division.
6 C2b	I can safely heat a sample of a chemical in a test tube.	**16** C5e I can measure the amount of gas produced in a reaction.
7 C2c	I can mark on a map of the world ten locations of earthquakes or volcanoes.	**17** C5h I can carry out a simple precipitation reaction.
8 C2e	I can distinguish, using experiments, between a sample of aluminium and iron.	**18** C6a I can identify samples of hydrogen and oxygen.
9 C2h	I can measure the volume of a gas produced in a reaction using a gas syringe.	**19** C6d I can test for chlorine gas with damp blue litmus paper.
10 C2h	I can measure the reaction time for a suitable reaction.	**20** C6g I can test a compound for unsaturation.

Intermediate: 2 marks 'Can-do tasks'

21 C1e   I can test for unsaturation.

22 C2a   I can make a sample of paint with thermochromic properties.

23 C2d   I can extract a sample of copper from a copper ore such as malachite.

24 C2d   I can purify a sample of impure copper using the electrolysis of aqueous copper sulfate.

25 C5a   I can investigate the mass changes during a thermal decomposition reaction.

26 C5b   I can set up a simple electrolysis circuit.

27 C5c   I can dilute a solution by a specified amount.

28 C5d   I can accurately deliver a known amount of liquid using a pipette.

29 C5h   I can prepare a dry sample of an insoluble salt by precipitation.

30 C6a   I can collect a sample of gas.

31 C6g   I can prepare a sample of a cold cream (emulsion).

Advanced: 3 marks 'Can-do tasks'

32 C1g   I can carry out an experiment to show that combustion of a hydrocarbon in a plentiful supply of air produces carbon dioxide and water.

33 C1h   I can do an experiment to find the energy output per gram of a liquid fuel.

34 C2a   I can use a natural product to permanently dye a piece of cotton.

35 C2b   I can make and test samples of concrete for their strength.

36 C2e   I can carry out an investigation to find the optimum conditions for corrosion of a named metal.

37 C2g   I can measure the rate of a reaction that produces a gas.

38 C2h   I can investigate a reaction to find a suitable catalyst.

39 C2h   I can use experimental results such as volume of gas produced against time to determine the rate of reaction.

40 C5b   I can set up an electrolysis experiment, controlling both current and time.

41 C5d   I can carry out a simple titration and get two consistent results within +/– $0.2\,cm^3$.

42 C5e   I can set up and perform an experiment to measure the amount of gas produced in a reaction.

43 C5h   I can identify an unknown ion by using a precipitation reaction and explain it using an ionic equation.

44 C6a   I can make a simple fuel cell (Nuffield sample scheme).

45 C6f   I can compare the hardness of two different water samples using soap solution.

Some of the 'Can-do tasks' produce a product, for example, producing a sample of fertiliser. This can be very useful as evidence that you have successfully completed a task.

Your teacher has to see that you have completed a task and record this on a record sheet. Remember, only the best eight can count so the maximum is $8 \times 3 = 24$.

Your teacher may give you a list of all the 'Can-do tasks' at the start of the course. You can then tell him or her when you think you have successfully completed one of them. They can then give you credit for this.

Remember, it does not matter if you fail to do a task or if you are absent. There will be many more chances throughout the course.

Finally, just how important is a 'Can-do task'? Every time you complete an advanced task it is worth more to your final result than scoring 4 marks on a written paper.

Good luck!

Science in the news

Do you read a newspaper or listen to radio or television news programmes? Do you believe everything you read or hear?

In February 2005, the news was dominated by the discovery that Sudan 1 contaminated many foods we commonly eat. Immediately, 350 products, including crisps, prepared meals, Worcester sauce, etc., were removed from sale and people were urged to return products that they had previously bought. Then a larger number of products were removed from sale.

The newspapers said things like:

> **Dr John Bell, chief executive of the Food Standards Agency** said *"Sudan 1 could contribute to an increased risk of cancer."*

A statement like this can be worrying, but just think for a moment.

If the risk was 1 in 10 000 and it doubled to 2 in 10 000 it would still be insignificant. However, if it was 1 in 4 and it doubled, then it would be 1 in 2 and that would be significant.

Newspapers then did not go on to report what Dr John Bell said next:

As part of your GCSE Chemistry, you need to do at least one 'Science in the news task'.

The task will be in the form of a question, for example:

'Should artificial food colourings be added to foods?'

With the question you will be given some 'stimulus' material to help you and approximately one week to do some research.

> *"However, at the levels present the risk is likely to be very small, but it is sensible to avoid eating any more. There is no risk of immediate ill health."*

What should you do with the stimulus material?

Read it through carefully and identify any scientific words you do not understand. Look up the meaning of these words. The glossary in this book might be a starting point. Then go through with a highlighter pen and highlight those parts of the stimulus material you might want to use to answer the question.

What research should you do?

You should be looking for at least two or three sources of information. These could be from books, magazines, the Internet or CD-ROMs. You could also use surveys or experiments.

You will need to include with your report a list of sources that are detailed enough so that somebody could check them. Some of your sources could look like this:

1   http://www.henryspink.org/feingold_food_programme.htm

2   Heinemann, *Gateway Science OCR Chemistry for GCSE*, pages 13–14

3   *Daily Telegraph*, 22 February 2005, page 2.

You can take this research material with you when you have to write your report about one week later. Do not print out vast amounts of irrelevant material from the Internet because you will not be able to find what you want when you write your report. Your teacher will probably collect in your research material to help them to assess your report but they will not actually mark it.

If you choose to do no research it does not stop you writing a report but you will get a lower mark.

Writing your report

You will have to write your report in a lesson supervised by the teacher. It has to be your own work. There is no time limit but if you need longer than the lesson allowed, all work must be collected in and stored securely until the next time.

Your report should be between 400 and 800 words. As you write your report you need to refer to the information you have collected. It is fine to copy a short section from a source providing it is relevant and you have given credit for the source. For example:

Dr Ben Feingold found that 50% of hyperactive children reacted to food additives. In 1973, at a meeting of the American Medical Association, he explained that excluding chemical food additives, e.g. food colourings, flavourings and preservatives from the diet of hyperactive children not only improved their health but also their hyperactive behaviour.

(http://www.henryspink.org/feingold_food_programme.htm)

You should be critical of the sources. You will soon find that everything you read in newspapers is not necessarily true. Make sure you answer the question. When you finish, read your report through carefully. Your teacher may give you details of the criteria they are using to mark your report.

Marking your report

Your teacher will mark your report against simple criteria and look for six skills, each marked out of a maximum of six. This makes a total of 36. Your teacher will explain these criteria to you.

This report is worth about 20% of the total marks. Hopefully, writing this report will make you more aware of science in our everyday lives.

Research study

The 'Research study' for GCSE Chemistry is similar to a 'Science in the news' study you may have already tried.

The 'Research study' for GCSE Chemistry involves looking at a scientific issue. You will concentrate on the work of scientists. They may be scientists working today or they may be scientists who worked in the past.

Your teacher will have a bank of tasks they can choose from. You only have to do one. If you do more than one the best mark will count.

Stimulus material

At the start of your 'Research study' you will be given some stimulus material. You should read this carefully. There are five questions that you will need to answer.

You will then be directed to do some research to extend the information you have. This research can be from books, CD-ROMs, the Internet, etc. You should carefully reference where the information has come from. Your references can look like this:

1) HYPERLINK "http://www.webelements.com/webelements/scholar/index.html" www.webelements.com

2) Heinemann, *Gateway Science OCR Chemistry for GCSE*, pages 75–77

3) Multimedia Science School 11–16 Alkali metals

Answering questions

In a later lesson, under the supervision of your teacher, you will have to write a report answering the five questions you were given. You can take in any notes you made during your research. The questions must, however, be answered in the lesson. Your notes may be collected by your teacher but they will not be marked. You should not answer the questions in advance.

The questions you are asked are graded in difficulty. The first one or two questions are straightforward and use the information you were given at the start. They are intended for candidates who will get a grade E–G. The last one or two questions will be much harder and often there are alternative acceptable answers. These questions are intended for candidates who will get A*–B overall.

The report you write to answer these questions should be between 400 and 800 words. Many of the best reports that are produced are brief, but they answer the questions clearly without including unnecessary material.

Your teacher will mark your report. A sample of these will be checked later by a moderator from OCR to make sure the marking is fair. Your teacher will mark your report against four criteria on a scale of 0–6. The total mark is 24.

The table summarises these criteria.

Criteria	Advice to you
The evidence you have collected	You should try to collect evidence from at least two sources
How you have used the evidence to answer the questions	You should show how you have used the evidence to answer the questions
How the evidence helps you to understand scientific ideas	You should show how the evidence helps to explain scientific ideas, e.g. how ideas have developed over time; how they are linked with social, economic and environmental issues
The quality of your report	You should be careful with your spelling, punctuation and grammar. Try to use correct scientific words

Your teacher may give you a set of 'student speak' criteria to help you.

Scientific ideas and how they develop

Throughout the work you are doing you should be aware of how scientific ideas develop over time. You will find examples in this book.

Where do you go from here?

Hopefully, having completed your course in GCSE Chemistry, you might want to study Chemistry further in the sixth form. It is important that you realise how scientific ideas have changed over time. It may well be that some of the ideas you have learned today may change as you study science in the future.

Chemistry is not a set of known facts that must be learned and passed on to future generations. Chemistry is a living subject that is likely to change as we find out more. Scientists have a responsibility to use this information for the good of everybody.

Good luck with your 'Research study'!

Data task

What is a 'Data task'?

During your GCSE Chemistry course you will probably do a task that involves analysing and evaluating some real data from an experiment. This is called a 'Data task'. You will also then do some planning of a further experiment.

Your teacher will have a number of 'Data tasks' they can give to you to do. You only need to do one. If you do more than one, your best mark will count.

An example of a *'Data task' is: 'How does the rate of electrolysis of dilute sulfuric acid change as the concentration of sulfuric acid increases?'* This links with the science in C3f Electrolysis.

Carrying out the task

You will be given some instructions to follow to do a simple experiment. You can do this individually or as part or a group. Alternatively, you can watch your teacher do a demonstration, or get some data from a computer simulation. You will need to collect some results and record these in a table.

There are no marks for collecting the results, but later on you are going to suggest improvements to the experiment. You cannot really do this unless you understand what was done in the first place.

Your results should be collected in by your teacher to keep them for the next lesson. If you didn't get any results, your teacher can give you a set. In the next lesson, your teacher will give you back your results and sheet of questions.

You can write your answers in the spaces given on the sheet teacher or you can write your answers on lined paper.

Writing up

This has to be done in a lesson supervised by your teacher. The question sheet will usually ask you to do the following:

1   Average your results.

2   Draw a graph to display your results. Remember your graph should fill at least half the grid. Make sure you choose a suitable scale for each axis and label each axis clearly.

3   Look for any patterns in your results.

4   Make some comments about the accuracy and reliability of your results. Look back at the table. Are the results the most accurate results you could get with the apparatus you have used?

For example, If you are using a hand-held stop watch it might show the time to the nearest one hundredth of a second, e.g. 10.17 s. But you would be better recording this as 10.2 s because you cannot use it more accurately. There is a delay when you turn the stopwatch on and off and this makes a reading to better than 0.1 s wrong. So times can be given accurately to 0.01 s.

If you are using a burette to the nearest $1\,cm^3$, you are not using it to the maximum accuracy. You should be able to read to the nearest $0.1\,cm^3$. If you have three very similar results, e.g. 32.5, 32.4 and 32.5, this indicates that your results are reliable.

Also, if you look at the graph you have drawn, are all the points you have plotted either on or close to the line or curve? Again, this suggests reliability. Any points that are away from the graph are called anomalous results. You should be able to identify anomalous results. You should show these clearly on the graph or in your writing. Remember that if the results you collected are, for example, 32, 33 and 154. 154 is an anomalous result and you should not include it. Instead you should ignore the 154 and average 32 and 33.

You may be given the opportunity to suggest what you could do to improve the experiment or get better results. This is called evaluation. Comments like 'take more readings' or 'do the experiment more carefully' are not worth credit, unless you qualify them.

5 At this stage, you should try to use some science to explain the pattern in the results you have found.

6 Finally, you will be asked to do some planning for a further experiment. This may be either to improve the experiment you have done or to extend the experiment to investigate another variable.

Marking your work

Your teacher will mark your Data task against a set of criteria. He or she may give you a set of 'student speak' criteria. There are five things to be assessed by your teacher on a scale of 0–6. This makes the total for the Data task a mark out of 30. This represents nearly 17% of the marks for the GCSE Chemistry award.

The criteria are shown in the table below.

Criteria	Advice to you
Interpret the data	Can you draw a bar chart or a line graph to display your results?
Analyse the data	Can you see a pattern? This should be expressed as: As _____ increases, _____ increase. You might then be able to go further and explain the relationship.
Evaluate the data	Can you comment on the quality of the data and suggest any limitations of the method used?
Justify your conclusions	Can you link your conclusions with science and understanding?
Ideas for further work	Can you give a plan which is detailed enough for another person to follow it up?

Good luck with your Data task!

Assessment of your practical skills

During your GCSE Chemistry course your teacher will have to make an overall assessment of your practical work. This is not based on any one practical activity, but is a general view of your practical work throughout the course.

There are two things your teacher will to looking for:

- How safely and accurately you carry out practical activities in science.
- How you collect data from an experiment, either individually or in a group with others.

Teachers are asked to use a scale of 0–6 and are given some help to do this.

They are told what is required for 2, 4 and 6 marks. They can give 1, 3 or 5 on their own judgements. If you have done no worthwhile practical work you may get 0.

The table summarises what is required for 2, 4 and 6 marks.

Number of marks	What is required?
2	You carry out practical work safely and accurately, but you need a lot of help doing the work.
4	You carry out practical work safely and accurately, but you need some help doing the work.
6	You carry out practical work safely and accurately, and you do not need any help doing the work. You are aware of possible risks and take this into account.

This assessment is worth about 3.3% of the marks available for GCSE Chemistry.

Don't worry about asking for help. The most important thing is you are able to complete the activity safely.

Enjoy the practical work in chemistry. If you go on to study Chemistry at AS and A2, the skills you have developed at GCSE will be very useful.

Good luck!

Glossary

acid rain rain with a pH below about 6 formed when pollutants such as sulfur dioxide and nitrogen oxides dissolve

actual yield the amount of product obtained in a chemical reaction

addition polymerisation polymerisation where monomers join together to form a polymer without any loss of atoms

alcohol a class of organic compounds whose molecules contain a hydrocarbon chain with an OH (hydroxyl) group attached

algal bloom excessive growth of algae, for example, during eutrophication

alkali metal element in Group 1 of the Periodic table

alkane a family of hydrocarbons containing only single carbon–carbon bonds. Alkanes have a general formula C_nH_{2n2}

alkene a family of hydrocarbons containing a carbon–carbon double bond. Alkenes have a general formula C_nH_{2n}

allotropes different forms of the same element, for example, diamond and graphite are different forms of carbon

alloy a mixture of metals or a metal and carbon (in the case of steel)

analgesic a class of compound which are used to relieve pain without inducing unconsciousness

anode a positively charged electrode

antioxidant substance that slowsdown the rate of oxidation of food

Aspirin an analgesic compound with the chemical name acetyl salicylic acid

atmospheric pollution contaminants of the environment that are a by-product of human activity. They include particles (smoke) and gases such as sulfur dioxide

atomic number the number of protons in an atom of an element

atom smallest particle of an element

automated process not under direct human control

backward reaction the reaction which takes place when the products of a reaction turn back into the original reactants, i.e. products reactants

baking powder supplies carbon dioxide during the baking process so cakes will rise. It contains sodium hydrogen carbonate

basalt an igneous rock formed when magma crystallises on the surface of the Earth

base a metal oxide which reacts with an acid to form a salt and water only

batch process non-continuous chemical process to produce a small quantity of product

bleach a solution usually containing chloride ions (Cl^-) and chlorate(I) ions (ClO^-) made by dissolving chlorine in sodium hydroxide solution

boiling point temperature at which a liquid rapidly turns to a vapour. Water has a boiling point of $100\,°C$ at normal atmospheric pressure

brine a concentrated solution of sodium chloride in water

calorimeter a piece of apparatus used for measuring heat quantities

carbohydrate a compound of carbon, hydrogen and oxygen which fits a formula $C_x(H_2O)_y$. Glucose, $C_6H_{12}O_6$, is an example of a carbohydrate

carbon monoxide a compound of one carbon atom and one oxygen atom, CO. It is formed by the incomplete combustion of carbon and carbon compounds. Carbon monoxide is colourless, odourless and poisonous

catalyst a substance that alters the rate of a chemical reaction without being used up

cathode a negatively charged electrode

cement a substance made by mixing powdered limestone with clay. When mixed with water it sets to a hard mass

CFCs a class of organic compounds called chlorofluorocarbons

chain reaction a continuing series of reactions where the first reaction produces particles which then become the starting material for further reactions

charge transfer the total amount of electrical charge passed though a substance

chlorination treatment with chlorine

chromatography technique used to separate dissolved substances in a mixture to identify them or test purity

colloid a state where very small particles of one substance are spread evenly through another

combustion burning of a substance with oxygen to release energy. Another word for burning

complete combustion when a substance burns in a plentiful supply of air or oxygen to release the maximum amount of energy

composite a material that is made up of other materials

concentration the quantity of a solute dissolved in a stated volume of solvent (often given in moles/dm^3)

concrete a construction material using cement, sand and aggregate (small stones) mixed with water

conductivity the ease with which a substance conducts an electric current

construction material material that is used in building

continuous process chemical process that produces product all of the time

convection current circulating movement of a heated fluid caused by differing densities

core the centre part of the Earth

corrosion the wearing away of the surface of a metal by chemical reaction with air and water

covalent bonding bonding in which a pair of electrons, one from each atom, is shared between two atoms

covalent type of bonding between atoms, usually non-metal atoms, involving a sharing of electrons.

cracking breaking down of long-chain hydrocarbon molecules by the action of a heated catalyst or by heat alone to produce smaller molecules

cross-linking the bonds joining different monomer chains

crude oil a mixture of hydrocarbons produced by the action of high temperatures and pressures on the remains of sea creatures over millions of years

crust the outer layer of the Earth

deforestation destruction of forests caused by excessive cutting down of trees

dehydration the process by which water is removed from a material or a compound

delocalised free to move, for example, delocalised electrons

denatured a description for the distortion which happens to protein molecule when heated

descaler solution used to remove limescale which becomes deposited on heating elements, taps and surfaces

detergent chemical that has a cleaning effect

dilution the process where more solvent is added to a solution in order to decrease its concentration

displacement when a more reactive element takes the place of a less reactive one; moving from one position to another

distillation the process by which water is removed from a material or a compound

drug chemical used medically for the treatment of diseases and injuries. Can also be 'abused' when used for non medical 'recreational' purposes

dry-cleaning cleaning of clothes carried out using an organic solvent

electrode substance used to conduct electricity to an electrolyte during electrolysis

electrolysis the decomposition of a compound by the passage of an electric current

electrolysis the decomposition of a compound by the passage of electricity

electrolyte a compound split up by an electric current when molten or in solution

electron negatively charged sub-atomic particle which exists outside the nucleus

electrostatically attracted attracted by the force between opposite (positive and negative) static charges

empirical formula the formula of a compound expressed as the simplest ratio of numbers of each type of atom in the compound

emulsifier (or emulsifying agent) a chemical that coats the surface of droplets of one liquid so they can remain dispersed in the other

emulsion mixture of two immiscible liquids where one liquid is dispersed in small droplets throughout the other

endothermic a reaction that takes in energy from the surroundings

energy level diagram a diagram which represents graphically the energy of a system before and after the reaction

E-numbers system for listing permitted food additives. All permitted additives are given an E-number, e.g. E124

equilibrium where a reaction and its backward reaction take place simultaneously, no overall change can be observed

essential elements elements that are needed by a living organism, for example, a plant

ester a sweet-smelling liquid formed when an organic acid and an alcohol react. Esters are used in perfumes and food. Methyl ethanoate is an example of an ester

ethanoic acid chemical name for acetic acid, formlar CH_3CO_2H

ethanol chemical name for ethyl alcohol found in alcoholic drinks, formula C_2H_5OH

eutrophication the process by which excessive quantities of nitrate ions pollute lakes and rivers

exothermic a reaction which gives out energy to the surroundings

explosion a very rapid reaction accompanied by a rapid release of gaseous products

fermentation breakdown of sugars to produce alcohol

filtration technique used to separate an insoluble solid from a liquid

finite resource a resource whose life is limited and whose supply will run out in the future

flame test test carried out by placing chemical in a Bunsen flame to determine the identity of the metal it contains

food additive a substance added to food to act as a colouring agent, preservative, emulsifier, flavour enhancer, etc

formula mass the average mass of a molecule of a substance (using relative atomic masses)

forward reaction a chemical reaction expressed in its conventional way where reactants turn into products, i.e. reactants → products

fossil fuel fuel produced from the slow decay of dead animals and plants at high temperatures and high pressures

fractional distillation method for separating liquids with different boiling points

fraction product collected on fractional distillation of crude oil. A fraction has a particular boiling point range and particular uses

free radical reactive particles which possess an unpaired electron

fuel cell an electric cell which produces an electric current

fullerenes isotopes of carbon discovered in 1985; they are made of ball-shaped molecules containing many carbon atoms

galvanizing the process by which a thin layer of molten zinc metal is applied to the surface of a piece of steel. This protects the steel from corrosion

glycerol a thick, syrupy liquid alcohol with a sweet taste, obtained from the fat in soap manufacture

granite an igneous rock formed inside the Earth by crystallisation of molten magma

graphite one form of the element carbon where the carbon atoms are present in layers; these layers are only weakly held close to each other

Group vertical column of elements in the Periodic Table

halide compound containing the ions of halogen elements

halogen element in Group 7 of the Periodic Table

hydration the addition of water to another substance with which it combines

hydrocarbon compound of carbon and hydrogen only

hydrogenation a chemical reaction where a hydrogen molecule joins with another compound, eg the hydrogenation of unsaturated oil to make saturated fat

hydrolysis a chemical reaction where a water molecule joins with another compound, eg the hydrolysis of ethane to make ethanol

hydrophilic a substance that has a liking or attraction for water

hydrophobic a substance that repels water

Ibuprofen a popular analgesic with anti-inflammatory properties

igneous rock formed when magma crystallises

immiscible describing liquids that do not mix, such as oil and water

incomplete combustion when substances burn in an insufficient amount of air or oxygen. It results in less energy release and possibly soot and/or carbon monoxide

indicator chemical used to test for acids and alkalis by change of colour

inert unreactive and unlikely to change chemically in the given circumstances

insoluble describes a substance that does not dissolve in a solvent

insoluble will not dissolve in the stated solvent under the given conditions

intermolecular force force of attraction between molecules

intermolecular forces between different molecules

ion exchange resin a polymer material which is capable of exchanging the ions in a solution with other ions which are loosely bound to the resin

ionic bonding bonding involving the transfer of one or more electrons from one atom to another, forming positive and negative ions which are held together by electrostatic attraction

ionic compound compound containing an ionic bond

ionic equation an equation which shows only those aqueous ions which actually change state as a result of the reaction under consideration

ionic lattice regular arrangement of ions in a solid ionic compound

isotope atoms of the same element and therefore with the same proton number, but with a different number of neutrons and therefore a different mass number

limescale the common name for the calcium carbonate which is deposited when hard water is boiled. Limescale can build up in central heating pipes and on electric heating elements

limestone a sedimentary rock formed from the remains of sea creatures. It is a form of calcium carbonate

limiting reactant in a reaction involving more than one reactant, the limiting reactant is the one which becomes used up first, causing the reaction to stop

lithosphere the crust and the uppermost layer of the mantle

LPG (liquefied petroleum gas) the gas which leaves the top of the fractional distillation column and is liquefied. It is an alternative to petrol or diesel in cars

magma rock between the crust and the core of the Earth

mantle a thick layer of dense semi-liquid rock below the Earth's crust

marble a metamorphic rock formed by the action of high temperatures and pressures on limestone. A form of calcium carbonate

mass number sum of the number of protons and neutrons in an atom

metallic bonding the forces that keep atoms together in a metal

mixed indicator an indicator which is made up of more than one pigment and which therefore gives a range of colours in different conditions

molar mass the average mass of a mole of a substance (using relative atomic masses)

molecular manufacturing the molecule by molecule building up of a product

molecule particle with two or more atoms joined together

mole the chemist's measure for a certain number of particles. A mole of particles will contain the same number of particles as there are atoms in exactly 12 g of the carbon-12 isotope

monomer small molecule that joins together with other molecules to produce a polymer

nanoparticle very small particle, about one millionth of a metre in diameter

nanotube very small particles arranged in tube shapes

negative electrode the electrode which is connected to the negative terminal of a DC power supply

neutralisation reaction in which an acid reacts with a base or alkali

neutron neutral sub-atomic particle originating inside the nucleus

non-renewable fuel a fuel that took a long time to form and cannot quickly be replaced

nucleon number sum of the number of protons and neutrons in an atom

optimum temperature (for enzymes) the temperature at which the activity of enzymes is at its greatest

ore a rock that contains a metal or a metal compound in sufficient quantity to make the extraction of the metal economically viable

oxidation reaction in which a substance gains oxygen, loses hydrogen or loses electrons; it is the opposite of reduction

oxidising agent a substance that takes electrons from another, causing it to be oxidised

ozone layer a layer of ozone gas lying within the stratosphere at about 20 miles above the Earth's surface

paracetamol a popular analgesic which has no anti-inflammatory effects

percentage by mass in a compound, the mass of a given element present expressed as a percentage of the total mass of the compound

percentage yield the fraction of the predicted yield that is actually obtained, expressed as a percentage (= (actual yield/predicted yield) × 100)

permanent hardness, of water hardness of water which is not removed by boiling . It is caused by dissolved calcium and magnesium sulfates

pH a measurement of the acidity of a solution, on a scale from 1 to 14

pharmaceutical drug chemical that is made to be used as a medicine

phenolphthalein a commonly used acid/base indicator which give a sharp end point in titrations since it is pink in alkaline conditions, and colourless in acidic

phosphorescent pigment pigment that stores energy when in light and can release this energy again in the dark and so glow in the dark

photosynthesis the process by which plants convert water and carbon dioxide into oxygen and glucose using the energy from the Sun

pollution the presence in the environment of substances that are harmful to living things

polymer long chain molecule built up of a large number of smaller units, called monomers, joined together by the process of polymerisation

polyunsaturated usually applies to fatty acids with two or more carbon-carbon double bonds.

positional chemistry placing molecules in the molecular manufacturing of a product

positive electrode the electrode which is connected to the positive terminal of a DC power supply

potential difference (electrical) a measure of the voltage difference between two points or electrodes

precipitate an insoluble product of a reaction taking place in solution which will therefore settle out of the solution

precipitate solid that appears when two solutions are mixed together

precipitation separation of a solid from a solution; the solid usually settles out

predicted yield the maximum amount of product that could be made during a chemical reaction, calculated using the chemical equation for the reaction and the relative atomic masses of the products

product substance that is formed in a chemical reaction. They appear to the right of the arrow in a chemical equation

proton number the number of protons in an atom

proton positively charged sub-atomic particle originating inside the nucleus

radable substances that can be broken down by such processes as decomposition by bacteria and can therefore be reused by living organisms.

rate of reaction the speed with which products are formed or reactants used up

rate of reaction the speed with which the products are formed and the reactants are used up during a chemical reaction

reactant substance that is used at the start of a chemical reaction. They appear to the left of the arrow in a chemical equation

recycled materials that are used again rather than disposed of

redox reaction a reaction involving both reduction and oxidation

reducing agent a substance which transfers electron to another, causing it to be reduced

reduction reaction in which a substance loses oxygen or gains electrons; it is the opposite of oxidation

relative atomic mass the mass of an atom measured on a scale where one atom of the isotope carbon-12 is exactly 12 units

relative formula mass mass obtained by adding together the relative atomic masses of all the atoms shown in the formula of a compound

respiration a process that takes place in living cells converting glucose and oxygen into water and carbon dioxide with a release of energy

reversible reaction a reaction where the products can easily be turned back into the original reactants

rhyolite a rock formed when lava crystallises. It is sometimes called pumice stone and is used as an abrasive

rock salt impure salt (sodium chloride) which is present as deposits in the ground

rust product formed when iron or steel are exposed to air and water. This brown compound is a hydrated iron(III) oxide

sacrificial protection an electrochemical method of preventing corrosion in iron or steel by attaching a more reactive metal to it

salicylic acid a starting material for the production of aspirin. Full chemical name is 2- hydroxybenzoic acid

salt (common salt) chemical name sodium chloride used for flavour enhancer in food and as a raw material in industry

saponification the chemical process of splitting a fat or oil with sodium hydroxide to form soap

saturated organic compound which contains only single covalent bonds, e.g. ethane C_2H_6

sedimentation settling out of solid particles from a suspension

single indicator single substance which in solution will give a colour change when the acidity or alkalinity of the solution is changed

smart alloy an alloy which can be restored to its original shape if deformed

sodium chloride the chemical name for common salt, formula NaCl

solubility the amount of solute which can be dissolved in a particular solvent under given conditions

soluble aspirin a form of aspirin which dissolves easily in water

solute the substance that dissolves in a solvent to form a solution

solution mining mining technique used to extract salt by dissolving underground deposits

solution what is formed when a solute dissolves in a solvent

solvent a liquid in which a solute dissolves

spectator ions the aqueous ions which are present but not involved in a precipitation reaction, and are not included in the ionic equation

stable octet full shell of eight electrons formed when atoms bond together

stratosphere layer in the atmosphere between about 10 and 50 km above the Earth's surface

strong acid an acid which ionizes completely when in aqueous solution

subduction dipping of one plate below another at a destructive plate boundary

subsidence a downward movement of an area of ground relative to surrounding land

superconductor material that conducts electricity with very little or no resistance

surface area the area of the surface of a solid object, usually measured in centimetres squared

tectonic plate very large plate of rock which floats and moves very slowly on the mantle of the Earth

temporary hardness hardness of water which is removed by boiling. It is caused by dissolved calcium hydrogen carbonate

thermal decomposition decomposition of a compound by heating

thermochromic pigment pigment that can change colour at different temperatures

tinning the process of making a tin plate coating on the surface of a piece of steel by dipping the steel into a bath of molten tin

titration an analytical technique used to measure the volume of one solution required to react completely with a given volume of another

toxicity a measure of how poisonous a substance is

transition element element in the central block of the Periodic Table

transition metal metallic element in the central block of the Periodic Table

ultraviolet light short wavelength, high energy electromagnetic radiation beyond the range of visible light

universal indicator mixture of two or more different acid/base indicators in one solution

unsaturated a molecule which contains at least one carbon–carbon double bond

unsaturated organic compound containing one or more double or triple bond between carbon atoms

volcano a tube from inside the Earth to its surface through which lava can escape in an eruption

washing soda common name for sodium carbonate, formular Na_2CO_3. IOH_2O used as a water softner

water hardness dissolved minerals, such as chalk, limestone and marble, in water make it difficult to produce a lather with soap. This is described as hardness

weak acid an acid which when in aqueous solution only ionizes partially. An equilibrium is set up between the original acids and its ions

yeast a single-celled fungus used in the brewing and bread making industries

Index

Revision Guides

Beat the rest - exam success with Heinemann

Ideal for homework and revision exercises, these differentiated **Revision Guides** contain everything needed for exam success.

- Summary of each item at the start of each section

- Personalised learning activities enable students to review what they have learnt

- Advise from examiners on common pitfalls and how to avoid them

Please quote S 603 SCI A when ordering

t 01865 888068 **f** 01865 314029 **e** orders@heinemann.co.uk **w** www.heinemann.co.uk

Inspiring generations

L554